917.1   Fodor's budget travel
F   Canada, 1986

DATE DUE

FODOR'S TRAVEL GUIDES

are compiled, researched, and edited by an international team of travel writers, field correspondents, and editors. The series, which now almost covers the globe, was founded by Eugene Fodor in 1936.

OFFICES
New York and London

FODOR'S BUDGET CANADA:
Editor: LANGDON L. FAUST
Area Editors: JOHN LEARNEY, SUSAN LEARNEY, ROGER NEWMAN, VALERIE ROSS, RALPH SURETTE, COLLEEN THOMPSON, KENNETH WINCHESTER, DAVID WISHART
Maps: DYNO LOWENSTEIN

SPECIAL SALES

Fodor's Travel Guides are available at special quantity discounts for bulk purchases (50 copies or more) for sales promotions or premiums. Special travel guides or excerpts from existing guides can also be created to fit specific needs. For more information write Special Marketing, Fodor's Travel Guides, 2 Park Avenue, New York, N.Y. 10016

FODOR'S

BUDGET TRAVEL CANADA 1986

FODOR'S TRAVEL GUIDES

New York & London

The following Fodor's Guides are current; most are also available in a British
edition published by Hodder & Stoughton.

Country and Area Guides

Australia, New Zealand
  & The South Pacific
Austria
Bahamas
Belgium & Luxembourg
Bermuda
Brazil
Canada
Canada's Maritime
  Provinces
Caribbean
Central America
Eastern Europe
Egypt
Europe
France
Germany
Great Britain
Greece
Holland
India, Nepal &
  Sri Lanka
Ireland
Israel
Italy
Japan
Jordan & The Holy Land
Kenya
Korea
Mexico
North Africa
People's Republic of
  China
Portugal
Scandanavia
Scotland
South America
Southeast Asia

Soviet Union
Spain
Switzerland
Turkey
Yugoslavia

City Guides

Amsterdam
Beijing, Guangzhou,
  Shanghai
Boston
Chicago
Dallas–Fort Worth
Greater Miami & The
  Gold Coast
Hong Kong
Houston
Lisbon
London
Los Angeles
Madrid
Mexico City &
  Acapulco
Munich
New Orleans
New York City
Paris
Philadelphia
Rome
San Diego
San Francisco
Stockholm, Copenhagen,
  Oslo, Helsinki &
  Reykjavik
Sydney
Tokyo
Toronto
Vienna
Washington, D.C.

U.S.A. Guides

Alaska
Arizona
California
Cape Cod
Colorado
Far West
Florida
Hawaii
New England
New Mexico
Pacific North Coast
South
Texas
U.S.A.

Budget Travel

American Cities (30)
Britain
Canada
Caribbean
Europe
France
Germany
Hawaii
Italy
Japan
London
Mexico
Spain

Fun Guides

Acapulco
Bahamas
London
Montreal
Puerto Rico
San Francisco
St. Martin/Sint Maarten
Waikiki

Contents

Introduction

Friendly, familiar, foreign, and near: Canada is the second-largest country in the world, stretching more than 5,000 miles between St. John's, Newfoundland, and Victoria, British Columbia, and another 2,500 miles from the American border to the North Pole.

Travel and tourism has become one of the most important industries in this vast land, employing one in twenty Canadians and accounting for $11 billion in annual revenue. The result is one of the world's most developed and sophisticated, yet personable, tourist businesses.

Best of all, Canada is a budget country. Even its major cities are less expensive than those in the U.S. It is a country rife with opportunities for the cost-conscious traveler: cozy inns and bed-and-breakfast lodgings, intimate restaurants, a multitude of low-cost transportation options, museums, galleries and buildings to visit, sports, arts, and magnificent scenery that cost little or nothing to enjoy.

By budget travel we mean moderately priced travel, not travel-on-an-attenuated-shoestring, for it is possible to visit Canada, even with its high cost of living, and have a wonderful, economical time.

In many ways, budget travel is a state of mind, a state which could be summed up as "look before you leap." The only sound approach to a budget holiday is to know exactly what you can afford, and keep to that figure by planning with care and spending with discretion. Ask yourself such money-saving questions as: Is there an off-season rate? Is there a weekend rate? Are there youth or other special discounts? Is there a special rate for reserving or booking in advance?

Where accommodations are concerned, small is not necessarily beautiful in Canada, nor is it necessarily cheap. Although inns and guest houses are usually among the best budget accommodations available, they can also be quite pricey. The one thing that will be certain in guest houses or small hotels is that you will meet with willing service, simple, clean rooms and, above all, friendly hosts. Private bathrooms and color televisions are pleasant luxuries, but they really are expendable, and more than compensated for by cheerful attention and lodgings with character. Where food is concerned our advice is look before you eat. Check the menu first for prices and just what is or is not included.

This book does not set out to cover all of Canada. For that, we recommend our major *Fodor's Canada* guide. In this book we have struck a balance between the major cities and some of the less-familiar regions that offer possibilities for the budget-minded. Divide your time between urban and rural Canada, with a maximum of time in the latter. Of course this guide includes some cities—Toronto, Vancouver, Montréal, Halifax, Calgary—they are places with a great deal to offer, especially in the way of entertainment. But cities have a way of separating you and your money in myriad unplanned ways. So include them in your itinerary, but balance them with a fair part of your trip in the countryside. If there is one thing Canada has to offer it is some of the most spectacular scenery in the world: snowcapped mountain peaks, surging seas of prairie wheat, fog-shrouded coastal outports, wild rivers, and tucked-away villages. These and other attractions are there, and all waiting to be visited for a budget outlay. All it takes is a bit of planning and the willingness to accept the comfortable ways of a friendly country.

We are always grateful to readers who write to us with their experiences and suggestions for improving our Guides. It is impossible to be totally accurate with information, given the speed at which the modern world changes, especially in the field of travel, but your letters will help us to get nearer to complete accuracy. Please write:
In the US. Fodor's Travel Guides, 2 Park Ave., New York, NY 10016.
In Europe. Fodor's Travel Guides, 9–10 Market Pl., London W1N 7AG, England.

Facts at Your Fingertips

PLANNING YOUR TRIP

WHERE TO START. Many a budget-minded traveler's regrets about spending too much cash while on holiday stem from not knowing enough to avoid wasting it. The best thing to do is to arm yourself with as much information as you can lay your hands on. You can then narrow your choice and work out a realistic budget that will stick.

The obvious place to start is the Canadian Government Office of Tourism nearest you:

Atlanta: 400 S. Omni International, Atlanta, GA 30303
Boston: 500 Boylston St., Boston, MA 02116
Buffalo: Suite 3550, 1 Marine Midland Ctr., Buffalo, NY 14203
Chicago: 12th Floor, 310 S. Michigan Ave., Chicago, IL 60604
Cleveland: Suite 1038, 55 Public Sq., Cleveland, OH 44113
Dallas: Suite 1600, 2001 Bryan Tower, Dallas, TX 75201
Detroit: Suite 1900, First Federal Bldg., 1001 Woodward Ave., Detroit, MI 48226
Los Angeles: 510 W. Sixth St., Los Angeles, CA 90014
Minneapolis: Chamber of Commerce Bldg., 15 S. Fifth St., Minneapolis, MN 55402
New York: Exxon Bldg., Room 1030, 1251 Ave. of the Americas, New York, NY 10020
Philadelphia: Suite 1810, 3 Parkway, Philadelphia, PA 19102
San Francisco: Alcoa Bldg., Suite 1160, 1 Maritime Plaza, San Francisco, CA 94111
Seattle: Suite 814, 600 Stewart St., Seattle, WA 98101
Washington, DC: NAB Bldg., Suite 200, 1771 N St. NW, Washington, DC 20036

A LOOK AT LIKELY COSTS. In many ways, budgeting is simplified if you can take a prepackaged trip. This is certainly the case in Canada, which is not a cheap country in which to travel owing largely to its size and corresponding cost of transportation. Fortunately, there is a wide range of package tours available, running the gamut from foliage bus tours of Québec to whale-watching cruises down the St. Lawrence River. Assuming you are going in an escorted group, we suggest the following rule of thumb.

Divide the number of days into the package price for the land portion of the tour. This should include lodging, most meals, transportation, escorting, and such standard incidentals as transfers and baggage handling. (We've excluded air fares because prices are more frequently quoted without them; fares vary enormously depending on season, charter or full fare, and so on.) If the price per day for the land portion comes out to $65.00 or more per day, the tour is not "budget" for the purposes of this book. If it comes out to around $50.00 per day, the tour is worth looking into further. If it comes out to around $40.00 per day, read on. Study the details carefully, and if they seem reasonable, this may be the tour that you are looking for.

However independent travel can be more flexible (and more fun), and if you take advantage of low season travel and accommodation rates, it needn't blow your budget. Montréal, Toronto, and Vancouver are cities with lively theater, concerts, and nightlife, and winter is the big season for these activities. Round-trip air fares are cheaper and hotels offer low-priced inclusive rates. Theaters, restaurants, and concert halls may offer reduced winter rates as part of a winter weekend package.

As you're on a budget holiday, we've assumed that you will have packed your suitcase with everything you need, that you will be passing up the more expensive forms of entertainment, and that shopping will be restricted. Bearing this in mind, an average day in Toronto, a popular tourist destination, would cost about $75.00. There are, of course, many ways in which you can reduce this further by exploring off the beaten bath, traveling out of season, and staying in hostels or guest houses.

A typical day in Toronto, per person

	Canadian Dollars
Hotel with breakfast, service and tax included (moderate)	$60.00
Lunch (table d'hôte)	20.00
Dinner (with wine)	40.00
Coffee in a café	2.00
Beer, 12 oz.	3.00
1 subway ride	1.00
Total	$126.00

As a general rule, medium-sized cities such as Edmonton, Halifax, and Saskatoon will be 10 percent cheaper than the larger centers. Rural areas within 250 miles of the U.S. border (southern Québec and Ontario, the Maritimes, the Prairies, interior British Columbia) will be as much as 20 percent cheaper.

WHERE TO GO. Unless you plan to travel on a packaged tour, with a fixed itinerary and schedule which you can't modify, it is advantageous to rough out your trip. This gives you the opportunity to decide how much you can cover comfortably in the time at your disposal. It also allows you to relate the extent of your travel to the limits of your pocketbook.

Highlights of Canada. The region most visited for its natural beauty and range of outdoor-oriented activities is the Canadian Rockies, especially the line of rugged peaks and emerald lakes stretching from Banff to Jasper in Alberta. National and provincial parks and private campgrounds offer a range of inexpensive accommodation. Other scenic areas include British Columbia's Vancouver Island, Alberta's Big Muddy Badlands, Georgian Bay in Ontario, Québec's Gaspé Peninsula, Cape Breton Island in Nova Scotia, and the shorelines of both coasts.

Niagara Falls was once the most popular tourist destination in Canada; it has been eclipsed in recent years by the city of Toronto with its variety of history and culture. Attractions range from the world's highest free-standing structure, the CN Tower, to Canada's largest zoo. Montréal, once Canada's largest city, still competes with Toronto in a number of things to see and do. Old Montréal, Mount Royal Park, and an exciting nightlife scene are prime attractions. Most European of all Canada's cities, Québec is a living museum of the 17th and 18th centuries; fine restaurants and historic charm abound here.

Many of the eastern cities still reflect their Loyalist past. Thousands of American Colonists, loyal to the King and Britain, fled to the Maritime Provinces during the Revolution. Here they prospered, and in turn are remembered in museums, monuments, and historic houses throughout the area. St. John, New Brunswick, is in particular a storehouse of Loyalist history. Halifax and St. John's are historic seaports that serve as good bases for exploring Nova Scotia and Newfoundland, respectively.

Manitoba's capital, Winnipeg, is the gateway to western Canada and a culture-conscious, cosmopolitan center, as evidenced by the Royal Winnipeg Ballet and the annual, weeklong Folklorama Festival in August. Regina and Saskatoon, in the heart of Canada's farming belt, are modest but attractive, with numerous parks and museums. Symbols of oil-fueled progress, Calgary and Edmonton rise sleek and shining above the Alberta prairie. As befits a boom town with plenty of money, Calgary has much newfound culture in the form of galleries, boutiques, playhouses, and restaurants.

Vancouver, with Howe Sound as a doorstep and the Coast Mountains for a backyard, boasts one of the world's most spectacular urban settings. Botanical gardens dot the city and numerous seaside trails lure strollers and beachcombers. Across the sound, on Vancouver Island, is a little bit of England in the form of Victoria, capital of British Columbia. From high tea in the aging Empress Hotel to double-decker tourist buses, the city exudes charm. The B.C. ferry system is the longest in the world and makes for an interesting island- and port-hopping holiday.

Ottawa, the nation's capital, was once known as the "Westminster of the Wilderness" because of its rural setting. Today it is a city of pomp and pageantry where the celebration of the past mingles with the day-to-day running of a country. Tulips carpet city parks and line the Rideau Canal in spring. In winter, the canal becomes the world's longest skating rink. Nearby are the rumpled hills of Gatineau Park, popular with cross-country skiers in winter and hikers the rest of the year.

Budget Areas. Some of the above areas—especially the large cities—are too expensive to stay in for more than an overnight stop. So, too, are the old and established resort areas such as Banff and the Laurentians, and the grand old CP hotels that dot the transcontinental line from St. John's to Victoria. But for every pricey "name" hotel there are several inns, motels, and bed-and-breakfast houses to be found. Particularly good values are to be found in the Maritimes away from the centers of Halifax and St. John. In Montréal and Québec, look for smaller "pensioner's" hotels or apartment buildings which also rent rooms or suites by the night. Toronto hotels are generally expensive, but the market is competitive, so watch for special discounts and package rates. Out West, a car is a great asset. Farm vacations in Saskatchewan, Manitoba, and Alberta are a good buy, particularly for large families with varied interests. The southern Canadian Rockies below Banff offers a cheaper and less crowded alternative to the traditional mountain parks.

WHEN TO GO. When you prefer to visit Canada will depend on what you like in the way of weather, sports, sightseeing, cultural events, and local color. While the country is too large to generalize about the best seasons, the area along the border with the United States is most pleasant during May and June or September and October. While the heat and humidity can make summer days uncomfortable in southern Canada, it is an essential requirement for travel in the North—at least for those who prefer mosquitoes and black flies to the bitter cold. The summer months are also comfortable in the Rockies. And British Columbia, tempered by its Pacific location, is a delight year-round.

Winter, all but intolerable in the North, brings a dry cold to the Prairies and generally heavy snow to the eastern forests. Autumn is most beautiful in the East, particularly the Laurentians of Québec. And spring, even though it is the most beautiful time for the orchards, suffers in appeal because of the melting snow and soggy spring skies—especially during April.

Special Events. Below are some of the special attractions that might influence you in choosing a date for your vacation. For further information and exact dates write to the relevant provincial tourist information office.

January. *Saskatchewan:* Winter Carnival in Humboldt. *Ontario:*

Winter Festival in Niagara Falls; Canadian National Figure Skating Championships in Toronto; Winter Carnival in Owen Sound. *Québec:* International Bonspiel (curling) in Québec.

February. *British Columbia:* Winter Carnival in Vernon; Boat Show in Vancouver. *Saskatchewan:* Winter carnivals in Estevan, Fort Qu'Appelle, Lloydminster, Melfort, and Prince Albert. *Manitoba:* Northern Manitoba Trapper's Festival in The Pas; Festival du Voyageur in St. Boniface. *Ontario:* Still more winter carnivals, in Sault Ste. Marie, Orillia, Burlington, Gravenhurst, Bracebridge, Huntsville, and Barrie; Spring Flower and Garden Show in Toronto. *Québec:* Perhaps the biggest and most famous winter carnival in North America takes place in Québec.

March. *British Columbia:* Music festivals in Powell River and Chilliwack. *Manitoba:* Royal Manitoba Winter Fair in Brandon; Manitoba Music Festival in Winnipeg. *Ontario:* Canadian National Sportsmen's Show in Toronto; Maple Syrup Festival in Elmira.

April. *Saskatchewan:* Men's World Curling Championships in Regina; Women's Curling Championships in Moose Jaw. *Ontario:* Spring Festival, Guelph; Niagara Blossom Festival in Niagara Falls. *Québec:* Maple festivals throughout the province (the world's largest producer of maple sugar and syrup), including St. Jean de Matha, Plessisville.

May. *British Columbia:* Victorian Days at Victoria; Rodeo at Cloverdale. *Saskatchewan:* International Band Festival in Moose Jaw. *Ontario:* Tulips turn Ottawa into a riot of color during the Festival of Spring; Shaw Festival in Niagara-on-the-Lake; St. Catharine's Folk Art Festival; Mennonite Auction Relief Sale in New Hamburg. *Québec:* Lumberjack Festival in Normental; Spring Festival in Pontiac; Festival of Birds in Lévis; Festival of the North Shore in Forestville; Floralies (international flower show; throughout the summer) in Montréal. *New Brunswick:* Festival of the Arts in Fredericton; Maritime Band Festival in Moncton. *Nova Scotia:* Apple Blossom Festival in Annapolis Valley.

June. *British Columbia:* Williams Lake Stampede; Salmon Derby in Howe Sound. *Alberta:* International Folk Festival at Red Deer; Rodeo Week in St. Albert. *Saskatchewan:* Western Canada Farm Progress Show in Regina; re-enactment of the trial of Louis Riel in Regina. *Manitoba:* Red River Exhibition in Winnipeg. *Ontario:* Shakespeare and other fine drama at the Stratford Festival (through October); International Air Show in London; International Caravan in Toronto; International Freedom Festival in Windsor. *Québec:* Shrimp Festival in Matane; Art Festival in Repentigny; St. Jean Baptiste Day celebrations throughout Québec (June 24). *New Brunswick:* Pioneer Days in Oromoncto; Grand Bay Days in Grand Bay; Kings Landing Dominion Day Weekend Salmon Festival in Campbellton; *Nova Scotia:* Festival of the Strait at Port Hawkesbury; Nova Scotia Tattoo at Halifax. Gathering of the Clans in Pugwash; Baddeck Handcraft Festival. *Prince Edward Island:* Natal Day Celebrations in Charlottetown. *Newfoundland:* Newfoundland Folk Festival in St. John's; St. John's Day Celebrations in St. John's.

July. *British Columbia:* Loggers Sports Days in Squamish and

Mission City; Nanaimo's Bathtub Race; Sea Festival in Vancouver; Julyfest in Kimberley. *Alberta:* Calgary Stampede, one of North America's oldest and greatest rodeos; Whoop-Up Days in Lethbridge; Edmonton Klondike Days; Rodeo in Red Deer. *Saskatchewan:* Gopher Derby in Eston; Pioneer Days in Saskatoon. *Manitoba:* Highland Gathering in Selkirk; Winnipeg Folk Festival; Trout Festival in Flin Flon; Manitoba Stampede in Morris; Northwest Roundup and Exhibition in Swan River. *Ontario:* Highland Games in Cobourg; Caribana in Toronto; Royal Canadian Henley Regatta in St. Catharines. *Québec:* Summer Festival in Québec; International Swimming Race in La Tuque; International Regatta in Valleyfield. *New Brunswick:* Loyalist Days Festival in St. John; Canada's Irish Cultural Festival in Chatham; Potato Festival in Grand Falls; Shediac Lobster Festival; Old Home Week in Woodstock. *Nova Scotia:* Antigonish Highland Games; Craft Festival in Lunenburg; Old Home Week in Parrsboro; Festival Acadien de Clare in Church Point; Bluegrass and Oldtime Music Festival at Ardoise, Hants County; Annual Piping Festival in Dartmouth. *Prince Edward Island:* Potato Festival in O'Leary; Irish Moss Festival in Tignish; Lobster Carnival and Livestock Exhibition in Summerside. *Newfoundland:* Summer Festival in St. John's; Killigrew's Soirée; Tourist Week in Port aux Basques; Regatta Day in Harbour Grace; Folk Festival at Castle Hill National Historic Site, Placentia Bay.

August: *British Columbia:* Pacific National Exhibition in Vancouver; International Air Show in Abbottsford; Peach Festival in Penticton; horse shows throughout the province, particularly Victoria, Vancouver, Duncan; International Regatta in Kelowna. *Alberta:* Festival of the Arts in Banff; Rodeo in Lloydminster. *Saskatchewan:* International Powwow on the Sioux Reserve near Fort Qu'Appelle; Rodeo in Regina. *Manitoba:* National Ukrainian Festival in Dauphin; Icelandic Festival in Gimli; Folklorama in Winnipeg; Opasquia Indian Days in The Pas. *Ontario:* Lake of the Woods Regatta in Kenora; Six Nation Indian Pageant in Brantford; Glengarry Highland Games; Canadian National Exhibition (fondly known as "The Ex") in Toronto; Miners' Festival in Cobalt; Canadian Open Old Time Fiddlers Contest in Shelburne; Fergus Highland Games; Royal Canadian Henley Regatta in St. Catharines. *Québec:* National Folklore Festival in Chicoutimi; Canots de la Mauricie International Classic in La Tuque; Blueberry Festival in Mistassini. *New Brunswick:* Acadian Festival in Caraquet; Miramichi Folk Song Festival in Newcastle; Handcraft Festival in Mactaquac. *Nova Scotia:* Highland festivals throughout the province, including Iona, New Glasgow, Trenton, St. Ann's; Atlantic Folk Festival in Hardwood Lands; Provincial Exhibition in Bible Hill; Nova Scotia Gaelic Mod at St. Ann's; Blueberry Harvest Festival at Amherst; International Air Show at Yarmouth. *Prince Edward Island:* Dundas Agricultural Fair; Oyster Festival in Tyne Valley; Le Festival acadien de la région Evangéline, Abram-Village; Charlottetown Old Home Week; Blueberry Social and Tea Party in Port Hill; Harvest Festival in Kensington. *Newfoundland:* Regatta Days in Stephenville and St. John's; Summer Games in the Burin Peninsula; Gander Day in Gander.

September. *British Columbia:* Big Dam Canoe Race in Hudson's Hope; Lillooet Rodeo. *Alberta:* Rifleman's Rodeo in Panoka; Blueberry Festival in Fort McMurray. *Saskatchewan:* Old Tyme Fiddling Championships in Swift Current. *Manitoba:* Pembina Threshermen's Reunion in Winkler. *Ontario:* Regional exhibitions in Ottawa, Kitchener, and Welland; Niagara Grape and Wine Festival in St. Catharines. *Québec:* Western Festival in St. Tite. *New Brunswick:* Lumberman's Days at Kings Landing. *Nova Scotia:* Fisheries Exhibition in Lunenburg; Joseph Howe Festival in Halifax; International Town Criers' Championship in Halifax.

October. *British Columbia:* Vancouver Oktoberfest. *Saskatchewan:* Kindersley Goose Festival Days; Tomahawk Rodeo at Cutknife. *Ontario:* Muskoka Cavalcade of Color; Oktoberfest in Kitchener-Waterloo. *Québec:* Snow Goose Festival in Montmagny. *Prince Edward Island:* Multicultural Festival in Charlottetown.

November: *Alberta:* National Farm and Ranch Show in Edmonton; Canadian Finals Rodeo in Edmonton. *Saskatchewan:* Agribition in Regina; International Short Film and Video Festival in Yorkton. *Manitoba:* Bonspiel of Champions in Boissevain. *Ontario:* Royal Agricultural Winter Fair in Toronto.

December. *Ontario:* Traditional Christmas celebrations at various historic sites in Toronto. *Québec:* Salon des Métiers d'Art in Montréal; Salon des Artisan in Québec.

TRAVEL AGENTS AND TOUR OPERATORS. Once you decide where you want to go, your next step is to consult a good travel agent. If you don't have one, the *American Society of Travel Agents,* 4400 MacArthur Blvd., N.W., Washington, D.C. 20007; or the *Association of British Travel Agents,* 53 Newman St., London W1P 4AH, England, will advise you.

Although travel today is becoming easier and more comfortable, it is also growing more complex in its details. As the choice of things to do, places to visit, and ways of getting there increases, so does the problem of *knowing* the answers to all these questions. A reputable, experienced travel agent is a specialist in these details, so he can be of great importance to your trip.

If you wish your agent to book you on a package tour, reserve your transportation and even your first few overnight accommodations, his services should cost you nothing. Most carriers and tour operators grant him a fixed commission for saving them the expense of having to open offices in every town and city.

If, on the other hand, you wish him to plan an individualized itinerary and make all arrangements down to hotel reservations and transfers to and from rail and air terminals, you are drawing upon his skill and knowledge of travel, as well as asking him to shoulder a great mass of detail and paperwork. His commissions from carriers won't come close to covering his expenses, and thus he will make a service charge on the total cost of your planned trip. This charge may amount to 10 or 15 percent, but it will more than likely save you money on balance.

STUDENT AND YOUTH TRAVEL. This is a special field in itself, full of possibilities for budget travel in Canada, for meeting all sorts of people, and for impromptu adventure and fun.

The Council on International Educational Exchange, 205 E. 42nd St., New York, NY 10017, is the basic agency for information on study, travel, and work programs abroad. More specifically academic is *The Institute of International Education,* 809 United Nations Plaza, New York, NY 10017. The *US Student Travel Service Inc.,* 801 Second Ave., New York, NY 10017, is a mine of information on all aspects of student travel.

Canadian agencies include the *Canadian Youth Travel Service,* 44 St. George St., Toronto, Ont. (with regional offices in Vancouver, Edmonton, Ottawa, Saskatoon, and Halifax); *Canadian Hostelling Association,* 333 River Rd., Place Vanier Tower A, Ottawa, Ontario K1L 8H9; *Club Voyages Inc.,* 5450 Côte des Neiges, Room 320, Montréal, Québec H3T 1Y6; *Canadian Bureau for International Education,* 141 Laurier West, Suite 809, Ottawa, Ont. K1P 5J3.

The *American Youth Hostels Inc.,* 1332 Eye St. NW, Washington, DC 20005, has low-cost overseas activities arrangements. Membership in the AYH makes you eligible for the entire network of youth hostels throughout the world.

In Britain, the *Youth Hostels Association* head office is located at Trevelyan House, St. Stephens Hill, St. Albans, Herts.

TRAVEL FOR THE DISABLED. One of the newest and largest groups to enter the travel scene is the handicapped. There are millions of people who are physically able to travel and who do so enthusiastically when they know they will be able to move about with safety and comfort. A growing number of travel agencies specialize in this market. Generally their tours parallel those of the non-handicapped traveler, but at a more leisurely pace, with everything checked out in advance to eliminate all inconvenience. Some important sources of information in this field are: *Access to the World: A Travel Guide for the Handicapped* by Louise Weiss (Facts on File, 460 Park Avenue South, New York, N.Y. 10016); *Travelability* by Lois Reamy (MacMillan, 101K Brown St., Riverside, N.J. 08370); also free on loan as a recording for the blind from Recording For the Blind, 215 E. 58 St., New York, N.Y. 10022 (BA135); the *International Directory of Access Guides* (Rehabilitation International, 1123 Broadway, New York, N.Y., 10010). There are also lists of commercial tour operators who arrange this kind of travel which are published by the Society for the Advancement of Travel for the Handicapped, 26 Court St., Brooklyn, NY 11242. Other information sources are the Travel Information Center, Moss Rehabilitation Hospital, 12th St. and Tabor Rd., Philadelphia, PA 19141; and Mobility International, 43 Dorset St., London W1.

Some of the specialized tour operators are:

Flying Wheel Tours, P.O. Box 382, Owatonna, MN 55060

In Britain, the *Royal Association for Disability and Rehabilitation,* 25 Mortimer St., London SW1, publishes a guide to Britain for the physically handicapped, which also includes information on other countries; contact them for more details.

WHAT TO TAKE. The first principle is to travel light. The restrictions, either by size or weight, imposed on air travelers act as an added incentive to keep baggage within the bounds of common sense. Don't try to pack at the last minute.

If you wear glasses or contacts always take an extra pair or set; at the very least have a copy of your prescription. Camera film, suntan lotion, maps (and a magnifying glass to read it), and insect repellent, if purchased before you go, will reduce those nuisance stops to pick up things you forgot.

Clothes. Canada's geographic and climatic extremes are great, so go prepared. All members of the family should have a sturdy pair of shoes with nonslip soles. Keep them handy in the back of the car. You never know when you may want to stop and clamber along a trail or explore a coastal tide pool.

Warm clothing is a must in all but midsummer, especially in the mountain region and the North. Remember to carry raingear (you'll need it in British Columbia), a sweater to protect you against cool evenings and air conditioning, something to cover swimsuits on your way to the beach or pool, and protective clothing for summer sun, which can burn tender skin even at these latitudes.

Carry raingear in a separate bag in the back of the car. If you're stopping en route, you'll find it's convenient to pack separately those few things you'll need for an overnight stay.

You'll be expected to dress for dinner in the better big-city restaurants. Montréal's social scene is particularly fashion-conscious.

TRAVEL DOCUMENTS AND CUSTOMS. Customs regulations between the United States and Canada are among the most liberal in the world. Passing from one country to the other is usually a simple matter of presenting some valid and acceptable form of identification and answering a few simple questions about where you were born, where you live, why you are visiting Canada, and how long you plan to stay.

The identification need not be a passport, although this is the most readily acceptable. You can use a driver's license, birth certificate, Social Security card, certificate of naturalization, or resident alien ("green") card. Persons under 18 who are not accompanied by an adult should bring with them a letter from a parent or guardian giving them permission to travel in Canada. Entry procedures for British citizens are similarly simple.

Canada allows British and American guests to bring their cars (for less than 6 months), boats or canoes, rifles and shotguns (but not handguns or automatic weaspons), cameras, radios, sports equipment, and typewriters into the country without paying any duty. It's a good idea to register any item of value upon entering Canada to prevent Customs problems when you return.

Some items are restricted, however. You need a contract for a rented car. And, if you are going to return home and leave behind a car you rented in the States, you must fill out an E29B Customs form. The family dog must have a certificate from a veterinarian to prove that it has no communicable diseases. Cats may enter without restriction. All plants must be examined at the Customs station. Most important, Canadian officials are diligent in pursuing smugglers of narcotics and other illegal items.

MONEY. The Canadian dollar, like the U.S. dollar, is divided into 100 cents, and coins and bills exist in the same denominations as in the U.S.—i.e., 1¢, 5¢, 10¢, etc. However the Canadian $2 bill, unlike its American counterpart, is found in everyday use. Actual exchange rates fluctuate from day to day. At the time we went to press, the Canadian dollar was worth about $1.20 U.S. and about 75 British pence. When possible, make currency exchanges in banks or reputable exchange offices, such as Deak-Perera in Vancouver (617 Granville St.), Toronto (10 King St. E. and 55 Bloor St. W.), and Montréal (1155 Sherbrooke St. W.). Exchange rates in stores and gas stations will likely be unfavorable.

Note: Prices listed in this book, unless otherwise indicated, are in Canadian dollars.

Travelers's checks are the best ways to safeguard travel funds. They are sold by various banks and companies in terms of American and Canadian dollars and pounds Sterling. Widely accepted American brands include *American Express, Bank of America,* and *Citibank.* Best known and most easily exchanged British traveler's checks are those issued by *Thos. Cook & Son.*

VISA, MasterCard, American Express, and other major credit cards are widely accepted in Canada.

MEDICAL SERVICES. Canada's health services are among the world's finest but, as in the U.S., they are expensive. Charges for adult in-patient care range from $100 to $300 per day, more in specialized hospitals. Visitors, who cannot enjoy the benefits of the various provincial medicare programs, are thus advised to obtain health insurance before leaving the United States or Britain. Blue Cross members, for example, can join the Canada Health Plan for Visitors to Canada offered by the Canada Council of Blue Cross Plans. Applications are widely available at Canadian drugstores, hospitals, travel agencies, and even in the Safeway chain of supermarkets, but application must be made within 10 days of arrival. The premium as of this writing is $2.50 a day single and $5.00 a day for family coverage. Under this plan, the visitor must report for health care to the emergency ward of a hospital should illness occur. Two additional sources of health insurance and medical information are the Canadian Government Office of Tourism and the International Association for Medical Assistance to Travelers (IAMAT), 188 Nicklin Rd., Guelph, Ont. N1H 7L5.

THE LANGUAGE. Officially, Canada is a bilingual country with two official languages: English and French. In practice, English is the dominant language in all provinces except Québec. To get to know the Québecois (or the Acadians of New Brunswick), a working knowledge of French is essential everywhere except in the large cities, and even in some urban quarters. The rural French-Canadians offer the double barrier of language and rural reserve, but a little French goes a long way with these basically friendly people. A glossary of basic French expressions is included in the back of this book.

GETTING TO CANADA

Air. Flying to Canada from the United States is relatively simple and convenient. New York is connected with Toronto, Montréal, Québec, Ottawa, Halifax, and other eastern cities. There are flights from Chicago to Winnipeg, Calgary, Toronto, Ottawa, and Montréal; and from Boston to Halifax, Yarmouth, St. John, Montréal, Toronto, and other cities. On the West Coast, regular flights leave from San Francisco and Los Angeles to Calgary, Edmonton, Vancouver, Toronto, and Montréal. Regional flights link Midwestern cities to Winnipeg and Regina.

The major air lines operating in Canada are *Air Canada, CP Air, Eastern Provincial, Quebecair,* and *Nordair,* It cannot be emphasized enough that fares vary tremendously. It pays to shop around for the best price well in advance of a planned vacation. Seat sales are generally offered on flights booked more than three weeks in advance with savings of up to 40 percent of regular economy fare. People over 65 are eligible to receive reductions on air, rail, and bus fares within Canada provided proof of age is supplied when tickets are purchased. Students between the ages of 12 and 21 can travel by air at reduced rates (on standby) by providing proof of age. Reductions are also common for children under the age of 12. A typical budget fare from New York to Montréal, round-trip, is about $170. Montréal to Vancouver, round-trip, can be almost as low as $300 or as high as $1,000.

Train. There are only three direct *Amtrak* connections with Canada: New York to Montréal, Chicago to Toronto, and Buffalo to Toronto. A variety of round-trip excursion fares are available, so inquire first from *Amtrak* or your travel agent.

Bus. The only bus company that makes long-distance runs from the United States to Canada is *Greyhound,* but its network of routes can get you from almost anywhere in the United States to any point in Canada. Inquire for information at your local *Greyhound* office. Sample fares are: New York to Montréal, $90 (U.S.) round-trip; San Francisco to Vancouver, $178 (U.S.) round-trip.

STAYING IN CANADA

ACCOMMODATIONS. Canada has a wide selection of accommodations ranging from hotels, inns, self-catering bungalows and apartments, motels, and guest houses to youth hostels and campsites.

If you do not have reservations, it is wise to begin looking for a suitable place to stay early in the afternoon and not run the risk of having to settle for potluck later in the day. If you have reservations, you should advise the establishment in advance if you expect to arrive late. Otherwise, some places will not hold reservations after a certain hour.

Reserve well in advance for hotels and motels in popular resort areas at peak seasons. Also, many cities, in any season, may be hosting large conventions or special events. Planning your trip early will give you time to make the best arrangements.

You can assume free parking at motels and country and resort hotels. But you will have to pay for parking at most city hotels.

Chains. In addition to the thousands of independent hotels and motels throughout the country, there are several popular chains in both categories. A major advantage of the chains is the ease with which you can make reservations—either one at a time en route, or all at once in advance. If you are staying at a member hotel or motel, the management will secure a booking at one of the affiliated hotels or motels at no extra cost to you.

Budget Motels. A relatively new alternative to the familiar—and increasingly expensive—hotel and motel chains is budget motel chains. These are designed to offer basic accommodations—a comfortable bed, clean bathroom, central heating, and air conditioning —without services, bar or restaurant, or fancy lobby. A double here can cost as little as $30.00. Most chains are regional and get more business from highway travelers than through reservations. For information and reservations, contact their central offices: *Rodeway Inns,* 8585 N. Stemmens Fwy., 400 South, Dallas, TX 75247; *Quality Inn,* 10750 Columbia Pike, Silver Spring, MD 20901; *Day's Inn,* 2751 Buford Hwy. NE, Atlanta, GA 30324. Also worth looking up are *Relax Inn* (Alberta), *Best Western Motels, The Inn Group* (Ontario), and *Wandlyn* (mainly Eastern Canada).

Vacation Apartments. If you are willing to do some of your own cooking and cleaning, you may wish to consider a vacation apartment as an alternative to hotels or motels. These are available (generally by checking local newspaper classified ads) in most major cities, especially Toronto. Accommodations run the gamut from modest studios to lavish penthouses put up for rent by vacationing or out-of-town owners. Talk to a travel agent or write the local tourist bureau for further information. Executive Travel Apartments

Ltd., 1101 Bay St., Suite 1805, Toronto, Ont. M5S 2W8 can arrange an apartment vacation for you anywhere in Canada.

Farm Vacations. Eight provinces have farm vacation associations, which distribute lists of guest farms, inspect facilities, and handle consumer complaints: *Alberta:* Alberta Country Vacations, R.R. 1, Chauvin, Alberta T0B 0V0; *Saskatchewan:* Saskatchewan Farm Vacations Assoc., Box 214, Allan, Saskatchewan S0K 0C0; *Manitoba:* Manitoba Farm Vacations Assoc., Box 23, R.R. 2, Morris, Manitoba R0G 1K0; *Ontario:* Ontario Farm Vacations Assoc., R.R. 1, Bruce Mines, Ontario P0R 1C0; *Québec:* Agricotours, 1415 Jarry E., Montréal; Québec H2E 2Z7; *New Brunswick:* New Brunswick Farm Vacations Assoc., R.R. 1, Harcourt, Kent County, N.B. E0A 1T0; *Nova Scotia:* N.S. Farm and Country Vacations Assoc., Centreville, Kings County, N.S. B0P 1J0; *Prince Edward Island:* P.E.I. Farm Vacations, R.R. 2, Winsloe, P.E.I. C0A 2H0.

An excellent source is John Thompson's *Country Bed and Breakfast Places in Canada* (Deneau and Greenberg, 1980), which lists more than 160 places from Gertie Legge's "Hospitality Home" in Heart's Delight, Newfoundland, to Emma and Les Bush's place near the British Columbia logging town of Ladysmith.

Home Exchange. For families or groups who are content to stay in one place during their vacation, a home exchange may be the answer. Several companies publish directories of families and individuals willing to swap homes with people for a specific period of time. The actual cost of accommodations may thus be reduced to nothing while travelers enjoy comfortable living quarters with amenities no hotel could offer. Often the trade includes the use of a car; almost always it means living in a place in a way the average hotel guest could never experience. There is no guarantee that you will find a listing in the area or during the days you would like, but the following directories provide hundreds of opportunities: *Vacation Exchange Club* (two issues, winter and spring, for $15): 12006 111th Ave., Youngtown, AZ 85363.

Hostels. The first Canadian youth hostel was established in 1933. Today, the Canadian Hostelling Association has more than 58 youth hostels and a membership of 30,000. The CHA is a nonprofit organization whose aims are to help all, but especially young people, to a greater knowledge and appreciation of the countryside, particularly by providing accommodations for them while traveling.

A hostel offers simple overnight accommodation. It is open to everyone and is a common meeting place for people from every nationality and background, particularly those interested in traveling off the beaten track. A hosteler may stay up to a maximum of three consecutive nights, though in some hostels this may be longer. In Canada, the cost of overnight accommodation ranges from about $7.00 to about $12.00 per person. Meals, where available, are extra. There is generally a fee differential for nonmembers. In 1985, the cost of CHA membership was: Junior (under 18), $9.00; Senior 1-year, $15.00; Senior 3-year, $40.00; Leader (Group), $25.00;

Family, $30.00; Life, $90.00. The CHA's national address is Place Vanier Tower A, 333 River Rd., Ottawa, Ontario K1L 8H9.

FOOD AND DRINK. Canada's cuisine, like its people, is a mix of the indigenous and the imported, the simple and the sophisticated. This combination resulted in a prize-winning effort in the 1976 World Culinary Olympics in Frankfurt, Germany. Competing with chefs from 21 countries, Canada placed second overall in the eight-day, round-the-clock contest (Switzerland placed first). Travelers have the chance to savor a dizzying variety of this fare in five food regions:

Seafood dominates the menus of restaurants in the four Atlantic Provinces—Nova Scotia, New Brunswick, Prince Edward Island, and Newfoundland. Lobster suppers are ubiquitous, and the delicacy turns up boiled, broiled, baked, steamed, in casseroles, and in salads, everywhere from hotel dining rooms (where prices range from $12.00 to $25.00 for a complete dinner) to church suppers ($8.00 to $15.00). Atlantic salmon and oyster stews are a close second in New Brunswick, usually served with baked beans and steamed brown bread. Prince Edward Island is noted for its juicy Malpeque oysters; Nova Scotia specialties include herring, clam chowder, and sea scallops. When Newfoundlanders talk about "fish" they mean cod, for it is a staple of that province's cooking. Trout, halibut, and hearty fish stews are popular throughout the Maritimes.

Montréal and Québec are the traditional gastronomic capitals of Canada and are both renowned for their French cuisine. Restaurants run the gamut from the provincial fare of Normandy (where many French Canadians originated) to classic haute cuisine served in an 18th-century setting of wooden beams and flickering chandeliers. Typical Québecois dishes include thick pea or cabbage soups, meat pies filled with pork (called *tourtière*), and for dessert, blueberry or other fruit pies. Montréal also has a good variety of ethnic restaurants: Chinese, Italian, Greek, Vietnamese, and Spanish.

Toronto's restaurants are the most varied in Canada. Where once only French cuisine was considered *haute,* the city now has a growing number of ethnic restaurants that reflect its cosmopolitan atmosphere. Excellent (and inexpensive) little restaurants can be found in the Kensington Market area and various ethnic neighborhoods that comprise the downtown core.

Such hearty fare as thick steaks and freshly baked breads made from high-quality grains are a mainstay of Manitoba, Saskatchewan, and Alberta. Cold northern lakes yield freshwater fish such as whitefish, pickerel, and a delicious local delicacy, Winnipeg goldeye. Ukrainian specialties of stuffed cabbage, potato dumplings, spicy sausage, and borscht enhance midwestern menus.

British Columbia's cuisine, like that of the Maritimes, is based on seafood. The sea provides King crab, oysters, shrimp, haddock, and salmon—usually served with produce grown in the province. Best bets for a wide selection of West Coast cooking are Vancouver and Victoria, where choices range from roast beef and Yorkshire pudding in the Empress Hotel to traditional Northwest Coast Indian recipes of salmon, prawns, fruit, and seaweed at Muck-a-Muck.

The general rule for metropolitan areas is to make reservations in advance wherever possible, especially for evening meals. Lack of reservations may not pose a problem for lunch, but remember that at dinnertime most travelers have settled in a particular place for the evening and will quickly fill up the nearby restaurants.

Restaurants serving fast foods have burgeoned in Canada during the last few years, to the convenience of some and the chagrin of others. These places combine prepackaged and portioned-controlled methods with high turnover to offer meals for as little as $3.00, and you can carry out the food or eat it on the premises. If you are a budget traveler, fast-food chains offer a familiar and often necessary product at reasonable prices. They may even allow you to catch your next bus or plane. Some of the more common chains in Canada include: *A & W* (266 outlets across Canada); *Burger King* (66); *Dairy Queen* (370, second only to McDonald's); *Harvey's* (100, food prepared and cooked in the restaurant); *McDonald's* (379); *Mr. Submarine* (137); *Pizza Delight* (145, mostly in Eastern Canada); *Scott's Chicken Villa* (250, Colonel Sander's *Kentucky Fried Chicken* chain); *Tote-a-Meal, de Petit Prince* (350, unique pressure-fried chicken and ribs); *Wendy's Old Fashioned Hamburgers* (80, a cut above other hamburger outlets). *Frites* stands abound in Québec; here you can find the classic Canadian hot dog ("all dressed") and French fries (served with vinegar).

Canadian wines, beers, and spirits are generally a good buy when dining out. *Labatt's* and *Molson* have the lion's share of Canada's beer market, but regional brands such as *Schooner* in the Maritimes and *Kokanee* in British Columbia are worth sampling. A 12-ounce glass of beer can range in price from $1.50 in a neighborhood restaurant or bar to $3.50 in a hotel bar.

Once a grapy imitation of European varieties, Canadian wines have come into their own in the last half decade. Particularly good are the Bordeaux-like reds and Chardonnay-like whites of the Niagara region, where almost 90 percent of Canadian wine is made. Inniskillin, Château des Charmes, and London Winery are excellent labels. Several good wines are also produced in British Columbia's Okanagan region, including Casabello (Fleur de Blanc), and Andrés (Similkameen Red and Richelieu Ehrenfelser). Wines range in price from $5.00 for a good table wine to $7.50 and up for a premium label. Mark-up in restaurants is usually 100 percent. Because of high federal and provincial duties levied on imported spirits, American and European wines are *not* a good buy in Canada.

"Native" beverages that may add to your enjoyment of a local meal are calabogus, a mixture of rum, molasses, and spruce beer (definitely not for the faint of heart), and a "wee swallie" of potent Newfoundland screech, a dark rum of dubious ancestry.

TIPPING. The service charges on hotel bills suffice, except for bellhops and porters (75 cents per bag or service). Whether you tip the hotel concièrge or innkeeper depends on whether he has given you any special service. If a service charge is included in a restaurant bill, it is customary to add the loose change or about 5 percent as a tip. If you do indulge in a taxi, tip about 10 percent. It is not customary to tip theater ushers, but barmen usually expect a tip.

SHOPPING. Quality and old-fashioned craftsmanship are the prizes to be found in Canada. But the days when you could acquire these at bargain-basement prices are long gone. And it's generally no good trying to bargain in Canada, except on antiques. But as you're on a budget, it's most unlikely that you'll find a real bargain that's also small enough to take home in your suitcase.

Some ideas for good inexpensive souvenirs to take home include examples of regional and native crafts. From Québec and the Maritimes: woodcarvings and fine woven goods; Ontario and the Prairie provinces: Mennonite, Ukrainian, and other ethnic crafts; British Columbia and the North: Indian crafts such as thick Cowichan sweaters and scarves, soapstone carvings, prints, and other artwork. Canadian beer and wine, food packs containing Québec maple syrup, Prairie honey, and Ontario cheese, and picture books depicting the country's spectacular scenery are other suggestions.

HOLIDAYS AND CLOSINGS. National public holidays in Canada are: New Year's Day (January 1); Good Friday (the Friday before Easter); Easter Monday (the Monday following Easter); Victoria Day (the Monday preceding May 25); Dominion Day (July 1); Labor Day (the first Monday in September); Thanksgiving Day (the second Monday in October); Remembrance Day (November 11); Christmas Day (December 25); and Boxing Day (December 26).

When a holiday falls on a Saturday or Sunday, it is observed on the following Monday. In recent years there has been a tendency to observe all holidays on the nearest Monday to the actual date. Remember, though, that many stores and attractions remain open on holidays even though banks, schools, and government offices may close.

In addition to the national holidays there are also a number of provincial holidays, most notably Québec's St. Jean Baptiste Day, the province's "fête national" (June 24).

ELECTRICITY. Canada's electrical system is the same as that of the U.S.: 110 volts, 60 cycles, alternating current (AC). American appliances can be used throughout Canada without adapters or converters.

MAIL. Stamps can be purchased at any post office in Canada, often from your hotel desk, or from coin-operated vending machines located in terminals, stationers, drugstores, and other shops. Post offices are usually open during business hours and sometimes on Saturday mornings.

If you expect to receive mail while traveling, you can have it addressed to you in care of your hotel, or care of general delivery at any post office on your itinerary. Letters should be marked "hold for 15 days" and should carry a return address.

There is no separate air mail rate for letters or postcards posted in Canada for delivery within the country or to the United States. Mail for distant points is automatically airlifted. The following postal rates are in effect.

Letters and Postcards

Within Canada	34¢ for the first ounce
To the United States	39¢ for the first ounce
Air Mail to all other countries	66¢ for the first ounce and for mailgrams

TELEGRAMS. To send a telegram to a destination anywhere within Canada, ask for assistance at your hotel, or go to the nearest CN/CP telegraph office. Overseas cablegrams can be dispatched by CN/CP.

TELEPHONE. Telephone rates and procedures are much the same as in the United States; coin-operated telephones are available almost everywhere. Local calls usually cost 25 cents and can be dialed directly. Long-distance rates are 35 percent lower on Sunday and between 6 P.M. and midnight on weekdays; 60 percent lower between midnight and 8 A.M. every day. Most phone books give samples of long-distance rates between various Canadian cities. For example, a long-distance call from Montréal to Vancouver, during business hours, costs about $1.00 a minute. Dialed after midnight, the rate drops to 40 cents.

USEFUL ADDRESSES. *United States Embassy:* 100 Wellington St., Ottawa, Ontario K1P 5T1 (613) 238-5335; *U.S. Consulates* also in Calgary, Halifax, Montréal, Québec, Toronto, Vancouver, and Winnipeg. *British Embassy:* 80 Elgin St., Ottawa, Ontario K1P 5K7 (613) 237-1530. *British Consulates* also in Calgary, Edmonton, Halifax, Montréal, Québec, Toronto, and Vancouver. *Canadian Government Office of Tourism:* Travel Information Service, 235 Queen St., 4th fl. E, Ottawa, Ontario K1A 0H6 (613) 996-4610; *Parks Canada:* Dept. of the Environment, Ottawa, Ontario K1A 1G2 (613) 997-2800; *Canadian Hostel Association:* Place Vanier Tower A, 333 River Rd., Ottawa, Ontario K1L 8H9; *Canadian Automobile Association* (affiliated with AAA; offices throughout Canada): 1775 Courtwood Crescent, Ottawa, Ontario K2C 3J2 (613) 226-7631.

TRAVELING IN CANADA

AIR. Canada is a huge country. Air travel has shrunk distances considerably, and the flying time between coasts is manageable.

However, service to smaller cities is often only once or twice a day. Therefore you may encounter time-consuming stopovers when trying to reach your destination.

As an alternative to long waits in airports, you may want to consider a fly/drive package. Most airlines, in conjunction with car-rental companies, offer these combination opportunities to most parts of the country year round.

Other flight packages offer plans for small groups and a choice of hotel accommodations. Some even offer campers and motor homes, if you're interested in roughing it a bit. Check into special children's rates as well. Book as far in advance as possible to take advantage of APEX fares.

The two major Canadian carriers are *Air Canada,* Place Air Canada, Montréal, Québec H2Z 1X5, and *CP Air,* 1 Grant McConachie Way, Vancouver, British Columbia V7B 1V1. Both airlines have an active travel information service; if you are interested in an area they don't serve, you will be directed to the carrier that does.

Regional carriers include: *Eastern Provincial Airways,* Head Office Box 5001, Gander, Newfoundland A1V 1W9; *Québecair,* Montréal International Airport, P.O. Box 490, Dorval, Québec H4Y 1B5; *Pacific Western Airlines,* 570 Fairy Road, Winnipeg, Manitoba R3H 0T7; *Norcanair,* Hangar #2, Mobile #3, Saskatoon, Saskatchewan S7M 5X4, *Nordair,* 1320 Graham Blvd., Tower of Mount Royal, Quebec H3P 3C8.

TRAIN. *Via Rail,* Canada's national passenger rail company, is proof that train travel is alive and well in North America. In 1982 Via Rail carried some 7.2 million passengers and is continuing its successful program of escorted and independent tours.

On the Canadian and Supercontinental cross-country routes, Via's distinctive blue-and-yellow trains have been rescheduled to permit travel through the most scenic parts of the Rocky Mountains in full daylight. Via also provides breaks in Winnipeg and Calgary, as well as on-board meal service while the trains are in the station. This schedule permits more convenient connections from the West to the Maritimes through Montréal.

Other Via Rail tours currently offered include *Cruising down the River* from Montréal (about $700, including roomette and hotel accommodations); the *Rocky Mountain High* from Vancouver, 9 nites through the Rockies by train, bus, and ferry (starting at under $1,000, including roomette, hotels, and sightseeing); and the *Panorama Reflections* from Winnipeg, 6 nights through valleys and prairie and across icefields to Lake Louise and Banff (from about $1,000, including sleeping car, hotels, and motorcoach).

A "mini-vacation" *Getaway* tour program now covers some 28 cities. Short excursions to Percé, Thunder Bay, Halifax, or Edmonton, for example, can be combined with a longer tour as time allows. Prices for all tours vary by season and by hotel selected.

Regional lines, many of them offering interesting scenic rail trips, include *British Columbia Railways,* P.O. Box 8770, Vancouver, British Columbia V6B 4X6; *White Pass & Yukon Route,* P.O. Box 4070,

Whitehorse, Yukon Y1A 3T1, *Ontario Northland Railway,* 195 Regina St., North Bay, Ontario P1B 8L3; *Algoma Central Railway,* P.O. Box 7000, Sault Ste. Marie, Ontario P6A 5P6.

Via's *Canrailpass,* good for unlimited travel on all or part of the Via system, continues to be popular among those travelers with many planned destinations on their itinerary. Prices range from $110 to $435, depending on length of validity, season, and portion of the system covered. A Canrailpass provides a coach seat. Sleeping car, "Dayniter," or Club Car accommodations are extra and can be booked separately in advance.

For information on rates, contact Via Rail Canada, Rail Travel Bureau, Central Station, Montréal, Québec H3C 3N3, or Via passenger service centers in Boston, New York, Buffalo, Detroit, Chicago, and San Francisco.

CAR. Extensive and well-maintained, Canada's highways skirt four Great Lakes, traverse the high spine of the rockies, and touch three oceans. Canada's most important road, the Trans-Canada Hwy. (#1), is the world's longest, stretching just under 5,000 miles from Victoria, British Columbia, to St. John's, Newfoundland.

Most of the Trans-Canada, as far east as Sydney, Nova Scotia, was constructed in 1962 after 12 years of widening old roads and building new stetches so that a single highway, now marked by signs with a white maple leaf on a green background, would cross the country from coast to coast. The finished road runs from Victoria through Kamloops, Calgary, Regina, Winnipeg, Montréal, Québec, Fredericton, and Halifax to Sydney. Ferries connect the highway with Prince Edward Island and Newfoundland extensions.

The second-largest Canadian road, the Yellowhead Hwy., follows the old Indian route from the Prairies and over the Rockies to the Pacific. It begins in Portage la Prairie, east of Winnipeg, and runs through Saskatoon, Edmonton, and Jasper National Park to Prince Rupert, British Columbia.

Dawson Creek, British Columbia, just over the Alberta border, is the southern terminus of the 1,523-mile Alaska Hwy., two-thirds of which is in Canada and most of which is unpaved. The Alaska Hwy. goes through Fort St. John and Fort Nelson before crossing the northern Rockies, where it rises to over 4,000 feet. It then enters the Yukon at Watson Lake, proceeding to the Alaska border via Whitehorse, Carmacks, and Dawson. The last stretch, in Alaska, terminates in Fairbanks. A budget-minded exploration of Canada's North is possible along this route, providing you take advantage of campgrounds and modest hotels and motels.

These primary arteries, along with the complex of roads in southeastern Ontario around Toronto and southern Québec around Montréal, bear most of the traffic in Canada. With connecting routes—such as the one between Calgary and Edmonton—they will take you anywhere you want to go.

Speed limits vary from province to province, but are usually in the 50–60 mph (80–100 kph) range outside the cities. The use of seatbelts is mandatory in most provinces, as are motorcycle helmets.

The price of gasoline varies more than the speed limit, but is generally more favorable than in the U.S. And Canada is much further along in adopting the metric system. Distances are shown in kilometers, and liquids, including gasoline, are sold in liters. (There are 3.78 liters in a U.S. gallon.) The price of gasoline ranges from 39 to 54 cents per liter. Ontario and Québec prices are the norm, dropping slightly in Manitoba, Saskatchewan, and British Columbia, but rising slightly in the Atlantic Provinces, the Yukon, and the Northwest Territories. The only "bargain" is Alberta, where the absence of a provincial tax lowers the cost considerably.

If you drive your own car into Canada from the United States, you should get a Canadian Non-Resident Inter-Province Motor Vehicle Insurance Liability Card, which is available from insurance companies in the States. (The card is not required if you intend to drive only in Ontario, Manitoba, Alberta, or British Columbia.) The best source for advice about automobile insurance is *The Insurance Bureau of Canada,* 181 University Ave., Toronto, Ontario M5H 3M7. Your driver's license, from whatever country, is valid throughout Canada.

Québec is the only province with toll roads (25 cents to 50 cents per gate on the Laurentian and Eastern Townships autoroutes).

In a number of places you will have to take a ferry to get where you are going by car, but ferry travel has become a popular form of transportation on both coasts and even on the Great Lakes.

Car rental. Although rental cars usually can be expensive, they do provide a measure of flexibility and independence, especially in urban areas. *Hertz, Avis,* and *Budget Rent-A-Car* all have outlets at major airports and rail terminals, and you can reserve your car before leaving home. Rates are comparable to those in the States.

More competitive rates are generally found in the following rental service: *Tilden Rent-A-Car,* 1485 Stanley St., Montréal, Québec H3A 1P6.

If you aren't too particular about the wheels you drive, check local listings in the city you're visiting for rental companies with names such as "Rent-A-Wreck" or "Rent-A-Dent." They offer healthy discounts on not-so-healthy cars.

If you want to drive from one major urban center to another but don't want to blow your budget on a car rental, try a "drive-away." Drive-away companies arrange for drivers to pick up a client's car at one point and deliver it to another (e.g., Vancouver to Toronto). To be a driver, you must be at least 21 years old and have a valid driver's license. In some cases, you may be required to leave a deposit, which is refundable upon delivery of the car. Frequently the drive-away company will help defray your gas expenses on the trip. Drive-away companies are listed in the Yellow Pages of the Toronto, Montréal, Winnipeg, Calgary, and Vancouver phone books. The major companies are: ACON, North American Auto Delivery, and Western Drive-Away Services.

BUS. Canada's two major carriers, *Voyageur* and *Greyhound,* offer several cost-cutting travel options. Greyhound's *Ameripass,* modeled after European rail passes, permits unlimited travel on any Greyhound line in North America. The passes are good for from seven to 30 days; the cost ranges from under $300 to nearly $500. If you're traveling in only one direction, say from Montréal to Vancouver, you can take advantage of Greyhound's *Cross-Canada Pass*, a 30-day, one-way rate of $99. For long-distance bus travel in Canada, another option is Voyageur's excursion discount plan. To qualify, you must leave any day except Friday and return within seven days. The regular $71.40 return rate between Toronto and Montréal, for example, drops to $55.45 if these conditions are met. A one-day excursion rate is also offered, providing you leave and return on the same day (Toronto-Montréal: $42 return). Write to other regional bus lines to inquire about similar savings: *Acadian Lines,* 6040 Almon St., Halifax, Nova Scotia B3K 5M1; *Gray Coach Lines,* 610 Bay St., Toronto, Ontario M5G 1M5; *Saskatchewan Transportation Company,* 2041 Hamilton St., Regina, Saskatchewan S4P 2E2; *Pacific Coach Lines,* 150 Dunsmuir St., Vancouver, B.C. V6B 1W9.

Urban transportation. Canada's two subway lines, in Montréal and Toronto, are modern, fast, and efficient. They are also, to the surprise and delight of American city dwellers, clean and safe. Fares range from 90 to 95 cents, as do those for buses and streetcars.

BOATS. Ferries, east and west, are more than a convenience; they are an essential means of transportation and a lifeline for many coastal communities.

In the Maritimes, ferries stitch together ports in Maine, Nova Scotia, New Brunswick, Prince Edward Island and Newfoundland. Passenger and vehicle ferry service is operated between Yarmouth, Nova Scotia, and Portland, Maine, by *CN Marine* and by *Prince of Fundy Cruises.* A one-way trip takes between 10 and 12 hours and costs about $45 each way (cars, about $70). Cabins, dining facilities, and entertainment are available on both ferries. Advance reservations must be made, especially during the summer. Contact Prince of Fundy Cruises, 468 Commercial Street, Portland, Maine 04101 (207) 775–5611. CN Marine may be booked through any CN office.

CN Marine also operates a service between Saint John, New Brunswick, and Digby, Nova Scotia (around $11.00; cars, $38.00); and between North Sydney, Nova Scotia, and the Newfoundland ports of Argentia (summer only) and Port-aux-Basques.

Passenger and vehicle service between Wood Islands, Prince Edward Island, and Caribou (near Pictou), Nova Scotia, is operated year-round by *Northumberland Ferries Limited.* The 14-mile crossing takes about an hour. CN's ferry between Cape Tourmentine, New Brunswick, and Borden, Prince Edward Island, costs only around $2.00 each way, $5.25 for automobiles.

British Columbia's most extensive ferry routes are between Vancouver Island and the mainland, especially Vancouver and Victoria. Service is normally cut back in winter. Detailed information on times and prices can be obtained within B.C. at most tourist information centers.

HITCHHIKING. This is, of course, the most inexpensive form of travel, though not very reliable. The law says that in most cases it is an offense to attempt to stop a car or truck to solicit a ride. However it does not specify that pointing your thumb in a certain direction constitutes soliciting. If you do hitchhike, make yourself seen without obstructing traffic. A clearly printed sign telling drivers your destination helps, as does a neat appearance.

CYCLING. This is almost as cheap as hitchhiking and you have a good chance of finding one for rent in many cities, resort areas, and college communities. Rail lines are experienced in handling bicycles; bus lines far less so. Established bike routes can be found in major cities. In the country, you're on your own. For information about bike trails throughout Canada, write the *Canadian Cycling Association,* Place Vanier Tower A, 333 River Rd., Ottawa, Ont. K1L 8H9.

LEAVING CANADA

CUSTOMS ON RETURNING HOME. If you plan to take along any foreign-made articles such as camera equipment, binoculars, expensive watches or jewelry, it is wise to put with your travel documents the purchase receipts or other evidence that the item was bought in your home country. Otherwise, on returning home, you may be charged duty. Customs always seems to take longer than anticipated, so arrive at the airport at least an hour before your flight is due to depart.

U.S. Customs. American citizens and other residents of the U.S. who visit Canada for at least 48 hours and who have claimed no exemption during the previous 31 days are entitled to bring in duty-free up to $400 (retail value) worth of foreign purchases. These items may be intended for personal use or as gifts for those back home, but *not* for resale. They all count, even if some are personal effects you have already worn.

All your purchases should accompany you across the border, and it is wise (and simpler when inspection time comes) to put everything, or as much as possible, into one bag or carryall. Also try to keep your purchase receipts together and handy, in the event you are asked to produce them.

Members of a family can pool their exemptions because each separate member, including all minors, is entitled to the $400 exemption.

Your $400 exemption includes the cost of one liter of wine or liquor per person over 21 years of age, but technically not if your papers (or passport) show you are from a "dry" part of the country.

You may take home 200 cigarettes and 100 cigars duty-free, but not if they're from Cuba.

Small gifts under $50 in value may be mailed home to friends duty-free, but not more than one package to any one address. Such packages cannot contain perfumes, tobacco, or liquor. Further information will be provided by the nearest U.S. Customs office or the U.S. Customs Service, Washington, DC 20229.

All U.S. residents who have spent less than 48 hours in Canada can bring into the U.S. duty-free merchandise worth a total of $25, including any of the following: 10 cigars, 8 ounces of tobacco, 4 ounces of alcoholic beverage, 4 ounces of perfume.

Great Britain. The following items which must be in accompanying baggage, are allowed to be brought in the country duty-free: Liquor or spirits: 1 liter; wine: 2 liters; cigarettes: 1 carton. Perfume and toilet waters: 50 grams. Cigarette lighters: 1 only; other articles not mentioned above to a value of $56.

Before departure, British citizens can obtain detailed customs information from their nearest office of the Customs and Excise, or can write: Secretary, HM Customs and Excise, King's Beam House, Mark Lane, London EC 3.

Australia. Each person 18 years of age or older is allowed duty-free admission of 200 cigarettes (1 carton), or 250 grams of cigars or other tobacco, and 1 liter of alcoholic beverages, including wine and beer. Travelers may bring back duty-free goods up to a value of $200 (Aus.), plus additional goods up to a value of $160 (Aus.) at a duty rate of 20 percent. Travelers under 18, if with a parent, may bring in goods to a value of $100 (Aus.) free of duty, with additional goods assessed at a rate of 20 percent.

Australian citizens wishing more detailed Customs information may query the office of The Comptroller-General, Department of Customs and Excise, Canberra, A.C.T., or the Collector of Customs office in any of the major cities.

DUTY-FREE is not what it once was. You may not be paying tax on that bottle of Canadian whisky, but you are certainly contributing to someone's profits. Duty-free shops are big business these days, especially in major Canadian airports, and markups are often around 100 percent. So don't be seduced by the idea that because it's duty-free it's a bargain. Very often prices are not much different from your local discount store and in the case of perfume and jewelry they can be even higher.

Ontario

For the traveler the best things in Ontario are free, or at least affordable: almost 70,000 square miles of freshwater rivers and lakes, practically half a million square miles of northern pine forests and rolling southern farmland, and sights and sounds in towns and cities as varied as nickel-rich Sudbury, genteel Scottish Kingston, rural Blyth, and cosmopolitan Toronto.

Ontario has dominated Canada since Confederation in 1867. It's synonymous with money and power (and arrogance, some would argue), and despite recent competition from oil-wealthy Alberta, it's likely to remain the political, cultural, and financial capital of the country.

The province's 8.6 million people make up a third of Canada's population and are as varied as the scenery. As Ontario is to Canada, so Toronto—the most populous city, and the province's capital—is to Ontario. Rich, powerful, diverse, Toronto is home to 2.1 million Italians, Chinese, Scots, Estonians, Hungarians, and native Canadians. In each of Toronto's neighborhoods the wide selection of ethnic restaurants and shops offers excellent value to the budget traveler, and almost no neighborhood is unsafe for accommodation.

EXPLORING TORONTO

Toronto boasts one of the world's safest, cleanest, and most efficient transit systems. But you can begin exploring the city with a walking tour guaranteed to leave you more pleased than tired. Start at the center of town in Nathan Phillips Square. Named after the mayor who backed the building of the new City Hall, the 9-acre site is active year-round. In summer it's filled with ethnic festivals, arts and crafts shows, and concerts. In winter, the reflecting pool becomes a popular skating rink, and crowds jam the area to welcome in the New Year. At any time you might find yourself in the middle of some organized march or political demonstration.

In front of you is the City Hall, which former mayor John Sewell used to call affectionately the "great gray clam." Completed in 1965 by Finnish architect, Viljo Revell, the structure is one of the boldest pieces of architecture in the city. City Hall offers conducted tours every day of the week. There is an information counter in the

TORONTO

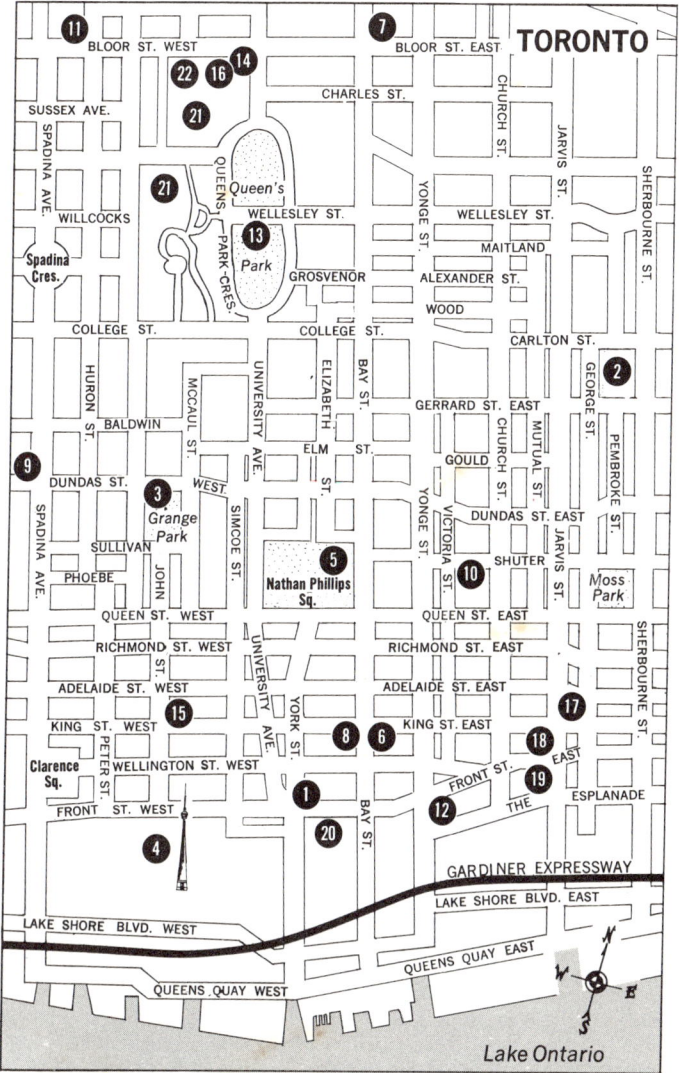

Toronto—Points of Interest

1) Air Terminal
2) Allan Gardens
3) Art Gallery
4) C.N. Tower
5) City Hall
6) Commerce Court
7) Cumberland Terrace
8) Toronto Dominion Centre
9) Kensington Market
10) Mackenzie House
11) Medical Arts Building
12) O'Keefe Centre
13) Parliament Buildings
14) Planetarium
15) Royal Alexandra Theatre
16) Royal Ontario Museum
17) St. James Cathedral
18) St. Lawrence Centre for the Arts
19) St. Lawrence Market
20) Union Station
21) University of Toronto
22) Varsity Stadium

front lobby. The bronze sculpture you see by the main entrance is Henry Moore's "Archer." Since it was unveiled in 1965, Toronto has developed a self-confident chic that's a far cry from the dull, Victorian, "Toronto the good" character it was known for before.

To your east looms the Old City Hall, itself a symbol of pre-1965 Toronto. This 1899 pile of Victorian Gothic stones, complete with clocktowers and gargoyles (said to be the architect's revenge on early city fathers), now houses traffic courts.

On the west side of the Square is the elegantly restored Osgoode Hall, since 1832 the headquarters of the Law Society of Upper Canada. On your way in you might have had some difficulty passing through the cowcatcher gates in the wrought-iron fence. White Corinthian columns and broad double stairs grace the main lobby, while the second-floor library boasts 40-foot vaulted ceilings and acres of leatherbound volumes.

At the northwest corner of City Hall Square, behind Osgoode Hall, a passageway leads past the New Courthouse and fountains to University Avenue, the city's broadest street. Here you will find the American Consulate, the birthplace of silent screen star Mary Pickford (555 University Ave.), and the Royal Canadian Military Institute—a private officers' club with an excellent collection of military paraphernalia.

Chinatown

Allow yourself to be lured by the pungent odors of Chinese cooking and turn either right or left from University Ave. along Dundas St. To your east lie restaurants; west there are more, plus the Art Gallery of Ontario. Its back entrance, overlooking a small leafy park, is called the Grange. Built in 1817, the Grange is a Georgian manor home, once belonging to members of Upper Canada's ruling Family Compact. Later it housed Toronto's first public art gallery.

Keep heading west on Dundas past the restaurants and shops of Chinatown to Spadina Ave., a veritable United Nations of ethnic diversity. One notable site is Switzer's Delicatessen (322 Spadina Ave.). As you work your way through the best corned beef sandwich in the city, reflect on the fact that "Red Emma" Goldman, the internationally famous anarchist and feminist, died in an upstairs bedroom. Between Dundas and College St., a block west, is Kensington Market. Originally Jewish, the market is now a medley of cultures—Portuguese, West Indian, Chinese, and Italian. Its stands, stalls and shops offer everything from fruit and vegetables, hundreds of local and imported cheeses and homemade halvah, to pots and pans, workboots, secondhand clothes, and Portuguese and West Indian records.

At Spadina and College are late-night jazz and blues clubs. To the north, looming above the Spadina—St. George circle, is a Gothic building that looks like it's from the set of Dracula. Constructed in 1875 as Knox College, the building later became Connaught Laboratories. Within its sinister-looking walls such benign work has taken place as the manufacture of the world's first penicillin and polio vaccine.

East along College, past Spadina, lies the University of Toronto. On the north corner of College and St. George is the former Central Public Library; across the street at 33 St. George St. is the Mac-Donald Mowat House, now the International Student Center. The house was once home to Canada's first prime minister, Sir John A. MacDonald, and later to Sir Oliver Mowat, premier of Ontario at the end of the 19th century.

East of St. George and north of College is the main campus of the 155-year-old University of Toronto. The leafy quadrangle of University College was begun in 1859. The small domed tower of the old Observatory building (now headquarters of the Students' Administrative Council) stands in front of Hart House, a Gothic-style student center built between 1911 and 1919 by the Masseys, one of Toronto's prominent families. Hart House features a paneled, Oxford-style Great Hall, a theater, gymnasium and the Arbor Room, an inexpensive cafeteria, where you can pause to refresh yourself before continuing your walking tour of the city.

Yorkville

The corners of Avenue Rd. and Bloor St. mark the edge of Toronto's most stylish shopping and coffeehouse district, Yorkville. An independent village until 1883, Yorkville was Toronto's bohemia in the 1950's and '60's with clubs featuring such then-unknown folksingers as Gordon Lightfoot, Joni Mitchell, and Neil Young. Some of Yorkville's architecture is new (Hazelton Lanes, Cumberland Terrace, York Square). Older buildings have been sandblasted or painted. Keeping in mind the budget traveler's credo that dreams are free, a walk through Yorkville's *very* expensive galleries and shops can pass a pleasant hour.

A side-trip: thirty minutes' walk northwest of Yorkville is Casa Loma, Toronto's own "Xanadu." It's testimony to the opulent bad taste of Sir Henry Pellat, a millionaire who spent upwards of 3 million dollars between 1911 and 1914 to equip his castle with gold-plated bathroom fixtures, an 800-foot-long underground passageway to the stables and a private elevator.

A fifteen-minute walk southwest of Casa Loma takes you to Markham Village, another area of boutiques, bookstores, and art galleries one block west of Bathurst and Bloor. At the corner of Markham is Honest Ed's, a budget store gone wild: bargains on everything from Band-Aids to salami.

Yonge Street

The first thing to note about Yonge St. is that much of it has seen better times. It might be stretching it to say that it's "the longest street in the world," but it does extend from Lake Ontario 207 miles to North Bay (as Hwy. 11) and then (by other names) a further 1,000 miles north and west. It was first laid out by Lieutenant-Governor

John Graves Simcoe about 200 years ago. The construction in 1978 of a massive, glassed-in shopping arcade, the Eaton Center, helped bring back some of the street's former class.

Maple Leaf Gardens, at Yonge and Carlton (College), is the home of the Toronto Maple Leaf hockey club. It also features wrestling, rock concerts, circuses, and the Bolshoi Ballet. South of College, Yonge St. turns into a strip of bargain book and record stores and raunchy movie houses. Two of the city's major department stores, Simpsons and Eaton's, are at the intersection of Yonge and Queen. On the northwest side is Eaton Center, housing the Metropolitan Toronto Convention and Tourist Bureau and Travel Ontario. Behind the Center and tucked away from the noisy commercial traffic is the tiny, pretty Church of the Holy Trinity, built in 1847 when a parishioner and benefactress willed the land to the Anglican Church in perpetuity. The Church hosts cheap weekday lunches, lectures, and concerts. East across Yonge St. along Dundas a block or two (at Bond St.) is Mackenzie House. Here the leader of Upper Canada's only rebellion (1837) died in 1861. The house has been restored to its 1850's finery and includes the flatbed printing press which Mackenzie's ghost is said to haunt.

Two of Toronto's major theater complexes are east of Yonge on Front St.: the O'Keefe and the St. Lawrence Center. From here looking west, you see lovely old Union Station, and beyond it, soaring 1,815 feet, the world's tallest free-standing structure, the CN Tower. From the tower's 1,100-foot-high observation pad and costly, revolving restaurant, you'll be rewarded with close to a 75-mile view on a clear day.

East of Yonge on Front St. is the 170-year-old St. Lawrence Farmers' Market, open Tuesday through Saturday and easily worth a visit, especially on a Saturday morning. Attached to the Market is another of Toronto's early city halls, the St. Lawrence Hall, built in 1844 and recently restored.

Less well known, and off the beaten tourist track are Toronto's neighborhoods: Rosedale, with its grand turn-of-the-century mansions; the Beaches, south of Queen St. and east of the Greenwood Racetrack, with its cafés and lakeside boardwalk; Little Italy stretching west of Bathurst St. (best shopping and restaurants are on College St. around Clinton, and St. Clair around Dufferin); Bloor West Village, a neighborhood of delis and cafés settled by Eastern Europeans, and the Danforth (from Broadview to Greenwood) whose restaurants, shops, and cafés are Greek.

PRACTICAL INFORMATION FOR TORONTO

Transportation

Virtually all major international airlines land at Toronto International Airport, 15 miles from the city's center. *Air Canada* and *Canadian Pacific* link Toronto to provincial and intraprovincial centers.

The cheapest way to get into the city from the airport is to take a *Gray Coach* **bus** to one of three points on the Toronto subway system: Islington station on the east-west Bloor line, $3.00 one way; Yorkdale station at the Yorkdale Shopping Center on the Spadina line, $3.25 one way; and York Mills station on the Yonge line; $4.00 one way. Buy your ticket before boarding the bus.

Slightly more expensive are the **airport buses** that will take you downtown to several major hotels for $6.50. **Cabs** and **limousines** will cost you anywhere from ten to twenty-five dollars, depending on your destination. But if you split the fare with other passengers, your ride might not turn out to be too costly after all.

BUS, SUBWAY, STREETCAR (THE TTC). The Toronto Transit Commission is public transit at its finest, and you can safely go anywhere you want. The subway runs across the city east and west and north and south (2 routes). Get a free transfer to connect you to the extensive system of buses and streetcars at each station so you won't have to pay again.

If you plan to use the TTC a lot, consider buying a Metropass. For about $40.00 you can travel as much as you want in a one-month period on all regular TTC routes. Single adult fares are 95 cents. You can buy eight tokens for $5.90 and 20 for $14.75. Exact change is needed for buses and street cars. Rates for children and Sunday/holiday passes are also available.

The subway runs from 6:00 A.M. to 1:30 A.M., but begins at 9:00 A.M. on Sunday. Buses and streetcars vary. Some run 24 hours a day. For specific information, call the TTC at 416–484–4544.

TAXIS. Taxis are plentiful but definitely not cheap, unless you're sharing. It will cost you $1.20 to step into a cab; then you'll pay $1.00 per kilometer. The biggest city-wide cabs are *Metro* (416–363–5611), *Diamond* (416–366–6868), *Co-op* (416–364–8161), and *Yellow* (416–363–4141).

CARS. If you're driving your own or a rented car in Toronto, you should be aware of some regulations. First, it's mandatory in Ontario that the driver and passengers wear seatbelts, or risk a $28

TORONTO SUBWAY NETWORK

Airport Bus Departure Point

YONGE ST.

MC COWAN
SCARBOROUGH CENTRE
MIDLAND
ELLESMERE
LAWRENCE EAST
KENNEDY
WARDEN
VICTORIA PK.
MAIN ST.
WOODBINE
COXWELL
GREENWOOD
DONLANDS
PAPE
CHESTER
BROADVIEW
SHERBOURNE
BLOOR-YONGE

DANFORTH AVE.

WELLESLEY
COLLEGE
DUNDAS
QUEEN
KING

FINCH
SHEPPARD
YORK MILLS
LAWRENCE
EGLINTON
DAVISVILLE
ST. CLAIR
SUMMERHILL
ROSEDALE

BAY
ST. GEORGE
SPADINA

UNIVERSITY AVE.

MUSEUM
QUEEN'S PK.
ST. PATRICK
OSGOODE
ST. ANDREW
UNION

BATHURST
DUPONT
ST. CLAIR WEST
EGLINTON WEST
GLENCAIRN
LAWRENCE WEST
YORKDALE — Airport Bus
WILSON   Departure Point

CHRISTIE
OSSINGTON
DUFFERIN
LANSDOWNE
DUNDAS WEST
KEELE
HIGH PARK
RUNNYMEDE
JANE
OLD MILL
ROYAL YORK
ISLINGTON
KIPLING

BLOOR ST.

Airport Express Bus departs from here

fine. Next, don't forget that in Toronto you must stop at all cross-walks marked *X* whenever a pedestrian is pointing his/her way across. Finally, be sure to stop behind the rear door of any streetcar that is letting out passengers.

Parking downtown is expensive, and you're better off leaving your car and taking public transit. If you do park, use a city-owned lot whenever possible (look for signs marked with a big green *P*), because the commercial ones are more costly. Outside the down-town area you should have no difficulty finding on-street metered and unmetered parking spots.

BICYCLES. Bicycles are an increasingly popular form of transpor-tation in Toronto: the city maintains designated routes. Bicycles can be rented at a number of locations, including *Brown's Sport and Cycle Ltd.,* 2447 Bloor St. W. (416–763–4176), and *Boardwalk Cycle,* 2210 Queen St. E. (416–690–0802).

FOR MORE INFORMATION

Your best bet for any information about Toronto is the *Metropoli-tan Toronto Convention and Visitors' Association* in the Eaton Cen-ter, 220 Yonge St., Suite 110, Toronto M5B 2H1 (416–979–3143).

Accommodations

You don't have to spend much to stay in clean, quiet, and central-ly located accommodations in Toronto. Prices are based on double occupancy as follows: *Inexpensive:* beginning at less than $55.00, and *Moderate:* $55.00 and $85.00. Reservations can be made through Accommodation Toronto (416–596–7117) or by phoning hotels directly.

Inexpensive

Anything you can get for $50.00 or less in Toronto is inexpensive. Tourist homes, private bed and breakfasts, Y's and hostels, motels and some hotels fall into this category. When making your selection it's important to consider location because, even if you have your own transportation, it's nice to be able to take advantage of public transit. Two numbers to note are the *Toronto Bed and Breakfast Association* (416–233–3887) and *Metro Bed and Breakfast* (416–964–2566) for full information on bed and breakfast establish-ments. Although not in the downtown core, the **Candy Haven Tourist House,** 1233 King St. W. (416–532–0651), is on the street-car line in the west end of the city. It's $25.00 a night and close to inexpensive restaurants, shops, and Lake Ontario. **The Karaba-now Guest House,** 9–11 Spadina Rd. (416–923–4004), is central-ly located near the university and within walking distance of Bloor St. shopping. It's an older Victorian building with a variety of nicely redecorated rooms; single rooms are priced from $30.00 a night, while a double room with shared bathroom costs $35.00. There are discounts in winter. The subway is literally outside your door. **The**

Linges, 46 Bellbury Cresc., in Willowdale at Highway 401 and Leslie Streets (416–493–0479) is a three-room bed and breakfast handy to the Ontario Science Centre and the lovely Edwards Gardens. Open all year. In the west end, near High Park, you'll find the **McKinnon Tourist Home,** 229 Grenadier Rd. (416–535–4956). A double room in this lovely old home will cost you $20.00 a night. Most of the 35 rooms in **The Whitehouse Hotel,** 76 Church St. (416–362–7491), have kitchenettes. Near the O'Keefe Center and the St. Lawrence Market, a variety of antique shops and offbeat eateries, The Whitehouse charges $50.00 to $75.00 **Journey's End–North York,** 66 Norfinch Dr., Downsview (416–736–4700), off Hwy. 400, is inexpensive and well maintained. It's excellent for families and only a few minutes from Canada's Wonderland, an amusement park. **Metro Inn,** 2121 Kingston Rd., Scarborough (416–267–1141), is remote but clean and affordable. The same applies to the **New Plaza Motel,** 4584 Kingston Rd. (416–284–9966). The **St. Leonard Hotel,** 418 Sherbourne St. (416–924–4902), is small (22 rooms) but well-maintained, near Allan Gardens and within easy access of the downtown core. A room with private bath will cost between $30.00 and $35.00 a night. No TVs, phones, restaurants, or air conditioning; free parking, though.

HOSTELS. Toronto Hostel, 223 Church St. Charges $9.00 for each non-member, $13.00 for members (416–368–1848).

Y'S AND RESIDENCES. YWCA's residence is at 80 Woodlawn Avenue E. (416–923–8454), 114 rooms. Single $27.00, double $24.00 each. That includes tax and a continental breakfast. Women only. **Tartu College,** 310 Bloor St. W. (416–925–9405 between 10:00 A.M. and 5:00 P.M.), is coed at $110.00 plus tax per person per week, $200.00 monthly, summer only. No daily occupancy.

SCHOOLS AND UNIVERSITIES. Campus Co-Op Residences (co-ed), 395 Huron St. (416–979–2161) are smack in the U. of T. campus area. The only catch here is that a one-month minimum stay is required, but it's excellent value. You can share kitchen and washroom facilities in well-kept older houses, with everyone pitching in with the upkeep. Cost: $40.00–$60.00 per week. May–August occupancy only. **Neil Wycik College Hotel,** 96 Gerrard St. E. (416–977–2320), offers 240 rooms from May to August, about $25.00 to $40.00. Right downtown and near practically everything, including the Eaton Centre and Maple Leaf Gardens, guests have the use of common kitchens, roof deck, and sauna. There are several **University of Toronto** colleges offering rooms from mid-May to mid-August. The average double-occupancy rate is under $22.00 a night, with student and weekly rates also available. Rates go down after the first week. Try any of the following: **Devonshire House** (416–978–2515), **Knox College** (416–978–4502, singles only), **New College** (416–978–8735), **Whitney Hall** (416–978–2532),

University College (416–978–8735), **Victoria College** (416–978 –3848), **Trinity College** (416–978–2523).

Moderate

Most hotel accommodations in Toronto fall into the *Inexpensive* or *Expensive* category. A few fall in between, like **The Brownstone,** 15 Charles St. E. (416–924–7381). About $60.00 to $70.00. You could not be closer to Yorkville and the center of town and still get a good night's sleep. The **Carlton Inn,** 30 Carlton St. (416–977 –6655), may not be the quietest hotel in the city, particularly when there's a hockey game next door at Maple Leaf Gardens. However, it features over 500 rooms with full amenities, an indoor pool, sauna, restaurants, and underground parking. Around $60.00 to $70.00. The **Executive Motor Hotel** is a little out-of-the-way at 621 King St. W. (tel. 416–362–7441). There are 72 clean rooms with TV; some rooms have water beds. Around $50.00 to $60.00, plus tax. **The Martyniuk Bed and Breakfast,** 56 Bellevue Ave. (416–365–0428), is located in the Kensington Market Area, a great place to shop and meander. Around $35.00 to $45.00, breakfast included.

Restaurants

Fifteen years ago visitors to Toronto complained that the city's eating establishments were strictly from hunger. Today, there are more restaurants per capita in Toronto than in any other Canadian city—more listings in its phone directory than Manhattan. The budget traveler can eat well and cheaply in Toronto. The following samples will give you an idea of where you can start. All prices are for full-course meals for two, exclusive of drinks, tips, and tax. Certain restaurants, as indicated, are not licensed to sell liquor. Price ranges are as follows: *Inexpensive:* less than $25; *Moderate:* $25.00–$45.00.

Inexpensive

You haven't visited Toronto until you've visited **The Bagel,** 285 College St. (416–923–0171), a city landmark. The Bagel serves Jewish dishes, everything from blintzes to the kind of boiled chicken Grandmother used to make. Unlicensed. Sit outside on a warm summer evening and enjoy a hugh spinach salad or a plate of mussels at the **Boulevard Café,** 161 Harbord St. (416–961–7676). The rice pudding is a good bet for dessert. Some South American dishes. **Bistro Europe,** 2390 Bloor West (416–769–0848), is a popular spot on the Bloor West Village shopping strip with pierogis, borscht, goulash and sandwiches. The **Continental,** 521 Bloor St. W., between Spadina and Bathurst (416–531–5872), is a mid-European diner frequented by university students. Unlicensed. If you're downtown you'll find imaginatively prepared tofu and soy dinners with sauces, salads, and desserts—making a virtue a pleasure—at **The Vegetarian,** 542 Yonge St. (416–961–9522) and 2849 Dundas West (416–762–1204). Recommended for 24-hour, inexpensive no-nonsense food is **Fran's,** 20 College St. (416–923–9867), and 21 St. Clair Ave. W. (416–925–6336). The **Ho Yuen** Restaurant, 135 Dundas W. (416–977–3448), is a dank and cramped basement that seats about 20 people and serves the best lobster in the city. Not to be confused with the other, more respectable **Ho Yuen** at 105 Elizabeth St. (416–977–3449), which is almost as good. Unlicensed. **Jake's,** 406 Dupont (416–961–8341), is a small restaurant featuring salads, hamburgers, tofu, and some other vegetarian dishes. A real bargain for lunch and supper on the U. of Toronto campus is the **Great Hall** at **Hart House** (416–978–2444). You can have a great meal that includes roast or stew for about $5.00. Vegetarian dishes available. The **Korona Restaurant,** 493 Bloor St. W. (416–961–1824), is another student hangout. Sausage, schnitzel, and goulash are house specialties. Unlicensed. The **Mars Restaurant,** 432 College St. (416–921–6332), is perhaps the best greasy spoon in town. Patrons who drive Cadillacs line up on Sunday morning for its huge bran muffins. The rice pudding competes well with the Boulevard's. Unlicensed. Budget French cooking at no-frills prices is available at the **Mount Pleasant Lunch,** 604 Mount Pleasant Rd. (416–481–9331). **The Old Fish Market,** 12 Market St. (416–363–0334), offers fresh fish daily, plus chowders and shrimp cocktails. Licensed. Attractive, and a bargain. There's a shellfish bar upstairs called **Coasters** (416–862–7129). **The Old Sod Restaurant and Tavern,** 2936 Bloor St. W., near Royal York Rd. (416–239–3812), is worth a trip to the west end for the Irish-Newfie pub atmosphere. Terrific stews and French fries. Try the soup of the day any day. **The Old Spaghetti Factory,** 54 The Esplanade (416–864–9761), is great for kids, especially inside the restaurant's streetcar dining area. Spaghetti and a variety of other pasta dishes aren't as good as those in Little Italy (College and St. Clair Sts.). **By The Way,** 400 Bloor West (416–967–4295) is tiny and the tables are usually taken up by students. But the felaffels and frozen yogurt are excellent. **The Parrot,** 325 Queen St. W. (416–593–0899), features excellent mushroom soup, and imaginative nouvelle cuisine entrees, such as chicken grilled with raspberry vinegar. What you save on calories here, you lose on such desserts as chocolate cheesecake and pecan pie. One of the best bargains in Toronto. At **Le Papillon,** 106 Front St. E. (416–363–0838), there are almost as many kinds of crêpes as flavors of Baskin-Robbins ice cream. **Le Petit Gourmet,** 1064 Yonge St. (416–966–3811), is small and always crowded. There's a garden outside with picnic tables. Choose quiches, salads, pâté, and pastries at the counter. Unlicensed. **Pearl's Roti Shop,** 868 College St. (416–532–9849) sells Caribbean sandwiches known as roti, which are pancakes stuffed with goat, curried chicken and lamb. Drinks include peanut punch. **Sher E Punjab Restaurant,** on Danforth across from the Chester subway stop, (416–465–2125), has formica tables, a close, steamy atmosphere, a wine and beer license, and a faithful clientele who claim the curries here are *pukka* (authentic). The king of the downtown delis is **Switzer's Delicatessen,** 322 Spadina Ave. (416–596–6900), with corned beef sandwiches in a class of their own. Kensington Market is around the corner. Like the Continental and Korona, **The Tarogato,** 553 Bloor St. W. (416–536–7566), is a popular student and artists' hangout. Schnitzel, cabbage rolls, and goulash are the best bets. **The Peking,** 251 College (416–979–2422). Decor includes photos of Mary Tyler Moore in the window—she shot a movie here—with murals as a backdrop. The Szechuan cooking is splendid and cheap. Licensed. **The United Bakers Dairy Restaurant,** 338 Spadina Ave. (416–593–0697), could be considered the dairy counterpart to Switzer's Deli. Scrambled eggs with onions and lox are salty but excellent. The giant poppy-seed cookies available at the counter will last your whole walking tour of Kensington Market. Unlicensed. **Young Lok Restaurant,** 122 St. Patrick St. (416–593–9819), is usually crowded and noisy, but always good. The informal atmosphere has you rubbing shoulders with bearded university professors and young Forest Hill lawyers.

Moderate

Arirang House, 716 Bloor St. W. (416–532–2727), offers pungent Korean food. BBQ beef and noodle dishes are specialties. Too bad the servings are getting smaller. **The Benes Inn Tavern,** 392 Eglinton Ave. W. (416–481–1853), offers dependable Hungarian cooking. The pastries are a Benes trademark. **The Market Grill,** 15 Market St. (416–366–7743). Fresh produce from the farmer's market upstairs, and simple Ontario cooking: roast pork with apple and mustard sauce, roast beef, fruit pies. Licensed. At the **Byzantium Restaurant,** 401 Danforth Ave. (416–466–2845), the cook will explain what each of the Greek dishes you see in the kitchen is; a waiter will bring your choices to the table. Large portions might include roast lamb, eggplant, spinach, and potatoes. **Bumpkin's,** 21 Gloucester (416–922–8655). French food for the thrifty is well prepared, and that means lines. **Capriccio Dining Room,** 580 College St. (416–535–2229), is more French than Italian now, but has a lovely, romantic environment, and the cooking is as delicate, savory, and rich as it always was. **Carlevale's Café** 158 Avenue Rd. (416–922–4787), is trendy with rather uncomfortable seats, but the menu includes artichoke salads, hot Italian sausage, fresh pasta. **The Cleopatra,** corner Bloor and Concord, just west of the Ossington subway (416–534–0702), has music and belly-dancing nightly, as well as the best Middle Eastern food for the money in the city. Spend the entire evening. **Ed's Warehouse Restaurant,** 270 King St. W. (416–593–6676), is an outrageously gaudy warehouse-sized eatery. Roast beef, the house specialty, is excellent. Frozen veg accompaniments are not. **Emilio's,** 127 Queen St. East (416–366–3345). The menu changes weekly but always includes fresh salads and huge sandwiches. Soviet poet Yevgeny Yevtushenko ate here. Licensed. At **La Folie,** 349 Queen St. W. (416–593–8812), there is a prix fixe menu, but two can still dine for around $30.00. Renovation chic means the atmosphere can be somewhat cool. **Le Select Bistro,** 328 Queen St. W. (416–596–6405), is another French eatery. The music and atmosphere are even better than the food—which is very good, from crudités to tarte aux prunes. **The Jerusalem,** 955 Eglinton Ave. W. (416–783–6494), offers a straightforward décor, but great Middle Eastern food—babaghanouj, hummous, grilled lamb—at moderate prices. **Michi,** 459 Church St. (416–924–1303), offers good Japanese food at reasonable prices. The sushi (raw fish) will leave you wanting more. **The Newfoundlander,** 185 Danforth Ave. (416–469–1916), boasts authentic Canadian screech (overproof rum), plates of cod 'n' potatoes, and music. **The Noshery,** 488 Eglinton Ave. W. (416–481–7281), presents multiculturalism at its noisiest. Here you can order Chinese, Jewish, Mexican, and, of course, North American food. Always popular with large families. Good Greek food at reasonable prices is available at **The Odyssey,** 477 Danforth Ave. (416–465–2451). One of the first renovated restaurants on the Queen West strip, **The Peter Pan,** 373 Queen St. W. (416–593–0917), is a fifties-style diner that's been pleasantly upgraded. Quiches, salads, and burgers. **The Pink Pearl,** 142 Dundas St. W. (416–977–3388), offers Cantonese food at its very best in a somewhat lavish environment. Lunchtime dim sum (meat and fish dumplings) is recommended. **Porretta's Pizza,** 97 Harbord St. (416–920–2186). Easily the best pizza in the city: thick, cheesy, with a delicate crust. Take out or eat among the ferns. Licensed. **The Rajput Dining Room,** 376 Bloor St. W., near Spadina (416–921–3679), features a dark interior, Eastern music, and a wide selection of Indian and Pakistani entrées from gentle Kashmiri chicken to hot Madras curry. If you want a heavy Polish meal, then the **Sir Nicholas Restaurant and Tavern,** 91 Roncesvalles (416–535–4540), is the place. The live dance ensemble and ostentatious décor are more likely to charm than to disturb you. Try roast duck with kasha, Polish liqueurs. At **Three Small Rooms,** 22 St. Thomas St. (416–979–2212), stay away from the largest of the rooms, **The Restaurant.** It's the city's best and one of its most expensive restaurants. But at two out of three, namely **The Grill** or **The Wine Bar,** you can have a splendid dinner for two and a glass of house wine for around $35.00. **The Treasure,** 150 Dundas St. W. (416–977–3778), offers great dim sum. Not as fancy as The Pink Pearl.

What to See and Do

Note: Call in advance to double check hours.

PUBLIC MUSEUMS AND GALLERIES

The **Art Gallery of Ontario,** 317 Dundas St. (416–977–0414), houses the world's largest public collection of Henry Moore sculpture. A major expansion program in 1974 also made possible the exhibition of the important Zacks Collection of 20th-century art. Altogether the AGO has more than 7,000 paintings, prints, drawings, and sculpture. Closed Monday. Admission: adults $3.50, students 12 and over, and seniors $1.50. Free on Thursdays 5:30–9:00 P.M. Behind the Gallery in the Grange Park is **The Grange,** an early

19th-century gentleman's home now fully restored in the style of the 1830's. Open Tuesday–Sunday 12:00 noon–4:00 P.M. as well as Thursday 6:00 P.M.–9:00 P.M. Admission included with Art Gallery admission. The **Canadian Museum of Carpets and Textiles,** 585 Bloor St. W. (Saturday and Sunday 12:00 noon–6:00 P.M.), is a gorgeous, scholarly, privately run collection of saris, Oriental carpets, batik—organized by enthusiasts. Located over Ed's Ice Cream Parlour, has no phone. Hockey fans might want to visit the **Hockey Hall of Fame** (416–595–1345) on the grounds of the Canadian National Exhibition to see such memorabilia as the Stanley Cup and other famous mementoes of hockey history. Admission: adults $2.00, students, children, and senior citizens $1.00. Also on the grounds of the Canadian National Exhibition is the **Marine Museum of Upper Canada** (416–595–1567), housed in officers' quarters dating from 1841. The exhibits include everything from an old Eskimo kayak to a tug in dry berth. Open daily. Admission: adults $1.50, children and seniors $1.00. The **McLaughlin Planetarium,** 100 Queen's Park (416–978–8550), next to the Royal Ontario Museum, offers a variety of stunning sound and light shows at selected times from Tuesday to Sunday. Admission: adults $2.75, children $1.75 (seniors free on Tuesdays). Call (416–598–1866) for times of special, higher priced shows. For a more sedate few hours, visit the **McMichael Canadian Collection** (416–893–1121) just outside Toronto and see a magnificently displayed selection of Canadian landscape painting and native art. Open daily 11:00 A.M.–5:00 P.M. Closed Mondays in winter. Adults $2.50; students $1.50; seniors $1.50, free Wednesday. The strikingly modern **Ontario Science Centre** at Don Mills Rd. and Eglinton (416–429–4100) houses over 500 fascinating exhibits that are great fun for adults and kids. Open daily 10–6. Admission: adults $3.00, youths $2.00, children 12 and under $1.00, seniors with I.D. free. The **Royal Ontario Museum** at Avenue Rd. and Bloor (416–978–3692) has one of the finest Chinese collections in the world, an Egyptian collection that includes mummies, galleries of European furnishings and musical instruments, and a gallery of Museology—a fascinating new display on the science of digging up, reconstructing and displaying objects from the past which makes it all seem like detective work. Open 10:00 A.M.–8:00 P.M. daily except Sunday, 10:00 A.M.–6:00 P.M. Adults $2.50, children, students, seniors $1.25, free on Tuesdays. Down the street is the **Sigmund Samuel Canadiana Gallery,** 14 Queen's Park Crescent (416–978–3711), featuring early Canadian furniture and antiques. Open daily. Admission is free.

PRIVATE GALLERIES

There are numerous private art galleries in Toronto, from the conventional to the avant-garde. Since most are closed Sundays and Mondays, you should call them before going. The **Albert White Gallery,** 25 Prince Arthur Ave. in the Yorkville area (416–923–8804), sells works by Henry Moore and other Europeans as well as some Canadian artists. **Aggregation Gallery,** 80 Spadina Ave. (416–364–8716), features the work of younger and lesser-known Canadian artists, while the **Carmen Lamanna Gallery,** 840 Yonge St. (416–922–0410), promotes experimental and conceptual art. **Gallery Moos,** 136 Yorkville Ave. (416–922–0627), is one of the older galleries in the city, exhibiting the works of established Canadians such as magic realist Ken Danby; prints at the back. For almost three decades Av Isaacs has promoted the works of such internationally acclaimed Canadians as Dennis Burton, Robert Markle, Graham Coughtry, and Joyce Wieland. **Glendon Gallery,** 2275 Bayview Ave. (416–487–6206). Concerts, art displays. Affiliated with York University. **Hart House Gallery,** 7 Hart House Circle (416–978–2453). Admission free; it's affiliated with the University of Toronto. Modern Canadian paintings are carried at the **Grunwald Gallery** 80 Spadina Ave. (416–365–3103). Visit the **Mira Godard Gallery,** 22 Hazelton Ave. (416–964–8197), for a selection of works by artists such as Andy Warhol, Alex Katz, Ben Nicolson. The **Sable Castelli Gallery** at 33 Hazelton (416–961–0011) carries such modern international masters as Warhol and Rauschenburg. The **Nancy Poole Studio** at 16 Hazelton Ave. (416–964–9050), shows Canadian works by the likes of magic realist John Boyle and Tony Urquhart.

SOME PRINCIPAL SITES AND ATTRACTIONS

Black Creek Pioneer Village, 5 Shoreham Dr., Jane and Steeles (416–661–6600), in the city's northwest corner is a restored mid-19th-century rural Ontario village. Livestock, craft exhibitions, and more than 30 buildings help create an authentic atmosphere. Admission: adults $4.00, senior citizens $2.00, students $1.75, and family rate $9.00. Free parking. Buildings are closed January and February. Just 32 km north of Toronto at Highway 400 and Major McKenzie Dr. is **Canada's Wonderland** (416–832–2205), a recently opened 370-acre Canadian version of Disneyland. Open from May to September, and weekends to October. Admission is a steep $15.95 for a one-day, unlimited-use adult passport. Children 3–6, half-price. **Casa Loma,** 1 Austin Terr. (416–923–1171), is worth a visit just to prove again that money and good taste don't necessarily go together, even where a 100-room "Dream Castle" is concerned. Open daily 10:00–5:00, adults $2.00, kids 6–12 50 cents, 13–18 $1.00. Of course you can't miss the **CN Tower,** 301 Front St. (416–360–8500), the world's tallest free-standing structure. Restaurants, discos, gift shops, a view from the top, and an amusement center are its pricey attractions. Admission to the main observation deck: adults $5.00, youths 12–17 $4.00, seniors $3.50, children (5–12) $2.50. Add an extra $1.00 to go a deck higher. **Colborne Lodge** (416–763–1534) at the south entrance to High Park, built in 1836 by John Howard, a Toronto architect, has been restored. The park was formerly part of the Howard estate. Open Monday–Saturday 9:30–5:00, Sunday noon to 5:00. Adults $1.50, seniors and children $1.00. In December, admission is 25 cents more. **Fort York,** Garrison Rd. off Fleet St. and Bathurst, near the Lake (416–366–6127), was destroyed in the War of 1812, then rebuilt, and now re-creates military life in Upper Canada as it was almost 150 years ago. Drills, parades, artillery exhibitions add to the color. Adults $3.00, children and seniors $1.50. Open daily. Almost everything is free at **Harbourfront** (416–364–5665), an 86-acre waterfront site that offers activities from strolling to restauranting or picnicking, to films, concerts, theater, and dancing. Ideal for an inexpensive evening. **Mackenzie House,** 82 Bond St. (416–366–1371), was the home of W. L. Mackenzie, radical newspaper publisher, first mayor of Toronto, and leader of the disastrous 1837 Rebellion in Upper Canada. Restored to the style of the 1850's, the house features Mackenzie's printing press in the basement. Adults $1.50, children and seniors $1.00. One of the most stunning pieces of recent Toronto architecture is the new **Metro Toronto Library,** 789 Yonge St. (416–928–5150). Designed by Raymond Moriyama, the brick-and-glass structure is spacious and full of light. A fountain greets you as you enter; plants hang from the different levels. Open daily. (Check.) The **Metro Toronto Zoo** on Meadowvale Rd., 2 km. north of Hwy. 401 (416–284–8181), is 700 acres, divided into geographic regions where animals roam in their faithfully re-created natural environments. Adults $4.00, youths and seniors $2.00, children (5–11) $1.00. Children under 5 free. Open daily throughout the year except Christmas Eve and Day. In winter you can bring your cross-country skis. Built on three artificial islands in Lake Ontario at the foot of Bathurst St., **Ontario Place,** 955 Lakeshore Blvd. (416–965–7711), offers a wide variety of inexpensive events from mid-May to mid-September, including outdoor concerts at the Forum. The **Parliament Buildings** at Queen's Park (416–965–4028) have free guided tours weekdays year round and summer weekends, and afford the opportunity to watch the provincial legislature when it's in session. The **Toronto City Hall** at Queen and Bay Sts. (416–947–7341) also has free conducted tours Monday to Friday. The **Toronto Islands** are another great place for children, with an amusement park on Center Island, bicycle paths, and ferry rides across. The **Ontario Science Centre,** 770 Don Mills Rd. at Eglington Ave. E. (416–429–4100), is the best playground in the city: computers, films, walk-in machines. Adults $3.00, students $2.00, children 12 and under $1.00. Open 10:00 A.M.–6:00 P.M.

Finally, there are a number of annual events that you won't want to miss if you're in Toronto when they're happening. These include **Caribana,** a July weekend of festivities on the Islands sponsored by the city's West Indian community; the **Canadian National Exhibition,** from mid-August to Labor Day; the **Royal Agricultural Winter Fair** in November; and **Toronto Caravan,** in June, a great display of multicultural events, located at pavilions throughout the city.

Entertainment

THEATER AND DANCE

A playwriting renaissance bloomed in Toronto around the Centennial (1967). Local theater continues to be as exciting as the off-Broadway big-budget productions. In Toronto there's the modern **St. Lawrence Center,** 27 Front St. E. (416–366–7723), home of the CentreStage Company, under whose name current productions are listed, and the **Royal Alexandra,** a restored Edwardian landmark at 260 King St. W. (416–593–4211), which features such stars as Peter O'Toole, Maggie Smith, Katharine Hepburn, and John Gielgud. Tickets to "Alex" are expensive and should be purchased early.

There are many small theaters in Toronto. A number have become influential under the auspices of dynamic artistic directors and talented actors, actresses and playwrights. Admission to most costs between $5.00 and $10.00. The **Berkeley St. Theatre,** 70 Berkeley St. (416–364–4170), is a converted firehouse, offering new Canadian works. One of Toronto's most important experimental theaters, the **Factory Theatre Lab,** has relocated at 94 Yonge St. (416–864–9971). **Theatre de P'Tit Bonheur,** one of the few French-language theaters in Ontario, is one of many theaters housed at Adelaide Court, 57 Adelaide St. E, a beautiful old renovated courthouse. The box office telephone number for all these theaters is (416) 363–6401. **Theatre Passe Muraille,** 16 Ryerson Ave. (416–363–8988), has housed the country's most innovative "collective creations," including *The Farm Show, Billy Bishop Goes to War,* and the irreverently satirical *Maggie and Pierre.* **Toronto Free,** 26 Berkeley St. (416–368–2856), is committed to the development of indigenous Canadian theater and has produced some of the country's leading theater talents. The oldest alternative theater in Toronto is George Luscombe's **Toronto Workshop Productions,** 12 Alexander St. (416–925–8640). TWP is oriented towards social and political commentary. The **Tarragon Theatre,** 30 Bridgman Ave. (416–531–1827), offers a selection of Canadian and classical plays. One exciting new theater is devoted to children's tastes: **Young People's Theatre Center,** 165 Front St. E. (416–864–9732), which is located in a beautifully converted former TTC stable, offers productions ranging from Shakespeare to the writings of contemporary children.

The National Ballet of Canada is headquartered in Toronto and performs at the O'Keefe Center during its annual season. It's certainly worth seeing the National, if you have a chance, but tickets sell out early and aren't cheap. If you're in Toronto during the summer months you can catch the company at Ontario Place for the $4.75 admission fee. **The Royal Winnipeg Ballet** comes to town every year, and this fine company is always a treat. Consult newspaper listings for details. Check the papers as well for information on some of the city's smaller dance companies. For under $10.00 you can catch avant-garde performance art at **The Funnel Theatre,** 507 King St. E. (416–364–7003), and the **Toronto Dance Theater,** 80 Winchester (416–967–1365). For the best deals in Toronto theater, look for **Five Star Tickets,** a discount ticket booth at the corner of Yonge & Dundas; unsold tickets for same-day shows are available here for half price.

FILM

Going to a movie in Toronto isn't cheap—to see a first-run movie costs around $5.00 for adults, $4.00 for youths 14–17, and $2.00 for children and seniors. But just as alternative theaters grew up in Toronto over the last 15 years, so did alternative film houses. Most show contemporary European films or repertoire classics. Some film theaters offer experimental programs.

Cinesphere is a theater at Ontario Place. During the summer, short stunning films are shown on its 6-story screen. The rest of the year Cinesphere offers a variety of North American and international feature films. Good rep and foreign films play at the **Revue Theatre,** 400 Roncesvalles (416–531–9959), adults $3.00, children, seniors $1.50. **The Funnel Theatre,** 507 King St. E. (416–364 –7003), presents highly experimental works by local film-makers and others. Admission: $3.50. **Harbourfront** (416–364–5665), the **Roxy Theater,** 1215 Danforth Ave. (416–461–2401), and the **Kingsway,** 3030 Bloor W. (416–236–1411), are all good inexpensive rep film houses, with everything from horror films to foreign movies.

MUSIC

The Canadian Opera Company performs at the O'Keefe Center in spring and early fall, though tickets are costly. The **Edward Johnson Building,** just behind the McLaughlin Planetarium at Avenue Rd. and Bloor (416–978–3744), is the home of the University of Toronto's Faculty of Music. It offers inexpensive year-round chamber music, recitals, and other concerts in its two theaters, Walter Hall and the Macmillan Theater. Nearby, the **Royal Conservatory of Music,** 273 Bloor St. W. (416–978–3797), is also a good bet. So too is the **Toronto Symphony Orchestra,** which has moved to the new Roy Thompson Hall. Under conductor Andrew Davis the TSO has become a world-class orchestra and features the finest visiting soloists. The orchestra's home in July and August is Ontario Place, where you can listen to lovely outdoor concerts. In fact, there is free summer music of all kinds in various parks throughout the city, as part of the **Summer Music Festival** (416–947–7251). **Tafelmusik** is an ensemble specializing in 17th century 'table music'. It performs at the St. Paul Centre, Trinity Church, 427 Bloor St. W. (416–964–6337). **Metropolitan United Church** at 51 Bond St. (416–363–0331) also runs a strong music program concentrating on organ and choral classical music. **Mariposa Folk Festival** is an annual early summer celebration of folk, ethnic music,

..rs, and blues. Call the Metro Tourist Board (416–979–3143) for schedule of events.

There are dozens of clubs in Toronto featuring jazz, rock and folk music. Often there's a small cover charge. **Club Blue Note,** 128 Pears Ave. (416–921–1109) specializes in rhythm'n' blues and Motown, and visiting acts typically include Martha Reeves and Junior Walker and the Allstars. Host George Olliver is a veteran bluesman and powerhouse dancer himself. **Albert's Hall,** upstairs at the Brunswick House, 481 Bloor St. W. (416–924–3884), offers Dixieland jazz, and the best in rhythm and blues. There's more jazz at **Cafe des Copains,** 48 Wellington East (416–869–1048), a rather pricey up-scale bistro, and the **Chick 'n' Deli,** 744 Mount Pleasant (416–489–4161). Check out the jazz at **Myer's Deli,** 69 Yorkville Ave. (416–960–4780), as well; it stays open later than any other Yorkville restaurant. **Harbourfront** presents a broad range of jazz, classical, and folk concerts, often free. **George's Spaghetti House,** 290 Dundas St. E. (416–923–9887), offers still more jazz; Moe Koffman is a regular performer. For the most current acts on the local punk and new wave scenes, visit the **Bam Boo lounge,** 180 Queen St W. (416–593–5771); the **Hotel Isabella,** 556 Sherbourne St. (416–921–4167) and especially **El Mocambo,** 464 Spadina Ave. (416–961–2558), where the Rolling Stones have recorded live. Cover in these clubs is $3.00 and up. The big pop venues are **Kingswood Music Theatre,** at Canada's Wonderland in Vaughan off Highway 400 (416–832–2205); **Maple Leaf Gardens,** 60 Carlton, (416–977–1641), and the **Masonic Temple,** 888 Yonge (416–922–6310) where BB King and Nena Hagen play when they come to town.

PUBS, PIANO BARS, AND DISCOS

There are so many places in Toronto to hang out, that the following list is only a sampling of some of the more popular and populous. Because they're popular, the best are pricey.

The **Brunswick House,** 481 Bloor St. W. (416–924–3884), is cheap and offers a very mixed music program with its beer. One of the most popular piano bars in town is the **Consort Bar,** King Edward Hotel, 37 King East, (416–863–9700), Toronto's most expensively renovated hotel, where the bar features the intelligent stylings of pianist John Arpin. There are five **"Dukes"** in Toronto, lovingly reproduced English pubs that offer pub-style food, like bangers and mash, and ploughmen's lunches, along with English stout and bitter. Downtown you'll find the **Duke of Gloucester,** 649 Yonge St. (416–961–9704), the **Duke of Richmond,** Eaton Center (416–598–4454), and the **Duke of Westminster,** First Canadian Place (416–368–1555). In the Yorkville area there's the **Duke of York,** 39 Prince Arthur Ave. (416–964–2441), and on North Yonge St., the **Duke of Kent,** 2315 Yonge (416–485–9507). Decidedly un- (or anti-) English is an Irish pub, the **New Windsor House,** 124 Church St. (416–364–9698). Great for Clancy Brothers sing-a-longs. **The Newfoundlander,** 185 Danforth Ave. (416–469

–1916), has authentic foot-stompin' Down East music on weekends. The **Pilot,** 22 Cumberland (416–923–5716), is a centrally located artists' and students' hangout. For Reggae try **Tiger's Coconut Grove,** 12 Kensington Ave. (416–593–8872). Not licensed. For the past 15 years the **Rooftop Bar** at the Park Plaza Hotel, 4 Avenue Rd. (416–924–5471), has been the meeting place of Toronto's media people. **The 22,** in the Windsor Arms Hotel, 22 St. Thomas St. (416–979–2341), is dark, intimate, and frequented by show-biz folk. Good piano music too.

SPORTS AND RECREATION

Toronto sports fans are among the most patient anywhere. For years they've supported professional teams that made money but lost games. Now patience is being rewarded—the *Argos* and *Blue Jays* are having good seasons. The *Maple Leafs* play **hockey** at Maple Leaf Gardens, 60 Carlton St. (416–977–1641) on most Wednesday and Saturday nights during the season. There are usually three games on Sunday. Standing room tickets are $6.50, others cost up to $20.00. The *Argonauts* play **football** at Exhibition Stadium from June to November, and it will cost you anywhere between $7.00 and $13.00 to see them. Call (416)–595–1131 for details. At Exhibition Stadium you can also see the *Toronto Blue Jays* of the American **Baseball** League. Tickets are less costly for baseball. **Horse Racing** fans have two tracks at their disposal in Toronto: *Greenwood Racetrack,* 1669 Queen St. (416–698–3131), a fifteen-minute streetcar ride from downtown, $2.75 grandstand, $5.50 clubhouse; and *Woodbine Race Track* on Hwy. 27 at Rexdale Blvd. (416–675–6110), home of the Queen's Plate. Post time for thoroughbred racing at both tracks is 1:30 P.M., for harness racing at Greenwood, 7:30 P.M. Toronto has many public 18-hole **golf** courses, including *Don Valley Golf Course,* 4200 Yonge St. (416–225–6821), and *Detonia Park Par 3,* Victoria Park Subway (416–691–6585). Twenty-five public parks have **tennis** courts, and there are a number of public **swimming** pools, including those in or near *Christie Pits, Don Valley, High Park, Monarch Park,* and *Sunnyside.* Before swimming in Lake Ontario, call the Public Health Department of Toronto (416–947–7401) for water conditions; lately pollution has closed the beaches. You can rent **sailboats** too. For information on this or other activities call *Metro Parks* (416–947–8186). They'll give you details on **skating rinks, horseback riding,** and **cycling** routes.

NORTHERN ONTARIO

Northern Ontario begins at the edge of the Canadian Shield— the 3.5-billion-year-old pink-and-gray granite rock face that curves across Central Canada. The landscape varies dramatically with waterfalls, rolling hills, and thousands of lakes, and then continues for miles as rock and pine forest, blueberry slopes, and more lakes. The Indians of the western part of the region were Ojibway; in the east, Huron (the same language group as the Indian princess Pocahontas who married pilgrim John Smith). The fierce enmity of the Iroquois was worsened by the arrival of European fur traders and missionaries. In 1639, a group of Jesuits established a mission, Ste. Marie-Among-the-Hurons, near Midland. By 1649, the mission was wiped out by the Iroquois, who horribly tortured several priests. (You can get the gory details at Martyr's Shrine, a neogothic religious center near a reconstruction of the original mission.) European settlement of most of the region didn't really begin again until the 19th century. Parts of the north are still basically frontier. For vast stretches, there's little in the way of tourist sites, accommodation, or fine dining. Except for the "metropolises" of the north—the poulations of Thunder Bay, Sault Ste. Marie, and Sudbury are all over 81,000—there's something impermanent-looking about the towns. Clustered along the Trans-Canada Highway (#17) the charmless prefabs, frame beer stores and gas stations will be abandoned when the miners, trappers, and lumbermen have exhausted the immediate area. Though civilization's pleasures are simple here, the natural beauties are prodigious, and your chief expense will be traversing the enormous distances between.

Exploring around Georgian Bay

Midland (population 12,132), a lake port town near the site of the 17th-century Jesuit mission to the Hurons, is the gateway to Georgian Bay and its Thirty Thousand Islands. Between Midland and Owen Sound lies Wasaga Beach (population 4,705)—the longest freshwater beach in the world, transformed into a Coney Island North. Its midway is visited each summer by 70,000 motorcyclists, pinball wizards, and screaming kids. Farther west lies Collingwood (population 11,240), once the end of an Indian portage trail, now a shipbuilding town. In the cave on nearby Blue Mountain, the last of the Petun Indian nation was wiped out by the Iroquois. Today Blue Mountain and the spectacular Beaver Valley area behind it are southwest Ontario's major ski sites.

East again, and north of Midland, the distinctive rock and lake scenery of northern Ontario begins. Per capita, Ontarians are more enthusiastic cottagers than anyone else, and this is cottage country. Georgian Bay and lakeside lots here cost as much as city houses— some, ten times the $20,000 a Chippewa chief was paid for the Muskoka district in 1815. By 1900, Muskoka had become a flourishing lumbering region. Northeast of Midland, and accessible via Hwy. 69, and then Hwy. 660 through Bala lies Gravenhurst (population 8,532), the district capital. Once supporting 20 sawmills, it was known as Sawdust City. Then wealthy tourists—including future American president Woodrow Wilson—began to arrive. Norman Bethune, hero of the Chinese revolution, was born here—his house is now a museum, featuring artifacts from the People's Republic of China. Gravenhurst was renamed and an opera house was built (now featuring Straw-Hat summer theater). Grand lodges went up throughout Muskoka. Lake steamers—like the *Sagamo,* now docked for tourist visits in Gravenhurst—opened the Muskoka Lakes to cottage builders. When the road builders came in the early 20th century, they blasted through the shield leaving dramatic rock cuts best visible on Hwy. 69 south of Gravenhurst and in the hilly county roads skirting Lake Rousseau. Muskoka's rivers, dammed and channeled for hydro power, now hide picnickers among the rocks; there are photogenic falls at Bala, Bracebridge, Port Carling (whose falls have been channeled into boat locks), near Dwight on the Oxtongue River, and around Magnetawan north of the Muskoka district. Of all Northern Ontario's tourist regions, Muskoka, the most southerly, is also the most developed. There are good restaurants, plays, shops, delis—and famous blueberry pies.

Algonquin and Haliburton

Algonquin Park, 2,900 square miles of protected wilderness, lies to the east of Muskoka, through the little town of Dwight. The park has been protected by government from the attractions and tribulations of Muskoka-type cottage development ever since it was founded in 1893; there are still timberwolves and bears here, dangerously ill-tempered ones too. No new cottages have been added to those clustering around Hwy. 60 for decades. Glass bottles and powerboats are fobidden in the park. There are nine road-accessible campsites; the rest are for canoers only. The park runs an excellent nature program for kids.

The Haliburton highlands are directly south of Algonquin. Here, rolling hills are more densely wooded than Muskoka's and the cross-country skiing is excellent. The Shield (name given to the shield-shaped pre-Cambrian rock mass in this area) breaks out of the woods at Bancroft, a uranium mining town and a rockhound's paradise. Eighty percent of Canada's mineral types occurs in the surrounding rock, including semiprecious zircon, beryl, rose quartz, and high-quality sodalite. Burleigh Falls, Buckhorn (with its Indian cultural center), Bobcaygeon and Fenelon Falls are pretty little resort towns. At Dorset, a 100-foot-high observation tower commands a view of Haliburton and Algonquin, and the road north.

Sudbury and Cochrane

The Sudbury (population 91,829) crater was formed by a meteorite 1.7 million years ago, leaving one of the world's richest nickel deposits. Today, it's a mining city with parks, a lively bilingual university and solid labor tradition.

Cochrane (population 4,848), north of Sudbury, is gateway to the Arctic: tourists and trappers board the Polar Bear Express for Moosonee (population 1,277) and Moose Factory, the old Hudson Bay Post on the Arctic tidewaters. Because of prevailing westerly winds, the lakes north and west of Sudbury aren't as damaged by acid rain from the nickel smelters as those east and south.

Sault Ste. Marie (Manitoulin and the Agawa Canyon)

A "clay belt" interrupts the Canadian Shield along the north shore of Lake Huron. Each August, the old farming town of Massey hosts a big county fair. North of the highway around towns like Eagle Lake the game fishing is legendary—the world's biggest muskellunge are caught here (28 kg. and up). Manitoulin Island, with its farms, beaches, waterfalls, lakes, museums, pretty little port towns, and flourishing Ojibway communities is accessible by ferry from Española. Many of Manitoulin's hotels, modest and moderate, and tent and trailer parks tend to fill up around the two Ojibway summer festival times. Sault St. Marie, a city of 81,355 people, is joined to the American "Soo" by the International Bridge over the St. Mary River. Picnicking beside the massive locks is a free attraction, though lock tours are also offered. The Soo, once jumping off point for voyageurs and fur traders, was a major military stronghold in the war of 1812. The ruins of Fort St. Joseph are being restored on St. Joseph's Island south of the city. Today the Soo is access point for the Agawa Canyon Tour, by Algoma Central Railway, up a deep winding canyon. The train crosses 130-foot-high trestle bridges and rounds stunning lakes. In most seasons, campers can arrange in advance with railway officials to be let off by the side of the tracks and picked up days later after real wilderness camping. Between Sault St. Marie and Thunder Bay lies some of Canada's most spectacular scenery, immortalized in the paintings of Group of Seven members Lawren Harris and A. Y. Jackson. The massive hills of the north shore of Lake Superior—world's largest freshwater lake—are serviced by good government-run camping parks. Some of the park sites—e.g., Lake Superior Provincial Park —have been chosen for the Indian pictographs (rock paintings) nearby. Two scenic detours are Aquasabon Gorge near Terrace Bay and Ouimet Canyon near Nipigon.

Thunder Bay

Thunder Bay (population 112,486) is where a billion bushels of the Prairie Provinces' wheat is stored in huge grain elevators before it's loaded in grain tankers for shipment down the St. Lawrence Seaway. The grain elevator towers are dwarfed by Thunder Bay's flat table-topped Mt. McKay (home of the Fort William Indian band, who operate its park campsite and ski run) and the Sleeping Giant, really the rock formations of Sibley Peninsula which look like a grave man, arms folded, lying on his back across the water from the city. The rock of the Thunder Bay area is rich in amethysts—semiprecious purple quartz. Thunder Bay is also ethnically rich. Its Finnish inhabitants run saunas and cross-country ski shops. There's good Italian pizza. Its founding French voyageurs revisit the city each summer when the reconstructed Old Fort William stages tourist pageants. The city commemorates its multiculturalism in the International Friendship Garden, and, too, in big family picnics in the parks along the cold but lovely Lake Superior shore and at Kakabeka Falls off the road to Kenora.

PRACTICAL INFORMATION FOR NORTHERN ONTARIO

Transportation

BUS. *Voyageur Colonial* buses connect most of the towns in Muskoka and Haliburton, and Voyageur and *Ontario Northland Transportation Commission* cross northern Ontario from Sudbury to Thunder Bay and beyond.

TRAIN. *Via Rail* cross the north but no longer stop at smaller communities. *Ontario Northland Railway* runs the Polar Bear Express, and also a slower train, for local trappers, to connect Cochrane to Moosonee. *Algoma Central Railway* heads north up the Agawa Canyon from Sault Ste. Marie.

CAR. The major highway north from Toronto is Hwy. 11; east-west from Sudbury to Kenora is Hwy. 17, the Trans-Canada. The roads are generally excellent, though smaller highways through the backhills can be treacherous in rainy or snowy weather. For 24-hour, year-round road conditions call (416) 248–3561.

AIR. *Nordair, Air Canada* and *CP* connect Toronto to major cities in the north; smaller lines such as *Austin Airways, Transair,* and *Bradley Air Service* fan out to smaller mining, trapping and lumbering communities.

FOR MORE INFORMATION

There are regional travel information centers in Sault Ste. Marie at 120 Huron St. and on Hwy. 400 at Barrie between Toronto and Muskoka. For local travel information the addresses are as follows. Bancroft: on Station St.; Bobcaygeon: 34 Bolton St.; Collingwood: First and High Sts.; Gravenhurst: 140 John St.; Kenora, 1500 Hwy. 17 E.; Lakefield, Water St.; Midland, 578 King St.; Sault St. Marie, 360 Great Northern Rd.; Sudbury, 1543 Paris St., 144 Durham St. S., and at the Civic Center; Thunder Bay, 520 Leith St. in the Pagoda.

Accommodations and Restaurants

Northern Ontario is "cottage country" and all summer long Ontarians and out-of-province visitors travel to the lakes and woods for sun, fish, and peace and quiet. There are numerous cottages, lodges, and restaurants in the near North catering to the tourist. In the farther North, the selection diminishes. Still, you don't have to be rich to find accommodations you'll enjoy, and you don't have to be a camper to afford a trip north. The following categories will help you decide where to stay and eat (prices are for 2 people).

Accommodations: *Inexpensive* (I) $50.00 and under, and *Moderate* (M) $50.00–$85.00. **Dining:** *Inexpensive* (I) $35.00 or less, and *Moderate* (M) $35.00–$55.00.

Near North

BALA. Try the *Grandview Cottages* (I) on Hwy. 169 by the Moon River (705–762–3942). Open May–October. *Trafalgar Bay Cottages* (M), Hwy. 169, P.O. Box 79 (705–762–3428), has 19 cabins and facilities, including fishing, tennis, and boating. Open May–October.

BOBCAYGEON area offers a variety of accommodations. *Pigeon Lake Cottages* (I), Mill Line Rd. (705–738–2333), has fireplaces and a beach on the lake. *Evergreen Point* (I), Walmac Shores Rd., R.R. 2 and Pigeon Lake (705–738–2826), has 8 cottages. Both of these places are inexpensive, both open May–October. *Nichols Cove Cottages* (M), Nichols Cove Rd. E., Box 341 (705–738–2173), on Pigeon Lake, *Lakeview Cottages* (I), on Front St. (705–738–2955), with a beach on Sturgeon Lake, are pricier.

BRACEBRIDGE. The choice of accommodations here is excellent. For example, *The Lofty Pines Motel* (I), on Muskoka Rd., Box 2279 (705–645–8755), is a bilingual (French and English) bed-and-breakfast spot that costs less than $50.00. *Holiday House* (M), 17 Dominion St. (705–645–2245), is recommended both for the hospitality it shows families with young children and for its dining room.

GRAVENHURST. If you're staying in this area, both the *Muskokan Motel* (I), on Bethune Dr., Box 448 (705–687–2274), and the *Oakwood Motel* (I), 1060 Muskoka Rd. S., Box 1869 (705–687–4224), offer no-frills value. On Lake Muskoka and Gull Lake there are many lodges and cottage resorts offering all kinds of activities. One of them is *The Pine Dale Inn Motel* (M), Pinedale Rd. (705–687–2822), with 21 rooms and one cottage overlooking Gull Lake. Also recommended is *The Welcome Inn* (I), 1165 Muskoka Rd. (705–687–3431). At these prices, you walk to the public beach. On the main street of Gravenhurst is *Sloan's* (I), 155 Muskoka St. (705–687–4611), the most famous restaurant in the Muskokas. It has home-cooked food and claims to serve "The World's Best Blueberry Pie." Across the street is *The Deli* (I), 144 Muskoka (705–687–4254), where you can stock up on picnic fare.

HUNTSVILLE abounds in places to stay, but the trick is to find what you want. *Sunrise Motel* (I), 33 King William St. (705–789–9673), is a 17-room motel near downtown, with an outdoor pool. *Sunset Inn* (I–M), 69 Main St. (705–789–4141), costs a little more but overlooks Hunter's Bay. *Bondi Village* (I–M), Muskoka Rd. 21 (705–635–2261), is a modestly priced resort with a beach on Lake of Bays. If you feel like splurging, take a log cottage with a fireplace at the very nice *Billie Bear Lodge* (M), on Muskoka Rd. 8, R.R. 4 (705–635–2441), on Bella Lake. You can eat at one of the many lodges in Huntsville, if you make reservations.

OWEN SOUND. The *Owen Sound Travellers Motel* (I-M), 740 9th Ave. (519–376–2680), the *Diamond Motel* (I), 713 9th Ave. E. (519–371–2011), the *Owen Sound Motor Inn* (M), 485 9th Ave. E (519–371–3011), and the *Key Motel* (I), RR3, Hwy 6/10 (519–794–2350) are all within budget consideration. In the Owen Sound area there are several inexpensive to moderately priced restaurants. The *Troubadour* is small, offering crêpes and a delicious cheesecake flavoured with anisette. *Pepi's Pizza* (I), on 2nd St. serves rich pizza with a light crisp crust. In Owen Sound's harbor is *Clarenville Floating Seafood Restaurant.* Get on the boat at 1st Avenue and 11th for surf 'n' turf in an interesting atmosphere. Also, there's the *El Ron Inn* (I), in Flesherton, whose dinner buffet has a good salad selection, solid entrées, pies, and is licensed.

Farther North

MAGNETAWAN. *Woodland Echoes Resort* (I) on Nipissing Rd. and Ahmic Lake (705–387–3866), is open May to October. It has a natural beach and offers boating, fishing and golf nearby. *Dunworkin Holiday Homes* (I), Old Nipissing Rd., Ahmic Lake (705–387–3760). Eight cottages overlook a beach.

MANITOULIN ISLAND. In Little Current try *The Anchor Inn* (I), on Waters St., Box 334 (705–368–2023). *Silver Birches Resort* (I–M), Hwy. 540 (705–368–2669), has an indoor pool, and overlooks the North Channel. *Gordon's Lodge* (M), on Hwy. 540B, Box 324 (705–282–2342), is in Gore Bay and offers beach front, fireplaces in the cottages, bicycle rentals and nearby golf plus 25 rooms and 8 cottages.

SAULT STE. MARIE and environs. Bargains are *Journeys' End Motel* (I), 333 Great Northern Rd. (705–759–8000); *Skyline Motel* (I), 232 Great Northern Rd. (705–942–1240); and *Adams Motel Flag Inn* (I), 647 Great Northern Rd. (705–254–4345). More expensive is the *Water Tower Inn* (M), 360 Great Northern Rd., (705–949–8111) with an indoor pool, whirlpool and exercise facilities.

For dinner, try *The Bavarian* (M), 647 Great Northern Rd. (705–949 –9278) which produces good schnitzel and torte. *Rico's* (M), 116 Spring St. (705–949–7337), is an Italian restaurant where the whole family can dine without breaking the bank. *Moviola Café*(M), 523 Queen St. E. (705–949–0335), is a popular spot to enjoy seafood, hamburgers and salads among pictures of movie stars. Sit at the bar or one of the ice cream parlour tables.

SUDBURY. *Loney's Sportsman's Lodge* (I-M), Box 475, Garson, is 34 mi. NE of town on Kukagami Lake Rd. (705–858–1281) and has rooms and cabins, many with fireplaces, plus cross country ski trails, a beach, and hunting and fishing packages. In town, try *Cassio's Hotel Ltd.* (M) 1145 Lorne St. (705–674–4203) and the *Northbury Hotel,* 50 Brady St. (705–675–5602). For something more central—and more pricey—there's the beautiful new *Peter Piper Inn*(M) at the corner of Larch and Minto Sts. (705–673–7801). Some rooms have saunas; there's also a Prime Ministerial suite— and a pool. The *Sheraton Caswell*(M), 1696 Regent St. (705–522– 3000), has an indoor pool and is close to Science North. The *Cardinal Motor Inn* (M), 1500 Regent St. S. (705–522–8900), and the *Senator Motor Hotel* (M), 390 Elgin St. (705–675–1273), are moderately priced. You can get real budget value in one of the residences at *Laurentian University,* Ramsey Lake Rd. (705–675– 1151), where a double room costs around $15.00 a night, or at the *Sudbury YWCA,* 111 Larch St. (705–674–2210), for about the same price. There aren't many great places to eat in Sudbury, and the good ones aren't that cheap. *The Peter Piper* (M) (*see above*) is recommended for fish, lasagna, and quiche. The décor is plants and wicker, and it's licensed. *Silver Beach Tavern* (M), 2929 Long Lake Rd. (705–522–5252), has cabbage rolls, steaks, fish and pasta. For good roast beef in an old English atmosphere, try *The Fox and Hound* (M), 187 Shaughnessy St. (705–675–2224).

TERRACE BAY is midway between Sault Ste. Marie and Thunder Bay and might be a good place to stop over. Both the *Imperial Motel* (I) on Hwy. 17, Box 338 (807–825–3226), and the *Norwood Motel* (I) on Hwy. 17, Box 248 (807–825–3694), have reasonable rates. The Imperial also has dining facilities.

THUNDER BAY has much to choose from when it comes to accommodations. The *Longhouse Village CHA Hostel* (I) on Lakeshore Dr., Box 2086 (807–983–2042), is rather remote (a bus will get you there—cab rides cost around $10). But it is easily the cheapest and friendliest deal in town. Swimming nearby. The *Lakehead University* residence (I), Oliver Rd. (807–345–2121), with rooms available from May to August, runs a close second. The *Lakeview Motel* (I), 391 North Cumberland St. (807–345–1171), *Bob's Motel* 235 Arthur St. W. (807–577–1343) which has an indoor pool, and the *Overpass Motel* (I) on Hwy. 17, R.R. 2 (807– 577–1525), are all under $50.00. *Ramada Inn Prince Arthur,* (I-M), 17 North Cumberland St. (807–345–5411), a central, tastefully restored hotel overlooking Lake Superior. The rooms are large, some hung with Inuit art, and the dining facilities are excellent (fresh fish, salad bar, cheese 'n' onion bread). The *Hoito* (I-M) 314 Bay St. (807–345–6323), is a restaurant founded by Finnish immigrants three generations ago. You'll enjoy fish soup and smorgasbord in a very basic basement environment. The *Scandinavian Deli* across the street has cheese, bread, smoked meats, and other delicacies. More (light) Finnish food (soups and pastries) at *Kanga's,* 379 Oliver Rd. (807–344–6761). It is even better known as Thunder Bay's best-appointed public sauna or Finnish steam bath.

Some Principal Sights and Attractions

The Near North

ALGONQUIN PARK. The bears, timberwolves, and 2,900 square miles of woods and lakes are the principal attractions. The *Park Museum* offers a history of the park, and the *Pioneer Logging Exhibit* tells the story of logging.

If you're in the **BOBCAYGEON** area in late July you won't want to miss the annual *Kawartha Lakes Ontario Open Fiddle and Step-Dance Contest.*

BRACEBRIDGE. Children will probably enjoy a visit to *Santa's Village* (705–645–2512) with its rides and animals. There are free sights too: two waterfalls in or near town.

Near **BURLEIGH FALLS,** in **BUCKHORN,** on the Curve Lake Indian Reserve, is *Whetung Ojibwa Crafts* (705–657–3661), open daily year-round, and selling everything from fur parkas to native prints.

MAGNETAWAN. There are three picturesque sets of rapids along the Magnetawan River, within a 20-minute drive of the town of Magnetawan. Drive along Hwy. 124 west of Hwy. 11.

On Hwy. 69 just south of **PARRY SOUND,** you'll find the *Reptile House,* R.R. 2, Otter Lake (705–378–2475), with its collection of live and stuffed snakes. Then cruise through the 30,000 Islands on the *Island Queen.* Call the *30,000 Cruise Line* office, 9 Bay St. (705–746–2311), for information. Parry Sound hosts an annual *Festival of Sound* (mostly classical music, with some Dixieland and pop) from late July to mid-August.

MIDLAND has many attractions including the *Huron Indian Village,* in Little Lake Park (705–526–8757), *Martyr's Shrine,* R.R. 1, Midland (705–526–6121), and *Ste. Marie-Among-the-Hurons* (705–526–7838)—historical monuments or re-creations of early Indian and French-Jesuit life. Near Midland the *Wye Marsh Wildlife Center,* R.R. 1, Midland (705–526–7089), is a wonderful bird sanctuary, while 30,000 Island cruises, leaving daily from the town docks, and sightseeing flights over the Islands are other popular local attractions.

Near **OWEN SOUND** are the 80-foot-high *Inglis Falls.* Drive half a mile west of Rockford (just south of Owen Sound) to the conservation area. For children, there's *Story Book Park,* about 2 miles south of Owen Sound. The *Tom Thomson Memorial Art Gallery,* 840 First Ave. W. (519–376–1932), has many works by the famous contemporary of the Group of Seven, and a collection of 19th- and 20th-century Canadian art. It's free to stroll down to the Owen Sound docks, although shipbuilding activity is slow. It's also free to take a stroll past the fish hatchery in nearby **CHATSWORTH.** The *Laughing Water Festival,* also close by, in **MEAFORD,** brings a drama festival to the local opera house. The town also boasts a good public beach at Memorial Park.

Farther North

MANITOULIN ISLAND has over 100 freshwater lakes, lovely port towns, waterfalls, and two Indian reserves. Archeologists suggest that Manitoulin was the site of one of North America's earliest native cultures. The twin towns **MOOSONEE** and **MOOSE FACTORY** were the site of the first Hudson's Bay Post. A few early 18th-century buildings and a museum explain the island's past. From mid-June to mid-September you can take a boat to *Fossil Island* to look at 350-million-year-old fossils. *St. Thomas Church* in Moose Factory is filled with Indian artifacts.

The oldest building in **SAULT STE. MARIE** is the *Ermatinger House,* 831 Queen St. E. (705–949–1488), built in 1814, and now restored. You can tour this oldest stone house west of Toronto. It was the home of a fur trader and his Indian wife, the daughter of an Ojibway chief. The Algoma Central Railway takes tourists up through the huge hills of the *Agawa Canyon.* Winter snow and ice make the trip even more beautiful. In the *Old Garden River Indian Reserve,* 16 km. east of town, visit the large Canadian-American trout hatchery. You don't have to go far to see the 30-meter-high *Crystal Falls* in Hiawatha Park, almost in the center of the Soo. *Superstack* will tell you when you're nearing **SUDBURY.** Symbol of the city and INCO, the giant metals corporation that put nickel and Sudbury on the map, Supterstack is a 380-meter-high chimney that is supposed to help solve the pollution problem. (It hasn't.) As well, Sudbury's new *Science North,* 100 Ramsey Lake Rd. (705–522–3700) is a hands-on science center with films, demonstrations and guided tours around an old nickel mine. Adults $4.00, children and seniors $2.00. *Laurentian University* (705–675–1151) is on Lake Ramsey, and tours of the campus, the *Doran Planetarium,* and the university *Art Gallery* are available. The *Flour Mill Heritage Museum* 514 Notre Dame Blvd. (705–674–2391), will give you an idea of what Sudbury was like in its premining days.

Dominating **THUNDER BAY** is the 600-meter flat-topped hill known as *Mt. McKay,* a ski-run in winter, a picnic park in summer. Take a Welcome ship cruise of the harbor and grain elevators along the waterfront. Call (807) 344–2512. You can also go by boat to *Old Fort William* (807–577–8461), or by car or city bus. The 170-

year-old fort, on the Kaministikwia River, has been restored to its glory days with 40 buildings, and it bustles with activities from baking to canoe-making. Open mid-May to early October. Adults $3.00, students $1.50, children under 6 free. The *Thunder Bay Museum,* 219 May St. S. (807–623–0801), offers a collection of Indian and pioneer artifacts, photographs, documents, and marine exhibits. Free admission. *Centennial Park,* at Donald and May Sts., has a logging camp, museum, almost 20 km. of hiking and skiing trails, and a children's animal farm. Admission is free. About 45 miles east, along the Terry Fox Courage Highway, are famous open pit amethyst mines. Head toward Nipigon and watch for signs.

Entertainment

SUDBURY. There are always events at Laurentian University, including *Sudbury Theater* presentations in Teacher's College Auditorium or Fraser Auditorium. In the nearly 2,000-acre *Bell Park,* Harris and York Sts., free summer festivities include band concerts, live theater, and rock music. Check the newspaper for details of performances by the Sudbury Symphony.

THUNDER BAY. The small (194-seat) *Magnus Theater,* 639 McLaughlin St. (807–623–1321), presents both new Canadian plays and classics from October to April. Throughout the summer there is dramatic entertainment at the *Chippewa Park Amphitheater* (807–344–8701).

EASTERN ONTARIO

To most people Eastern Ontario is just Ottawa and Kingston. But while they're rewarding destinations in their own right, there's much to explore in the rocky lakelands and fertile farm country in between. This was the first part of the province to be settled. Kingston was capital of Upper Canada in the first half of the 19th century. Less wealthy than the industrial-commercial Toronto-Hamilton axis, Eastern Ontario has more inexpensive accommodations, old towns, and historic sites.

Exploring Eastern Ontario

Begin your trip east with a stopover in Peterborough (population 60,620) where the Trent-Severn Waterways and the Otonabee River meet. Peterborough is an older city, leafy and genteel, the hometown of famed Canadian writer Robertson Davies, who for many years edited the local newspaper. It's a city of beautiful parks, like Crary Park and the Riverview Park and Zoo near the campus of Trent University. The huge hydraulic lift locks in the Trent Canal are one of the dominant sights of Peterborough and account for its other name, "Lift Lock City." *Liftlock Cruises* (705–742–9912) tours the locks three times daily. There are some imposing turn-of-the-century homes in Peterborough, including Hutchison House, a 19th-century doctor's residence. The Peterborough Summer Festival (late July to early August) includes music, theater, and aquatic events. A lively Farmer's Market operates on Saturday mornings.

A few kilometers north of Peterborough, on Hwy. 28, is the delightful little town of Lakefield (population 2,374). England's Prince Andrew attended the private boys' school there. Lots of antique stores line the main drag, which also passes the century old Anglican Christ Church. The Warsaw Caves, tunnels scooped out by prehistoric rivers, are nearby.

Now head south to Hwy. 2 and Trenton (population 15,085), where the Trent-Severn Canal System begins. The canal system is almost 400 km. long, with 44 locks, connecting to Georgian Bay on Lake Huron. Trenton is a pretty town of boats and bridges. There are bargains on the weekend at the Quinte Flea Market.

Farther east on Hwy. 2 lies Belleville (population 34,881) on the Bay of Quinte. After gold was discovered north of town in 1860 Belleville dubbed itself "Gateway to the Golden North." Today, "golden north" refers to the lakelands of Hastings and Presqu'ile, a rolling peninsula of small historic towns which juts south of Belleville into Lake Ontario.

Kingston (population 52,616) stands where Lake Ontario flows into the St. Lawrence, at the southern end of the Rideau Canal. Its 150-year-old gray limestone buildings make it handsome, if staid. This former military stronghold and capital of Upper Canada doesn't dwell on its past. Today it's a university town and headquarters of Canada's Royal Military College. The close-cropped cadets in their scarlet-and-black uniforms and pillbox hats rub shoulders with tourists at Old Fort Henry or the Fort Frederick Museum. Some cadets perform the Ceremonial Retreat pageant each Wednesday and Saturday at the fort. Catch the 45-minute tour train from the Bureau of Tourism, 209 Ontario St. The train takes you to the city's major attractions, including the Agnes Etherington Art Gallery, the 100-year-old Grant Theater, the fort, and the town's fine old neighborhoods. Princess St. is good for browsing. At 23 Ontario St. is the Pumphouse Steam Museum.

Traveling along Hwy. 2 east of Kingston you'll pass the Thousand Islands area, one of the oldest and most beautiful resort regions in Canada. Boat tours of the islands leave from Kingston and from Gananoque (population 4,863) farther east. Gananoque has antique stores and renovated alleys of boutiques, plus a restaurant that's more a cultural institution: The Golden Apple Inn (613–382–3300), which serves authentic "Canadian cuisine," relishes, chutneys, homemade rolls, fresh vegetables and good meat (but prices are a bit higher than our moderate range).

Head north from Gananoque along Hwy. 15, then dip south to Lanark (population 773), an old lumbering town on the Clyde River, founded by Scottish settlers in 1821. A subsequent influx of immigrants from Ireland during the Potato Famine gave the town the Irish-Scots character it has today. Three shops along the main street (George St.) offer good bargains: a sweater factory outlet, a discount shoe store, and an antique, reproduction pine, nut, and fudge emporium.

Perth (population 5,660), a few kilometers southeast on the River Tay, has the dubious distinction of being the home of "The Big Cheese." Back in 1882, Perth contributed a 22,000-pound Cheddar to the Chicago World's Fair. The cheese broke the first railway flatcar it was loaded on. Perth's Last Duel Park is named after the last fatal duel to take place in Ontario in 1833, and at the old Burying Ground you can see the grave of Robert Lyon, one of the duelists. The history of Perth and environs is presented in the Archibald W. Campbell Memorial Museum, 11 Gore St. Best bargains in the area: cheese, jam, seasonal fruit sold at the roadside.

Ottawa

Ottawa is the third-largest city in Ontario (population 295,163), but it outstrips the largest, Toronto, in terms of the scorn, affection, and jealousy heaped upon it by the rest of Canada. That's because in 1858 Queen Victoria annointed it—a backward lumber town at the junction of the Rideau and Ottawa rivers—capital city of the new Dominion. Today, Ottawa is known by nicknames such as "Disneyland on the Rideau." The difference is, in this Disneyland, many of the tourist attractions are absolutely free.

The best place to start your walking tour is at Parliament Hill. This 29-acre plot of land, 150 feet above the Ottawa River, was acquired by the capital's founders, who hired architects Thomas Fuller and Chilion Jones to design the Neo-Gothic Parliamentary complex. The centerpiece of their design is the 291-foot-high Peace Tower. You may hear the Tower before you see it. The gun is fired at noon Monday through Saturday and at 10 A.M. Sunday. The Tower's 53-bell carillon is led by the 22,400-pound Bourdon Bell, which strikes each hour. At 10 A.M. every summer day (weather permitting) pipes and drums sound for a 30-minute-long changing of the guards ceremony (the Canadian Grenadiers and the Governor-General's Foot Guard). The Senate, House of Commons, and Opposition offices are all behind the tower in the Center Block. The public is welcome to observe parliamentary debates in the limestone and oak-paneled House of Commons inside. The liveliest debates are in the daily Question Period. Also worth a visit are the crimson and gold Senate Chambers, and the domed Library with its white marble statue of Queen Victoria.

Rambling around the grounds of Parliament Hill you'll find statues of Canada's founding fathers—including Thomas D'Arcy McGee, shot by American-Irish Fenians in 1868; Canada's first prime minister, Sir John A. MacDonald; and Sir Wilfred Laurier (the country's first French-speaking prime minister). Across Wellington Street are the National Press Building, The United States Embassy and, a block south of Wellington, the Sparks Street Mall. In the mall, cars have been replaced by pedestrians, fountains, sidewalk cafés, and sculpture. The Mall runs between the grand old Château Laurier Hotel and the heroic bronzes of Canada's War Memorial at its east end, through Kent Street farther west. At 150 Kent, at the National Film Board of Canada's gallery of photography, there are free films and slide shows.

The Rideau Canal runs through quiet Ottawa neighborhoods to join the Ottawa River just below the Château Laurier. A set of steps descends the steep gorge where manual locks lift the boats 79 feet from the river up to the canal. In winter civil servants skate along the canal, briefcases in hand. Behind the canal is the modern National Arts Center, and across Elgin Street at the corner of Slater is the National Gallery. Inside the Gallery are reconstructed medieval cloisters and a collection of Van Gogh, Picasso, and Canadian artists and sculptors.

North of the Arts Center on Rideau St. lie the flowers, sausages, fruit and vegetable stalls of the Byward Market. The neighborhood also has offbeat boutiques and restaurants. Sussex Dr. curves near the market, past the Château Laurier and heads past renovated Victorian buildings housing art galleries and cafés, then continues past Nepean Point Park, Notre Dame Basilica (at the corner of St. Patrick St.) and the Canadian War Museum. Then Sussex Dr. skirts the monument-studded park above the Ottawa River. It passes the rather modest Prime Minister's Residence (24 Sussex Dr.) and grander Rideau Hall (the Governor General's Residence) across Sussex at MacKay St. Rideau Hall's grounds are open to the public.

The gardens of the Central Experimental Farm on the outskirts of town are more rewarding: here, among 1,200 acres of flowers, shrubs, trees and vegetables, the government of Canada conducts cross-breeding projects. The public is free to wander on weekdays.

PRACTICAL INFORMATION FOR EASTERN ONTARIO

Transportation

CAR. Hwy. 7 is the central route between Toronto and Ottawa. Hwy. 2 runs along Lake Ontario. Parallel to Hwy. 2 is the 401, big, busy and best taken only if you're in a hurry.

BUS. *Voyageur Colonial* is the major bus service for eastern Ontario. In Toronto the number to call for information is (416) 979–3511.

TRAIN. *Via Rail* runs day, express and overnight services from Toronto to Ottawa. Call (416) 366–8411 in Toronto for details.

AIR. Uplands Airport in Ottawa is serviced by national and international carriers. From Toronto to Ottawa you can take *Air Canada* or *Canadian Pacific.*

FOR MORE INFORMATION

You can get information on **Eastern Ontario** by writing *Ontario Travel* at Queen's Park or by calling toll free 1–800–268–3735; in Toronto call (416) 965–4008 weekdays, (416) 364–4722 weekends and holidays. Brochures, maps, and pamphlets are available by mail, or can be picked up at the Ontario Travel Office in Toronto's Eaton Center. In **Kingston** and environs contact the Kingston *Bureau of Tourism,* 209 Ontario St. (613–548–4415). For **Ottawa** information contact *Canada's Capital Visitor's and Convention Bureau,* 222 Queen St. (613–237–5150 or 613–237–5158). Other regional tourist office include Belleville, 183 Pinnacle St.; Lakefield, Water St.; Perth, 80 Gore St.; Peterborough, 393 Water St.; Trenton, 97 Front St.

Accommodations and Restaurants

During the busy summer months, prices won't be cheap in an area where tourism contributes largely to local economies. This doesn't mean that traveling in Eastern Ontario has to be prohibitively expensive. The following categories will help you decide where to stay and eat. (Prices are for 2 people): **Accommodations: *Inexpensive*** (I) $65.00 and under, and *Moderate* (M) $65.00–$90.00. **Restaurants:** *Inexpensive* (I) $30.00 or less, and *Moderate* (M) $30.00 to $45.00. Three pamphlets from the provincial government's Ontario Travel in Toronto are especially helpful to the budget traveler: the *Guide to Country Inns and Dining;* the *Accommodations Guide,* which includes some inexpensive cabins and hostels; and the *Farm Vacations Guide.*

BELLEVILLE. *Baron's Motor Inn* (I), 325 N. Front St. (613–962–5367), is a modest motel with an indoor pool. *Queen's Motor Inn* (I–M), 400 Dundas St. E. (613–966–1211), also has a popular dining room with a menu featuring German cooking.

GANANOQUE. You can rent cottages on the St. Lawrence River. *Blink Bonnie Motor Lodge* (I–M), 50 Main St. (613–382–7272), has a quiet location and an indoor pool. Also recommended is *Country Squire Family Inn* (I-M), 715 King St. E. (613–382–3511), with outdoor pool, billiards room, and a newly renovated restaurant. Don't forget to have a meal in the charming, old *Golden Apple Inn* (M but can run higher), 45 King St. W. (613–382–3300).

KINGSTON. Contact the *Kingston Area Bed and Breakfast Association,* 10 Westview Rd. (613–542–0214). *The Prince George Hotel* (I-M), 200 Ontario St. (613–549–5440) is a restored 19th century hotel with a lively bar downstairs and pretty rooms upstairs.

On the waterfront. *Beaver Motel* (I–M). Hwy. 15 (613–546–6674), has 22 quiet rooms in a scenic setting with outdoor pool. A pleasant suburban motel is the *Walnut Grove Motor Inn* (M), 2327 Princess St. (613–546–2691), which boasts an outdoor pool, efficiency units and picnic areas. Kingston is a university town and caters to students' appetites. One cheap, cheerful, licensed health food restaurant is *The Sunflower,* 20 Montreal St., no meat. The *Firehall Dining Room* (M), 251 Ontario St. (613–548–8888), a restored 1840's firehall, is a university student favorite for steak and salad. Lamb, steak and homemade pastries are served in the courtyard of *Chez Piggy* (M but can run higher), 68R Princess St. (613–549–7673), a restored stone livery stable circa 1810.

MEAFORD. *Trollers Motel* (I–M), 168 Sykes St. (519–538–3030), has six cottages and a six-room motel. While in Meaford, try the well-prepared lakefish at the *Fisherman's Wharf* (M), 12 Bayfield St. (519–538–1390). *The Backyard Cafe* (M), 27 Nelson St. (519–538–4455), serves fresh salads, chicken, and fish; it's beloved by local theater-goers.

PETERBOROUGH. The *Otonabee Motor Inn* (M), 84 Lansdowne St. E. (705–742–3454), is recommended for its outdoor pool and beach front on the Otonabee River. There are boat launching facilities. On the outskirts of the city try the *Blue Jay Motel* (I) on Hwy. 7, R.R. 7 (705–743–2160). *The Farmer's Kitchen Products* (I), 137 Hunter St. (705–745–4226), is a natural-food bar. *The Cheese Shop* (I), 118 Hunter St. W. (705–745–9221), is a local favorite for take-out sandwiches and coffees from around the world. *Moncrief Dairy* (I), 226 Charlotte St. (705-745-5645), offers good, inexpensive lunches.

OTTAWA. Although there are numerous **hotels and motels** in Ottawa, they aren't cheap. For instance the famed Château Laurier's is *not* recommended for budget-minded. There are a number of moderately priced hotels and motels, however, like the recently renovated *Hotel Roxborough* (M), 123 Metcalfe St. (613–237–5171), and the *Parkway Motel* (M) at 475 Rideau St. (613–232–3781). Always reliable, and very central—just down the block from the National Gallery is the *Lord Elgin* (M), 100 Elgin St. (613–235–3333). It's a large hotel with small but clean rooms, favored by businessmen. The inexpensive range includes the *Churchill Arms Motel* (I), 815 Churchill Ave. (613–729–3118) and the *Nicholas Street Jail Hostel,* 75 Nicholas St. (613–235–2595). A former jail converted by the Canadian Association, it's a fairly comfortable, very friendly and highly unusual place to stay right near the center of town. Dormitory accommodation for Youth Hostel members costs less than $10.00 for members, less than $13 for nonmembers. Open during the summer, maximum stay 3 nights. A $5.00 refundable deposit is required. Reservations and payment should be made in advance to the Ottawa YM/YWCA, 180 Argyle St. (613-237-1320). There are many amenities, including pool, gym and cafeteria, and special weekly and group rates. A double room is in the "Inexpensive" range. Check out the residences at *Carleton University,* 1237 Colonel By Dr. (613–231–3610). Open from mid-May to the end of August, double rooms are around $30.00 for two per night. Reservations are required. Located in the city center, the *University of Ottawa,* 648 King Edward Ave. (613–231–7055), also requires reservations. Its double rooms cost slightly more. Like Carleton it offers weekly rates as well.

There is a wide variety of **restaurants** in Canada's capital catering to diplomats and reflecting the proximity of French Québec. Even today on the Québec Hull side of the Ottawa River the food tends to be better than Ottawa's—and that means very good indeed. Some of Ottawa's most pleasant restaurants are in the Byward Market. Ranging from inexpensive to moderate, these include *Café du Marche* (M) (613–233–5175), a café in the main Market Building, 55 George St., specializing in crêpes; the *Cafe Bohemian* (M) at 89 Clarence St. (613–238–7182). *Cafe Casa Blanca* (M), 87 George St., in the market (613–233–3190), is a licensed restaurant serving delicious Moroccan couscous and lamb. *Live-Eaticus* (I), 129 Bank St. (613–234–9607) is a vegetarian eatery. *Le Café* (I) in the National Art Centre, Elgin St. at Confederation Square (613–996–5051), overlooks the canal and is a good bet for lunch. The *Khyber Pass* (I-M), 271 Dalhousie (613–235–0881), serves Afghanistani cooking closely related to Indian curries. Other international restaurants located throughout the city and priced in the moderate category include the *Café Colonnade,* 280 Metcalfe (613–237–3179), famous for pizza, and *Mamma Teresa,* 300 Somerset St. W. (613–236–3023), where Mamma does veal and cheese, or vermouth, or wine sauce. It's possible to blow your budget at both, or to enjoy a moderate meal. Strictly off limits to budget watchers at dinner is *Chez Jean Pierre* (M at lunch only), 210 Somerset St. (613–235–9711). French cuisine correctly and deliciously prepared. *Pinetree Village* (I-M), 354 Elgin St. (613–232–6126), is recommended for Chinese food, especially its chicken dishes. The *Wan Wah* (I-M), 1098 Bank St. (613–235–0670), is for the more adventurous, serving squid and seaweed. *Hungarian Village* (M), 164 Laurier St. W. (613–238–2827), has good paprikash. At the crowded tables of *Topkapi Restaurant* (I-M), 142 Metcalfe (613–232–5992), you'll get shish kebabs and chicken in yogurt. For inexpensive meals try *Mother's Pizza and Spaghetti Parlour,* 745 Montreal Rd. (613–744–0121).

What to See in Eastern Ontario

BELLEVILLE. The *Hastings County Museum* (613–962–2329) housed in Glanmore, a restored Victorian mansion at 275 Bridge St., is worth visiting for its large collection of lights and lamps.

GANANOQUE. Visit the *Gananoque Museum* on King St. (613–382–4663) to see extensive exhibits of military artifacts. Open

June—September, afternoons daily except Sundays. At *The Tinker's Dam* on King St. W., family entertainment includes puppet shows, a craft market, and a café (open all year, daily). A 1 ½- or 3-hour *Boat Cruise* through the Thousand Islands winds past grand old summer resort homes with a stop at *Boldt's Castle.* Call *Gananoque Boat Lines* (613–382–2144) or *Ivy Lea Cruise Boats* (613–659–2293) for details.

KINGSTON. Begin your tour at the *City Hall,* 216 Ontario St., a domed limestone building built in 1843–44. *Bellevue House,* 35 Centre St., was once the home of Sir John A. MacDonald, Canada's first prime minister. Restored to the period when Sir John lived there, it's full of MacDonald memorabilia. Open all year, daily except holidays. Free. On *Brock Street,* the town center in the 1800's, you can see period shops still operating today, including *Cooke's Old World Shop,* a gourmet grocery store with dark-wood fittings still in business after a century. *Old Fort Henry* (613–542–7388) used to be Canada's mightiest citadel, and today it re-creates the military life of the 1800's, complete with marching soldiers, cannon, and a *Sunset Retreat.* Located at the junction of Hwys. 2 and 15, the Fort is open daily from mid-May to mid-October, while just across the bay is *Royal Military College* (613–545–7209), Canada's premier military school. At the corner of Barrie and King Sts. is the *Murney Tower Museum,* a hugh limestone Martello tower, now a museum. From July through Labor Day it's open daily. Admission 50 cents. The city's 1849 pumping station at 23 Ontario St. has been restored and is now the *Pumphouse Steam Museum* (613–546–4696), housing the largest collection of steamgenerated pumps, engines, and models in the world. Open daily from mid-June to Labor Day. Admission $1.00. The *Marine Museum* (613–542–2261), at Ontario and Union Sts., offers a history of Great Lakes shipping from the late 17th century on. Open daily from mid-May to mid-October. Because Kingston was the birthplace of organized hockey, it's appropriate that the city house the *International Hockey Hall of Fame,* at York and Alfred Sts. (613–544–2355). Open weekends from mid-September to mid-June, and daily from mid-June to mid-September. Two museums explore the area's lumbering history: the *MacLachlan Woodworking Museum,* 1316 Princess St., open from mid-June to Labor Day, Tuesday through Saturday, and a museum called the *Bell Rock Mill,* 34 km. north off Hwy. 38, opperating saw, planing, shingle, flour and grist mills. Open April–November, Monday–Friday; Victoria Day–Labor Day, daily except Tuesdays and Wednesdays. At *Queen's University* campus, visit the *Agnes Etherington Art Center* (613–547–6551). It's at University and Queen's Crescent. The center contains over 3,000 works including a substantial collection of 20th-century Canadiana. Open all year, daily, except Mondays. For entertainment the university has much to offer (call 613–547–5940 for information). One favorite student pub is *Muldoon's* (613–544–6881) in the Hotel Frontenac; local M.P. Flora MacDonald sometimes leads Gaelic songfests here.

Dollar Bills, downstairs in the Prince George (613–549–5440), is another lively student tavern.

PETERBOROUGH. *Peterborough's Centennial Museum and Museum of the Trent-Severn Waterways* (705–743–5180) has exhibits of minerals and artifacts that tell the history of the region. The Peterborough *Art Gallery,* at 2 Crescent St. (705–743–9179), exhibits chiefly Canadian works. For plays, try the *Arbor Theater* (705–748–3111), at Trent University. Best pub: the *Jolly Hangman,* on campus. *Art Space,* 190 Hunter St. W. (705–745–0976), shows works by avant-garde local artists. At *Kawartha Downs* raceway, there's harness racing all year round. To the southeast of Peterborough is *Lang Grist Mill* and *Hope Saw Mill* (705–295–6694), with 20 restored colonial buildings, including a school and blacksmith's. To get there, drive east on Hwy. 7, then south on Cty. Rd. 34. You can swim and fish in the river, and have tea at the *Keene Hotel* in the village. at *Serpent Mounds Provincial Park* are 2,000-year-old burial mounds left by Indians—plus swimming sites in Rice Lake.

OTTAWA. Practically the whole city of Ottawa is an attraction, from its parks and shops to its embassies and historical buildings. For tourist information call 613–237–5150. OC TRANSPO (Ottawa-Carleton Regional Transit Commission, public transport) will take you on a quick tour of all the major attractions like the *War Memorial, Lower Town* (the original city), *Sussex Drive* (where the Prime Minister lives at #24), and the Governor General's residence at Rideau Hall nearby; *Rockcliffe,* Canada's most prestigious neighborhood, various embassies, the *Rideau Canal,* and finally *Parliament Hill.* Get off the bus on "The Hill" and take a free guided tour of the *Center Block,* open from 9:00 A.M. to 9:00 P.M. daily during the summer, to 4:30 the rest of the year. If Parliament is in session, you might care to sit in on *Question Period,* beginning at 2:00 P.M. from Monday to Thursday, at 11:00 A.M. on Friday. In order to avoid the lineups to the public gallery, try to obtain a pass from your local M.P. before going.

There are lots of **museums** worth seeing on Ottawa. (Some are free; none costs much.) The *National Gallery of Canada,* at Elgin and Slater Sts. (613–992–4636), houses Canadian and European art, and regular exhibitions. Open daily all year except Christmas Day; from September to April it's closed Mondays. The *National Library and Public Archives,* 395 Wellington St. (613–995–7969), features Canadian historical documents, recordings, films, and photos. Open daily all year. Kids enjoy the *Canadian War Museum,* 330 Sussex Dr. (613–992–2774), and the *National Postal Museum,* 180 Wellington St. (613–995–9904), with its reconstructed post office and philatelic displays. There are two former prime ministerial **residences** worth seeing. Sir Wilfred Laurier and, later, William Lyon Mackenzie King lived at *Laurier House,* 335 Laurier Ave. E. (613–992–8142). The house has been restored to the King era, with many of his personal effects on display. King's summer home at

Moorside, *Kingsmere,* is a 10-minute drive on the Gatineau Pkwy. from Hull. It's open from late May to Thanksgiving. The genuine Gothic ruins were taken by King when he was in London during the Blitz.

The *National Arts Centre,* in Confederation Square (613–996–5051), is really the center of the city's cultural life. With two **theaters,** a studio for smaller dramatic events, an opera house and two restaurants, there's no shortage of entertainment year-round. Featuring programs of dance, film, puppetry, theater and opera, the NAC is also the home of Ottawa's National Symphony Orchestra.

Ottawa is not an after-hours city; it seems that bureaucrats really do lead dull lives. However, there are some moderately priced clubs and bars, including *La Brasserie* (613–232–5713), an open-air beer garden by the canal at the National Arts Centre. It offers live entertainment Monday–Saturday nights. *Vines,* 54 York St. (613–563–4270), is a wine bar in the basement of the Old Fish Market. For a taste of Québecois culture, cross the river to Hull and pay a visit to the *Brasserie Bon Vivant,* 462 Boulevard St. Joseph (819–771–8990). Some of the best folksingers in Québec appear there, and the food is plentiful and inexpensive.

Ottawa is very much a **sports** town, both professional and recreational. During the season, *Ottawa Roughriders CFL* football can be seen at Landsdowne Park (613–563–4551). *Ottawa 67's* play Major Junior A hockey. There's year-round harness racing at *Rideau-Carleton Raceway* (613–822–2211) and *Connaught Park* (613–771–6111). But the real fun is participating in some of the many inexpensive recreational activities the capital has to offer. Biking and boating are two of the big ones. Rent a bicycle at *Rent-a-Bike* (613–233–0268), at the Château Laurier, or at *Dow's Lake Boathouse* (613–232–2023) and spend the day cycling along the many kilometers of carefully laid-out bicycle routes throughout the city. Or rent a boat at *Dow's Lake Boathouse* or *Hog's Back Marina* (613–733–5065) and go canoeing, sailing, rowing, or pedaling. Free, naturalist-led *Nature Walks* are available year-round in areas just outside the city like the Gatineau Park. Call (613) 992–4231, or ask for a schedule at 16 Metcalfe St. or at 161 Laurier Ave. W., 7th floor. Winter is one of the best times to visit Ottawa. There's cross-country skiing and a year-round ice rink at the *Nepean Sportsplex,* 1701 Woodroffe Ave. (613–226–6554). Skating in winter on the frozen Rideau Canal is a must. You can rent skates at the *Park Lane Hotel,* 111 Cooper St. (613–238–1331). If you'd like to cross-country ski, call *Fresh Air Experiences,* 1291 Wellington St. (613–729–3002) for equipment, or rent at ski areas in Gatineau Park and Mont Cascade, both on the Québec side of the Ottawa River.

SOUTHWESTERN ONTARIO

The part of Ontario that curves around Lake Ontario, known as
The Golden Horseshoe, is the most developed and wealthiest region
in the country. Here are flat, fertile farmlands, little old towns with
flourishing flea markets and sleepy local museums, and the long
beaches of the Lake Erie and Lake Huron shores. Budget travelers
should be warned of crowded hotels and campsites near the area's
popular theater festivals—Stratford's Shakespearean festival,
Niagara-on-the-Lake's Shaw, and even around the Straw Hat Theater festivals at Blyth and Grand Bend. The food is the best in the
province, especially if you haunt the farmers' markets for local
sausages, cheeses, jams, and pies. There's little in the way of
wilderness here; southwest Ontario has been farmed, and even
fought over, since before the War of 1812. To reach southwest
Ontario simply head west from Toronto.

Exploring Hamilton

"I just flew in from Hamilton" goes the local joke, "and boy, are
my arms dirty." Known as "Pollution City" because of its two
massive steel plants, Hamilton (population 411,445) is actually a
surprisingly gracious garden city. The old neighborhoods around
Aberdeen, Markland, and Ravenschiff Sts., where the early steel
magnates built their mansions, make a rewarding walking tour.
Hamilton's famous Botanical Gardens ring Burlington Bay; despite
its pollution, the waterside is still home to wild ducks and blue
herons, and the gardens are splendid. Gage Park in the east end
of town features a Children's Museum. It seems that some of Hamilton's residents are big on sports—the Football Hall of Fame is
here—while some go to Hamilton Place's art gallery and theater,
and to outdoor concerts at Dundurn Castle instead. The castle was
built by Sir Alan McNab, one of the venal Scots who founded the
city. Though he became a prime minister of Upper Canada, he
shamelessly admitted, "Politics? Railways are my politics!"

Niagara Falls and Niagara-on-the-Lake

There couldn't be two more dissimilar towns than these. Niagara
Falls (population 70,960) has been a honky-tonk tourist trap and
kitsch capital since the 1820's. That was when tourism promoters
sailed a cargo of "furious animals" over the Falls to their deaths
in order to lure crowds. Later, as daredevils crossed the Falls by
tightrope, or went over in barrels, hawkers sold tourists white stones
as "congealed mist" and bottled water guaranteed to burn (it
didn't). One of Napoleon's relatives came here after her wedding,
launching the town's honeymoon tradition. Today's 10 million annu-

al visitors and honeymooners stroll the city's lavish gardens—most are in the park system that skirts the Niagara River, and have their photos taken by the 158-foot-high Canadian (Horseshoe) Falls. You'll blow your budget if you visit the city's many other sights—wax museums, marinas, and rides under the Falls. But the gardens are free. Niagara-on-Lake (population 12,186) just 20 minutes north by car, is a quaint, genteel Loyalist community of white clapboard houses and hundred-and-fifty-year-old shops (many now turned into boutiques and cafés). The Shaw Festival is headquartered in a modern brick complex at one end of the main drag, Queen Street. Some houses in the neighborhoods on either side of Queen Street date from the 1820's—try Johnson, Prideaux, and King. For a brief time—1791–1796—Niagara-on-the-Lake was capital of Upper Canada. By the War of 1812, the capital had been moved to York (Toronto)—wisely, for this town was occupied by American troops. In 1776, and again in the War of 1812–14, the settlers of this entire region defended their right to be British colonials as opposed to free Americans; as evinced by the string of old forts from Fort George outside Niagara-on-the-Lake, and Old Fort Erie (south of Niagara Falls) to Fort Malden in the western end of the province just outside Windsor.

Farther West

West of Niagara-on-the-Lake are Ontario's vineyards; St. Catharines (population 124,018) is the site of an annual grape and wine festival. Along the Lake Erie shore are resort and fishing towns (Lake Erie's plentiful fish are still considered safe, though the government advises eating them no more than once a month). Inland are old farming communities such as St. Thomas (in the tobacco belt), Ingersoll (site of a cheese making museum), and London. Stately and conservative, situated on the banks of the River Thames, London (population 254,280) has a major university. A renovated opera house, art galleries, boutiques, and cafés enliven the downtown area around Richmond, King, Adelaide, and Dundas Sts. The oldest buildings in town are Eldon House (1834) and the Labatt Pioneer Brewery, dating from about the same period.

Windsor

Windsor (population 192,083), west of London, was once a crossover point for runaway slaves. Many freed slaves settled around Dresden, including the Rev. Josiah Henson, model for novelist Harriet Beecher Stowe's character Uncle Tom. In the 1920's Windsor again became a crossover point—this time for Canadian rum being smuggled past U.S. Prohibition laws to American gangsters. Today, this city still directs its attention to the Detroit shore of the Windsor River. A network of parks plus the Windsor Art Gallery (a converted warehouse) face the water. Fort Malden, Bob-Lo Amusement Park, and some of the province's best boat and birdwatching are all found along the river shore to the south of town.

North of Windsor

Lake Huron, north of Windsor, is lined with long sweeps of beach. Grand Bend is one busy center, as windsurfers vie for space by the yachts. Bayfield (population 649) is quiet and quaint, worth a detour for its sidewalk cafés and renovated old hotels. The streets of Goderich (population 7,340) are laid out like spokes of a wheel round a central park. Locals claim this town on bluffs above Lake Huron has the best sunsets in the world. The best place to view them is from the park on the promontory by the old county jailhouse.

Inland is theater festival country—at Blyth and, of course, at Stratford (population 26,262). The Avon River's swans, willows, and riverside Victorian neighborhoods are lovely attractions the budget traveler can enjoy for free.

Kitchener-Waterloo

Originally named Berlin by its German founders, Kitchener was renamed during World War I. Neither it nor the adjacent municipality of Waterloo (total population 189,734) has lost much of its German flavor. Kitchener supports a flourishing Oktoberfest with more than 20 Festhallen. On the town's main drag, King St., is a 23-bell glockenspiel. Every Saturday morning Mennonites from the surrounding farms come to market to sell shoofly and schnitz pies, kochkäse (cheese cooked with caraway), and excellent sauerkraut. On Queen St., near the market, there's a Viennese-style pâtisserie, famous for its coffee and chocolate-rum balls. Musically, too, Kitchener is very German and supports a symphony, 600-voice vocal concerts, and a small ballet company.

German culture is supplanted by Scots as you head northeast from Kitchener toward Elora (a quaint old gray-stone town built on a picturesque gorge (population 2,666),), Fergus (home of the annual Fergus Highland Games, population 6,000), and Guelph (population 71,207). Guelph's downtown is dominated by the twin spires of the Church of Our Lady of the Immaculate Conception modeled on the great cathedral at Cologne. Some of the buildings on the grounds of the University of Guelph and surrounding neighborhoods are build of gray limestone which adds to the town's Edinburghian atmosphere.

Head back to Toronto via the Rockwood Conversation Area. The action of the Speed River has carved weird shapes out of the rock. Tiny Rockwood has an excellent bakery, fudge factory, and French restaurant; it's a dormitory for trendy Toronto expatriates.

PRACTICAL INFORMATION FOR SOUTHWESTERN ONTARIO

Transportation

BUS AND CAR. The Queen Elizabeth Way (QEW) follows the western rim of Lake Ontario from Toronto through Hamilton to Niagara Falls. The major highway linking Toronto and Windsor is the MacDonald Cartier freeway (Hwy. 401). Of course, roadside diners and motels off this highway tend to be pricier than those off parallel Hwy. 2; Hwy. 3 which skirts the Lake Erie shore; and Hwy. 7, which goes through Stratford, Kitchener-Waterloo, and Toronto. *Voyageur Colonial* and *Gray Coach* lines are among the major bus carriers.

FOR MORE INFORMATION

Ontario-wide tourist offices are open all year at 5629 Falls Ave. in Niagara Falls; 110 Park St. E. in Windsor, and at Blue Water Bridge in Sarnia. Regional and local tourist office addresses are as follows: Chatham, 48 Fifth St.; Fergus, 160 David St. S.; Fort Erie, 68 Goderich St.; Guelph, Trafalgar Sq.; Hamilton, 100 Main St. E.; Kitchener, 67 King St. E.; London, 300 Dufferin Ave.; Niagara Falls, 5433 Victoria Ave. and at Table Rock House; Port Dover, Harbour St.; St. Catharines, 132 King St.; Windsor, 80 Chatham St. E.

Accommodations and Restaurants

You won't have any trouble finding a place to stay or eat in the "Golden Horseshoe," Canada's most populous and prosperous region. As usual, your main concern will be to get good value without feeling you've had to compromise. Again, the following categories should be a guide (prices are for 2 people):

Accommodations: *Inexpensive* (I) less than $60.00 and *Moderate* (M) $60.00–$80.00.

Restaurants: *Inexpensive* (I) less than $35.00, and *Moderate* (M) $35.00–$50.00.

GUELPH. There are several pleasant and surprisingly modestly priced places to stay in Guelph. Try *George Wiatr's Woodlawn Motel* (I), 281 Woodlawn Rd. W. (519–826–5850) with quiet rooms and swimming nearby. Also recommended for their recreational facilities are the *Parkview Motel* (I), 721 Woolwich St. (519–836–1410), or the *Rockhaven Motel* (I), 780 York Rd. (519–824–7500).

Offering more services and facilities is the *College Motor Inn* (M), 716 Gordon St. (519–836–1240). For good homemade pâté, moussaka, lasagna, and other Mediterranean dishes, try *The Bookshelf* (I-M), 41 Quebec St. (519–821–3333). Licensed for beer and wine. *The Baker St. Bistro* (I), 76A Baker St. (519–836–8750) serves good salads and moussaka.

ELORA. Near Guelph in Elora are two Mill St. restaurants worth trying. At the *Elora Mill Restaurant and Inn* (M but can run higher) (519–846–5356) the view of the river and waterfalls may be more spectacular than the food. But the *Café Floré* (M) at the other end of Mill St. (519–846–5631), under the watchful eye of master chef Florio, offers great salads, Basque chicken, beef bourguignonne, and pastries. The best tables overlook the river. Licensed.

In **ENOTTVILLE,** on Hwy. 6 between Guelph and Fergus, the *Golden Beaver* (M) (519–843–3927), small and unpretentious-looking, serves good Canadian food. Unlicensed.

HAMILTON. In downtown Hamilton there are the venerable Royal Connaught Hotel and the Holiday Inn but these exceed our moderate price range. The "budget" traveler will do better at the *Manhattan Motor Hotel* (I), 737 King St. E. (416–527–2708) and the *Beach Motor Inn* (I) 400 Beach Blvd. (416–547–8906). The *YMCA* (I), 79 James St. S. (416–529–7102), is true budget value. Right downtown, it's open year-round; you should book in advance. *McMaster University* (I), on Main St. W. (416–525–9140), isn't as central as the Y, but its residences are cheap, and you can use such university facilities as the pool, tennis courts, cafeteria, and communal kitchens. The *Cobblestone Lodge* (I), 684 Main St. E. (416–545–9735), is a lovely old tourist home not far from downtown, near public transport and quiet tree-lines streets. Reserve in advance. Hamilton has a pretty good selection of restaurants. The *Aero Chinese Tavern and Steak House* (M), 650 Barton St. E. (416–544–5022), and the *Pagoda Chop Suey House* (M), 85½ King St. E. (416–522–6766), offer reliable Cantonese food, as well as North American dishes. *Shakespeare's Steakhouse* (M but can run higher), 181 Main St. E. (416–528–0689), claims to be the best steakhouse in town, but it's pricey. The *Ben Hur Steakhouse and Seafood Restaurant* (I), 15 Plains Rd. W., Burlington (416–639–7902), has a châteaubriand special for two for $13.95 total that's worth trying. The fish isn't always as tasty. Not to be outdone, the *Hacienda Steakhouse* (I), 150 Centennial Pkwy. N. (416–561–0725), offers a châteaubriand special for two for $12.95. Two can have baby salmon at the same price. The *Trocadero Restaurant* (M), 525 Barton St. E. (416–527–3894), is one of the most popular Italian restaurants in the city, and *Martin's Steak House* (M), 946 Barton St. E. (416–549–8829), is a busy and informal steak restaurant that also serves good charbroiled burgers and French fries. *Pappas Restaurant and Tavern* (M), 309 Main St. E. (416–525–2455), offers a Greek menu that includes roast lamb, pork and chicken, feta and olive salads. For excellent Polish and Ukrainian food try *Sir Stefan's*

(M), in the west end of the city at 436 Aberdeen Ave. (416–528–0878). Downtown, *Lisbon Place* (M), 300 James St. N. (416–522-2137), is a good bet for seafood, European and Canadian food. Also downtown, the *Black Forest Inn* (M), 255 King St. E. (416–528–3588), will charm you with its Bavarian atmosphere and menu. For an inexpensive corned beef sandwich and soup try *Switzer's Deli City and Bagel Bin* (I), 1685 Main St. W. (416–527–4000). Unlicensed. Just west of Hamilton in Ancaster, the setting at the *Old Mill* (M), 548 Old Dundas Rd. (416–648–1827), is more spectacular than the food, but it's affordable.

In the **KITCHENER-WATERLOO** area there is a good selection of inexpensive motels to choose from. In Kitchener, *Evergreen's Motel* (I), Fisher Rd. exit off Expressway to Highland Rd. N. (519–743–4161) is well-appointed and close to picnic areas. *Pioneer Motel* (I), 4391 King St. E. (519–653–3229) is directly across the street from a pioneer theme park. *Sherwood Motor Hotel* (I), 2830 King St. E. (519–893–6122) has an outdoor pool and reliable coffee shop. In the moderate range in Kitchener you'll find the *Conestoga Inn* (M), 1333 Weber St. E. (519–744–5242), and the *Valhalla Inn* (M), on King St. (519–744–4141). In Waterloo, *Olde Heidelburg House* (I), Hwy. 86 and County Rd. 15 (519–699–4413), has 16 rooms with TV and Mennonite cooking in the dining room. The residences at the *University of Waterloo* (I), University Ave. (519–885–1211), are open to visitors from mid-May to mid-August. Use of university facilities is included. Book in advance. The *Kitchener Farmers' Market,* in the Market Square Mall downtown, is a great place to buy bread, sausages, fruit and vegetables, and much more, if you want to picnic. *The Rathskeller* (I), 151 Frederick St. (519–578–6670), serves affordable German food. At the *Valhalla Inn* (M), mentioned earlier, you can try Sunday brunch in the Black Walnut Dining Room. *Angie's Kitchen* (I), 47 Erb St. is famous for its home cooking and pastries. No reservations.

PORT DOVER. If you're staying in Port Dover on Lake Erie, the *Erie Beach Hotel* (I), Box 9, Walker St. (519–583–1391), is a very good value. You should certainly have a meal in the dining room, famous for its fresh lake fish, great salads, and desserts. Prices are impressively inexpensive.

BAYFIELD. The *Little Inn of Bayfield* (M), Main St., Box 102 (519–565–2611), is a charming 13-room hotel on Lake Huron. The *Oakwood Inn* (M), on Hwy. 21, Box 400 (519–238–2324), has rooms and cottages for rent also on Lake Huron in the **GRAND BEND** region.

LONDON. Inexpensive accommodations in London begin at the *University of Western Ontario,* 5 km. from the center of town. Call (519)679–3991 for information on the residences, rooms available from May to August. The *YM-YWCA* (I), 433 Wellington St. (519–432–3706), has both inexpensive rooms and meals, and is centrally located. There are a number of inexpensive hotels and motels, including *Journey's End Motel*(I), 1156 Wellington Rd. S. (519–685 –9300), handy to entertainment, and the *Motor Court Motel* (I), 1883 Dundas St. (519–451–2610) with waterbeds and fireplaces. *The Rainbow Motel*(I–M), highways 2 and 4 (519–685–3772), has 23 clean rooms and outdoor pool. *The Village Café* (I), 715 Richmond St. (519–432–2191), is another good bet for hamburgers and salads. *Poacher's Arms* (M), 241 Queen's Ave. (519–672–4088), serves English dishes including rabbit and steak & mushroom pie. The *Shanghai Restaurant* (I), 304 Springbank Rd. (519–471–4420), offers good, cheap Chinese food.

NIAGARA FALLS has as much right to be known as "Motel City" as "Honeymoon City." On Lundy's Lane you'll find an endless row of affordable motels, including the *A-1 Motel* (I), 7895 Lundy's Ln. (416–354–6038); *Canuck Motel* (I), 5334 Kitchener St. (416– 358–8221); *Detroit Motor Inn* (I), 13030 Lundy's Ln. (416–227– 2567); and *Fiddler's Green Motel*(I), 7720 Lundy's Ln. (416–358– 9833). The 130-room *Michael's Inn*(ranges from I to higher than M), 5599 River Rd. (416–354–2727), offers a splendid view of Niagara Gorge and the Rainbow Bridge. If you're lucky you might be able to get one of the hotel's least expensive rooms. There definitely aren't as many restaurants as motels in Niagara Falls, but there are quite a few. Some are good value, including the *Old Stone Inn*(M), 5425 Robinson St. (416–357–1234), a renovated flour mill where steak, lamb, rabbit, and some Italian dishes are featured, and *Casa d'Oro*(M), 5875 Victoria Ave. (416–356–5646), frequented by the business crowd at lunchtime. The *Jade Garden* (M), 5306 Victoria Ave. (416–356–0336), is a popular Chinese restaurant.

NIAGARA-ON-THE-LAKE is not cheap to stay in, although the *Royal Anchorage Motor Hotel* (I–M), 186 Ricardo St., Box 233 (416–468–2141), and the *Gate House Inn*(I), 142 Queen St., Box 1364 (416–468–2205), and the very old, 10-room *Angel Inn*(I), 224 Regent St. (416–468–3411) are affordable. The historic *Oban Inn* (M), 160 Front St., Box 94 (416–468–7811), overlooks the Niagara River. It has rustic charm and surprisingly moderate rates. Make sure you book well in advance. The Oban also serves hearty British fare in its dining room, but meals can be costly. More affordable are the beer, egg, and cheese dishes at the publike *Angel Inn*(I), Queen and Regent Sts. (416–468–3411). *The Buttery* (I), 19 Queen St. (416– 468–2564), offers simple, inexpensive snacks and meals.

STRATFORD. You can find clean, inexpensive rooms in one of the lovely old homes that rents to guests during tourist season. For information write the Stratford and Area Visitors' and Convention Bureau, 38 Albert St., Stratford, Ontario, N5A 3K3, or call (519) 271–5140. *Traveller's Motel*(I), 784 Ontario St. (519–271–3830), is a reliable local motel. The *Queen's Hotel*(I–M), 161 Ontario St., Box 115 (519–271–1400) is older, but offers a number of rooms in the inexpensive range. Picnicking is a very popular Festival pastime, and *Leslie Cheese House* (I-M), 423 Erie St. (519–271–3160), is a good place to pick up an exotic box lunch for two. *The Old Prune* (M), 151 Albert St. (519–271–5052) has a garden patio and Quebec-style dishes.

WINDSOR. You will have no trouble finding motel accommodations under $50.00. *The Journey's End,* 2955 Dougall Ave. (519–966–7800); *Madrid Motor Hotel,* 2530 Ouellette (519–966–1860); and the *Cadillac,* 2498 Dougall (519–969–9340) are all in the inexpensive category. A little more costly are the *National Traveller Hotel* (M), 675 Goyeau St. (519–258–8411), and the *Continental Motor Inn* (M), 3345 Huron Church Rd. (519–966–5541). *Chez Vins* (I-M), 26 Chatham St. E. (519–252–2801), is a bistro with tasty soups, salads, and daily specials. Taped and live music too. If you like chicken, then try the *Chicken Court* (I), 531 Pelissier St. (519–252–7226), for fried, broiled, or barbecued fowl at great prices. *The Himalaya* (I), on Ouellette St. (519–258–2804), is a curry diner with a reputation.

What to See and Do in
Southwest Ontario

BAYFIELD. See Lake Huron Shore.

BLYTH. There is an innovative theater festival here during the summer, from June through mid-September. For information, contact the Blyth Festival, Box 10, Blyth, Ont. N0M 1H0 (519–523–9300). For information on other neighboring attractions, see Lake Huron Shore.

DRESDEN. On Park St., the *Uncle Tom's Cabin Museum* combines a museum with the restored home of Rev. Josiah Henson. He was a runaway American slave who went on to found Ontario's first vocational school—emphatically *not* an "Uncle Tom." The small museum shows Underground Railroad and slavery artifacts. Nearby around **PETROLIA** are remnants of a 19th-century oil boom: *The Oil Museum of Canada* on Hwy. 21, *Petrolia Discovery* (a reconstructed 19th-century rig still operating), and some grand old homes from boom times.

ELORA is a quaint town, fast becoming a tourist trap, on a gorge above the Grand River. Here are numerous craft shops, cafés, restaurants, and antique stores. The last covered bridge in Ontario is nearby at **MONTROSE,** on the road to Elmira, a Mennonite community. In **ELMIRA,** there's a famous store, the *Sap Bucket,* at 20 Church St. E., for expensive but genuine Mennonite quilts and crafts.

FERGUS is the home of the *Fergus Highland Games* each August. There are also old swimming holes along the Grand River.

GUELPH is dominated by *Our Lady of the Immaculate Conception Church* (modeled on Germany's Cologne Cathedral). Below the church there's a Saturday morning *Farmers' Market.* Nearby at **ROCKWOOD** is the *Rockwood Conservation Area*—a park with strange rock formations and good birdwatching—and the *Halton County Radial Railway Museum.* A streetcar and electric railway museum, it's 15 km (9 miles) north of Hwy. 401 via Guelph Line; open weekends only and run by tramcar-enthusiast volunteers.

HAMILTON. There are two walking tours to take around Hamilton which will give you a sense of the Steel City's gritty magnificence. First is through the *Royal Botanical Gardens,* on Plains Rd. off Hwy. 403. Across Burlington Bay you can see the *Dofasco Steel* plant. In the Gardens themselves are nature trails, a rose garden, and boat rentals (caution: the waters of Burling Bay are very polluted). Hamilton's second great walking tour is past the grand old houses of Aberdeen, Markland, and Ravenschiff Sts. off James St. on King St., across from City Hall. *Hamilton Place* combines a free *Art Gallery* and huge *Theater* (416–525–7710 for ticket information). Behind Hamilton Place is *Jackson Square,* a huge indoor plaza with a bustling *Farmers' Market* and a new *Library* whose auditorium occasionally features free lectures and folk concerts. *Whitehearn,* an historic house on the opposite side of City Hall, costs around $2.00 admission and features extravagant Victorian furniture and a small collection of doll furniture too. For kids, there's the *Canadian Football Hall of Fame* in City Hall Plaza, and the *Children's Museum,* more of a playground really. It's worth the small admission price for children ($1.00), but adults will appreciate more a stroll in the surrounding Gage Park.

KITCHENER-WATERLOO are twin cities in the heart of Mennonite country. The Saturday morning *Kitchener Farmers' Market* is famous for Mennonite crafts and delicacies. It's on King St., across from the *Glockenspiel,* a 23-bell clock with Snow White, instead of a cuckoo, appearing each day at noon. Some historic buildings in the Kitchener-Waterloo area include *Woodside National Park,* on Wellington St. off Lancaster (519–742–5273). Woodside is refurbished in 1890's style when it was home to the family of William Lyon Mackenzie King, Canada's longest-serving and most eccentric prime minister. The *Joseph Schneider House,* at 466 Queen St. S. (519–742–7752), dates from 1820. In Waterloo, the *Seagram's Museum,* Erb and Caroline streets, celebrates the arts of booze: distilling, and blending. The comprehensive exhibits are housed in a century-old warehouse. *Doon Pioneer Village,* just outside of town at **DOON,** off Interchange 34, offers displays, activities and picnicking.

Along the **LAKE ERIE SHORE, PORT COLBORNE** has some of the world's longest locks—great for watching ships heading up the

Welland Canal—and a small *Historical and Marine Museum* chock full of glassware and old ship gear, housed in a former Loyalist estate at 280 King St. **PORT DOVER** is a fishing town famous for its Lake Erie perch, which you can buy at fish 'n' chip joints or at the *Erie Beach Hotel* (519–583–1391). *Rondeau Provincial Park* has nature trails and *Point Pelee Park,* a 4,000-acre wilderness, is a noted bird sanctuary.

On **LAKE HURON SHORE,** north from Lake St. Clair is **GRAND BEND,** a beach resort with ships bobbing in the harbor and the *Huron County Playhouse.* North on Hwy. 21 is **BAYFIELD,** an old town of restored inns, shops, and cafés. The sunsets over Lake Huron near **GODERICH** are best viewed from the *Huron Historic Jail* (now a museum) on cliffs above the water. Nearby are the *Blyth Summer Theater Festival* (519–523–9300) and **BLYTH's** famous leather and suede factory outlets. Hiking is good at *Falls Reserve Conservation Area* and you can camp or picnic overlooking Lake Huron at *Point Farms Provincial Park* north of Goderich.

LONDON. *Museum of Indian Archaeology* (open all year) and *Lawson Indian Village* (open May 24–Nov. 1), 1600 Attawandaron Rd., is a good introduction to Ontario Indian history. Adults $1.00. The city also hosts the *Centennial Museum* at 325 Queens Ave. (519–432–7166), which has traveling exhibitions. The city is build around the Thames River, much like its English counterpart. Over-looking the river are the *London Regional Art Gallery* at the corner of Queens Ave. and Ridout St. (519–672–4580), and *Springbank Park,* where families cruise the Thames aboard the paddlewheeler *Tinkerbell,* and kids play in *Storybook Gardens.* The main shopping and private art gallery streets are King St., Dundas, and Richmond, where *Theater London,* 471 Richmond (519–672–8800), an opera house, has been restored to its 1901 grandeur. Among the older buildings in town are *The Royal Canadian Regiment Museum* at Wolsley Hall (519–679–5275), boasting an extensive gun collec-tion, and the *Labatt Pioneer Brewery* (519–673–5050) at the end of Simcoe St. W., a replica of the city's first (1828) brewery. *Fanshawe Park* has a full *Pioneer Village* (519–451–2800).

The main attractions at **NIAGARA FALLS** are the 51-meter-high Falls and the city's extensive garden and park system which extends the length of the Niagara River from Fort Erie to Niagara-on-the-Lake. Parks Commission naturalists guide tourists among the po-tholes, tunnels and other rock formations of the *Niagara Gorge.* *Queen Victoria Park,* along the Niagara Parkway by the brink of the Falls (416–356–3053), has 500,000 daffodils in spring; like it, *Oakes Garden* and *Oak Hall,* Portage Ave., is a free horticultural park. It can be budget-breaking to visit the city's commercial tourist attractions: *Skylon Tower,* 5200 Robinson (416–356–2651), with revolving restaurant; the new *Pyramid Place* amusement park, 5400 Robinson (416–357–4442); *Marineland and Game Farm* at 6757 Portage Rd. (416–356–8250); *Louis Tussaud's Waxworks Museum,* 4915 Clifton Hill (416–354–7521); *Ripley's Believe It or Not Mu-seum,* 4960 Clifton Hill (416–356–2238); and the *Guinness Museum* *of World Records,* 4943 Clifton Hill (416–356–2299). The *Maid of the Mist* sails from the foot of Clifton Hill and River Rd. right up to the Falls. Call (416) 358–5781 for information. You can stroll along a boardwalk beside the Falls at the *Great Gorge Trip* and *Daredevil Exhibit,* 4330 River Rd. (416–356–0904).

NIAGARA-ON-THE-LAKE, the first capital of Upper Canada (1791–96), today hosts the *Shaw Festival* (May to September). The main theater complex is at the south end of *Queen Street,* restored to its 19th-century charm with the 1886 *Niagara Apothecary Shop,* and numerous fudge, jam, cheese, woolens, and antique stores. The *McFarland House* is south of town on the Niagara Parkway— Georgian brick home of the early 1800's. Best old streets to walk around town are Rideaux, Front, King, and Johnson; there's an old frame cottage at the corner of Johnson and Gate Sts. which was once home to runaway slaves. To return to Toronto via Lake Ontario, call the *Royal Hydrofoil Cruises* (416–468–2195 or 366–2223 in Toronto).

ST. CATHARINES, just west of Niagara, is known for its *Grape and Wine Festival* each September, and its *Royal Henley Regatta,* North America's largest rowing event, held in August. The local art gallery is *Rodman Hall,* 109 St. Paul Cres. (416–684–2925), a 30-room mansion on 5 acres of park. In the nearby town of **VINELAND** is *Tivoli Miniature World,* Box 90, Vineland Station (416–562–7455), where kids can wander among replicas of the Kremlin and Loire Valley châteaux. *Ball's Falls Conservation Area,* just outside **JORDAN,** was established around two 18th-century log cabins and a scenic gorge and waterfalls picnic spot.

STRATFORD is famous for its renowned *Shakespearean Festival* —but not all the festival's entertainments are classical or even dramatic. There are jazz, folk, and even pop concerts too. Call (416) 363–4471, toll-free from Toronto, for information, or write Stratford Shakespearean Festival Foundation of Canada, Stratford, Ontario, Canada N5A 6V2. The *Gallery Stratford* in an old pumphouse at 54 Romeo St. N. (519–271–5271), has good traveling collections. You can rent canoes or paddleboats to splash about on the Avon River. Check the *Visitors' Bureau* at 38 Albert St. (519–271–4040) for news of *Summer Music Concerts in Market Square.*

WINDSOR'S *Art Gallery* (519–258–7111) and *Dieppe Park* are both located on Riverside Drive looking across the Detroit River to Detroit. The *Ontario Travel and Information Center* is nearby at 110 Park St. E. *Ouellette St.* is known for good shopping, *Jackson Gardens* for their nighttime illumination, and *Ojibway Park* for its unique garden of wild flowers and grasses. One of the oldest buildings in town, the 1812 home of Col François Baby now houses the *Hiram Walker Historical Museum* at 254 Pitt St. W. (519–253–1812). South of Windsor, in **AMHERSTBERG** is *Fort Malden,* 100 Laird Ave. (519–736–5416), and the *North American Black Histori-*

cal Museum (519–736–7353). The town itself is being renovated too, and its tarmac streets replaced with original cobblestone and Victorian streetlamps.

Entertainment in Southwestern Ontario

There's plenty to offer, much of it free, but be warned—cultural events can be pricey.

ELMIRA hosts a *Maple Syrup Festival* in Spring, when—water permitting—spectators line the Elora Gorge to watch white-water kayaking.

GUELPH's *Spring Festival* draws top international musicians for classics and jazz. Call (519) 821–7570 for ticket information.

HAMILTON. *Hamilton Place* (416–525–7710) is increasingly popular on major tour routes. *Bannister's* is a favorite discothéque at King and John Sts. *Paddy's Tavern* on Main St. W. (416–527–2410) is a popular student pub. There are summer *concerts* on the grounds of *Dundurn Castle* (416–522–5313). You can bet on the horses at *Flamboro Downs* (416–627–3561), and in nearby Brantford each August the local Mohawk Native community hosts a *Six Nations Pageant.* Hamilton's *Tiger Cat Football* games are well attended—get tickets in advance for Ivor Wynne Stadium (416–544–7978).

KITCHENER. Call (519) 578–1570 to see what's on at the *Center in the Square*—at 101 Queen St. W.—the *Kitchener-Waterloo Symphony,* the 600-voice choir of *Kitchener Sings,* or the *Black Walnut Ballet.* In Spring, about a month after the sugaring-off season in the sugar maple bushes outside of Kitchener, the town of New Hamburg hosts the *Mennonite Relief Sale.* In Autumn, Kitchener is taken over by *Oktoberfest* revelers. In Waterloo, on the campus of the University of Waterloo, there's a newly opened *Museum and Archive of Games*—almost 1,000 all told.

Along the **LAKE ERIE SHORE,** there's a lively commercial fishing port, beach and pinball arcade at Port Dover, and in *Pinafore Park* in St. Thomas, summer evenings come alive around the bandshell.

Along the **LAKE HURON SHORE,** there's *summer theater* at Blyth—where the Blyth Festival offers original Canadian drama—(call 519–523–9300 for ticket information) and at *Grand Bend's Huron County Playhouse* (519–238–8451).

LONDON. Richmond St. is lively, with the renovated *Grand Theater* at 471 Richmond (519–672–8800) and *Sorrenti's Wine Bar* at #476. In Winter, skaters flock to *Victoria Park's* illuminated rink—especially on New Year's Eve.

The city of **NIAGARA FALLS** lights up the Horseshoe Falls each evening and in summer there are *fireworks.* May brings the *Niagara Blossom Festival* to the region; in fall, St. Catharines hosts the *Grape and Wine Festival.*

For information on **NIAGARA-ON-THE-LAKE's** *Shaw Festival* and *concerts,* call (416) 361–1544 from Toronto or (416) 468–3201 in Niagara for program details.

For information on **STRATFORD's** *Shakespearean Festival,* call (416) 363–4471 in Toronto or (519) 273–1600 in Stratford. In addition there are *concerts* in Civic Square.

WINDSOR celebrates its centuries of happy proximity to Detroit with an *International Freedom Festival* in early July. The Black community also throws an *Emancipation Day Parade.* For information on what's playing at the *Cleary Auditorium,* 201 Riverside Dr., call (519) 252–6579. Bistros, rock clubs, and supper clubs around town include *Jason's,* 25 Chatham St. E. (519–253–7992); *Chez Vins,* across the street (519–252–2801); *The Other Place* at 3067 Dougall Rd. (519–969–6011), a bar with backgammon and music; *Coco's* in the Richelieu Inn at 430 Ouellette St. (519–253–7281), a lively disco; and *Top Hat Steak and Supper Club* (519–253–4644), a popular cabaret—though *not* inexpensive.

Québec

Québec is that huge province that spreads north of the Eastern United States. The largest of the ten provinces of Canada, it offers a wide variety of interests to its visitors. Mountains and forests, lakes and rivers, farmlands and quaint old villages seemingly sleeping under the white-and-blue Québec flag offer a vivid contrast with the bustling life of Montréal, and the old French atmosphere of Quebec City, the capital. But the natural beauty of the land is not its only charm. Québec is French, and rich in history and culture. It also maintains a legendary sense of warmth and hospitality towards its visitors for whom there is a large choice of activities, and a guarantee that they will be treated in an open, friendly way, whatever language they may speak.

Québec has been divided into 18 tourist regions, spreading from the Magdalen Islands in the St. Lawrence Gulf to the Ottawa Valley bordering the Province of Ontario, and from the Eastern Townships and the Richelieu Valley on the U.S. border, to the vast, almost uninhabited James Bay region, site of the powerful hydroelectric development on the La Grande River. But between these extremes are easily accessible points of major interest where you can expect to spend a lovely and unforgettable time at reasonable cost. These center around Montréal and the Laurentians region, and around Quebec City.

EXPLORING MONTRÉAL

With a population of over 1 million (3 million for Greater Montréal), Montréal is the second largest French-speaking city in the world. It is situated on an island and built around a mountain, Mount Royal, which is visible for miles. It houses the head offices of two of the world's greatest railways—The Canadian Pacific and the Canadian National—both of which operate hotels, telecommunications, ships, and trucks. It boasts two international airports: Dorval, which handles all domestic and U.S. flights, and Mirabel, which handles all other international flights as well as transfer flights and air cargo. The city itself offers a network of ultramodern express traffic arteries and an underground Métro system, recognized as one of the world's most sophisticated and effective. Linked up with hotel accommodations, parking garages, exhibition facilities, office

space, and panoramic lookouts, it is enhanced by beautifully decorated indoor stations featuring works by Québec's most talented
artists and offers an intriguing underground city of miles of intercon-
necting arcades and malls, lined with shops, restaurants, theaters,
and other services. In inclement weather, a whole city is within
comfortable reach, with rapid and inexpensive transport at every
turn, and no need to venture outdoors.

Like many other cities, Montréal is best discovered on foot. For
that purpose, it can be divided into 6 main areas where you can
profit inexpensively from your stay while discovering the varied
charms of this unique city. These are Old Montréal, St. Denis Street,
Center Town, Man and His World, the Olympic Village, and Mount
Royal.

Old Montréal

Bordered by Notre Dame St. and Montréal Harbor, Old Montréal
starts at Place d'Armes, where ends the financial district. The Paul
Chomedey de Maisonneuve Monument (he was the founder of
Montréal) dominates the area. In front is the beautiful Notre Dame
Basilica, with its magnificent works of art. This is the usual starting
place of walking tours of Old Montréal and a required stop of bus
tours. Strolling east from there, you will come to Place Jacques
Cartier, facing the City Hall and dominated by the Nelson Column.
Lined with terraces and featuring a flower market all summer, this
spot is the heart of Old Montréal. There are centuries-old stone
buildings reconditioned to modern needs and housing inns, restaurants, apartments, and boutiques. Note: in this district all street
names are painted on red plaques affixed to corner buildings.

St. Denis Street

New life has sprung up along this street with the construction of
the Québec University Campus. This campus in itself is unique. It
was erected in modern, red-brick style, around two façades of the
St. Jacques Church facing St. Denis St. and St. Catherine St. Inside
is an efficient network of stairs and escalators surrounding an open
area complete with flowers, plants and a cascade of running water.
After visiting the university, take a run down St. Denis Street with
its numerous bars, restaurants, terraces, and little boutiques. St.
Denis is just east of St. Lawrence Street, which divides Montréal
between East and West.

Center Town

Center Town spans the area between Dominion Square and
Sherbrooke St. and houses all the main hotels of Montréal. Its focal
point is the corner of St. Catherine and Peel Sts. Using St. Catherine
St. as your main artery, you get a wide choice of sights ranging from
great department stores to chic boutiques, from elegant restaurants
to smoked-meat palaces, from lively discothèques to cozy little bars.

MONTRÉAL

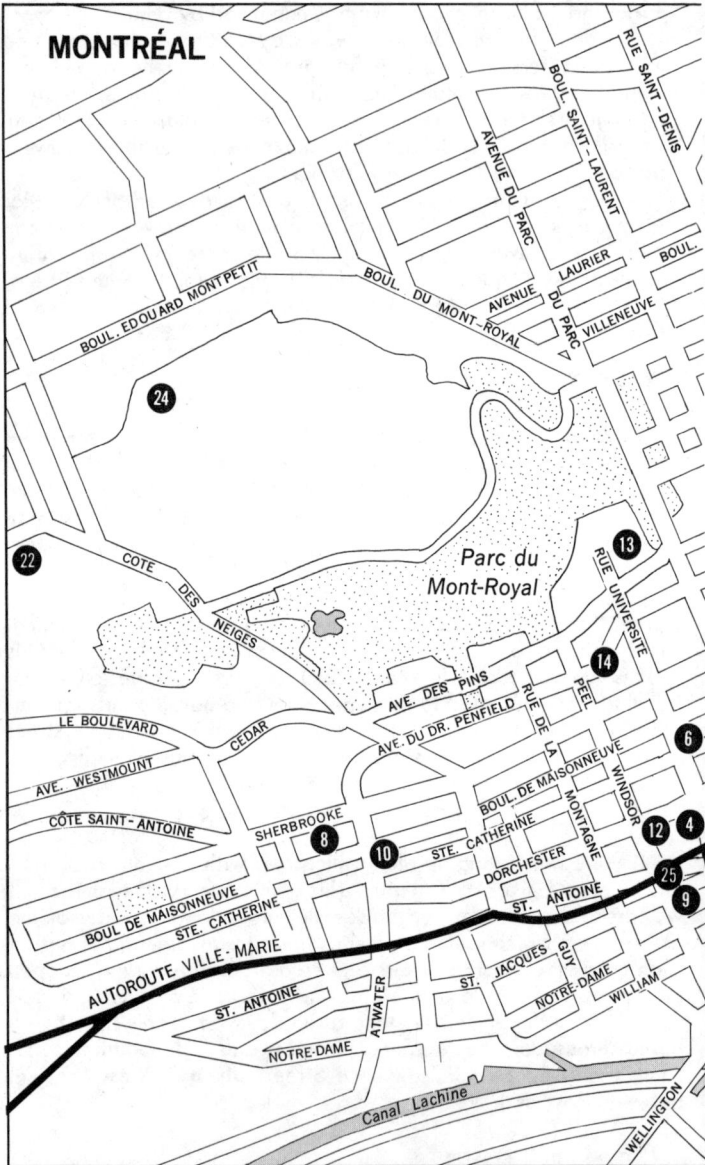

Parc du Mont-Royal

Streets and labels on map: RUE SAINT-DENIS, BOUL. SAINT-LAURENT, AVENUE DU PARC, LAURIER, BOUL., DU PARC, VILLENEUVE, BOUL. EDOUARD MONTPETIT, BOUL. DU MONT-ROYAL, AVENUE, CÔTE DES NEIGES, RUE UNIVERSITÉ, PEEL, LE BOULEVARD, CEDAR, AVE. DES PINS, RUE DE LA MONTAGNE, AVE. DU DR. PENFIELD, AVE. WESTMOUNT, CÔTE SAINT-ANTOINE, SHERBROOKE, BOUL DE MAISONNEUVE, WINDSOR, STE. CATHERINE, DORCHESTER, ST. ANTOINE, BOUL DE MAISONNEUVE, STE. CATHERINE, AUTOROUTE VILLE-MARIE, ST. ANTOINE, ATWATER, ST. JACQUES, GUY, NOTRE-DAME, WILLIAM, NOTRE-DAME, WELLINGTON, Canal Lachine

Montréal—Points of Interest

1) Aquarium
2) Bonsecours Market
3) Botanical Garden
4) Central Station
5) Chateau Ramezay
6) Christ Church Cathedral
7) City Hall
8) Congregation Notre-Dame Mother House
9) Dow Planetarium
10) Forum
11) Garden of Wonders
12) Marie-Reine-du-Monde Cathedral

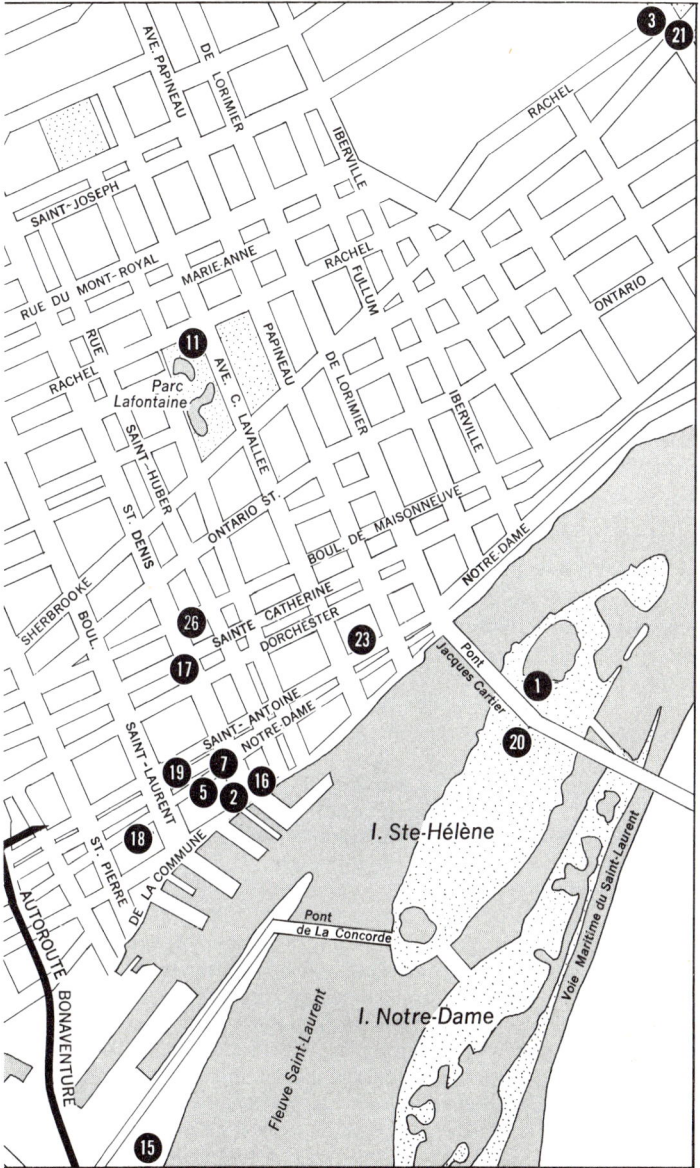

13) McGill Stadium
14) McGill University
15) Museum of Contemporary Art
16) Notre-Dame-de-Bonsecours Church
17) Notre-Dame-de-Lourdes Church
18) Notre-Dame Church
19) Old Court House
20) Old Fort
21) Olympic Stadium
22) Oratoire St. Joseph
23) Post Office
24) Quebec University
25) Radio Canada Building
26) University of Montréal

In this area you'll find the Montréal Museum of Fine Arts, the McCord Museum, McGill University, Mary Queen of the World Basilica, and a wide range of art galleries. And at all times of the day or night, St. Catherine St., from Bleury to Crescent St., is a sight to remember.

Man and His World

Man and His World is the perpetual extension of Expo '67, the great event that marked the 100th anniversary of Canada. It is a permanent (summer months only) exhibition of international pavilions and the showplace of countless fiestas and performances. The whole exhibition spans three islands of the St. Lawrence River and can be reached by two bridges, the Jacques Cartier and the Concorde Bridges, as well as by a métro station on Ste. Helen's Island, the main of the three. Of the other two, Notre Dame Island features picnic grounds and a bicycle track, and La Ronde Island an entertainment park.

The Olympic Village

The Olympic Village and Stadium stand at the corner of Pie IX Boulevard and Sherbrooke St. This sports complex was constructed for the 1976 Olympics, but designed to accommodate athletic competitions and other sports events. The design of the stadium seating areas assures 70,000 spectators a clear view of the competition. The Stadium also houses kitchens, restaurants, bars, offices, libraries, post offices, communications outlets, and a sports museum. In summer it features the Expos, Montréal's baseball team. A tunnel links the Olympic Park to Montréal's Botanical Garden, offering some 23,000 species and varieties of flora. Special sections feature perennials, fruit trees, medicinal plants, shrubs, and aquatic plants.

Mount Royal

Wooded slopes, rolling lawns and manmade Beaver Lake help make 530-acre Mount Royal Park a favorite year-round recreation area. The mountain, a former volcano, rises 763 feet above sea level, affording a panoramic view of the city. The park's 100-foot illuminated cross is a landmark that can be seen for 50 miles. It commemorates the wooden cross planted there in 1643 by religious explorer Paul de Chomedey, sieur de Maisonneuve, after Montréal (then named Ville Marie) was spared from a great flood. The park features lovely promenades as well as a nature museum which holds exhibitions in an old stone hunting lodge. In winter, Beaver Lake becomes a skating rink. There are also ski trails, toboggan hills, and horsedrawn sleighs.

Mount Royal also houses, on its northern slope, the University of Montréal Campus and the famed St. Joseph's Oratory. This shrine, founded more than a half century ago, attracts millions of visitors each year.

PRACTICAL INFORMATION FOR MONTRÉAL

Transportation

AIR. Montréal has flights arriving at Dorval Airport and Mirabel from all over the world.

CAR. Most Americans use their cars to get to Québec. The highways are well marked—white lettering on green for highways, white on blue for toll auto routes. The signs are in French with distances marked in kilometers. The first part should be no problem —in Québec, all routes lead to Montréal. As for the kilometers, they are easily transposed in miles by using the 5-to-8 formula: 8 kilometers equal 5 miles.

TAXI. Minimum fare is $1.20, plus 70 cents a km. From Dorval to downtown around $20.00. From Mirabel around $50.00.

PARKING in Montréal is relatively easy, but can be costly in hotels and privately owned lots. The Municipal lots, easily recognizable by the Montréal crest featured on their rates signs, are your best bet.

BUSES. Buses can take you downtown from Dorval Airport for $5.50 or from Mirabel Airport for $8.00. Montréal Urban Transport buses supply service all over the island: single tickets 90 cents; 15 tickets $11.00. The subway takes transfers from buses and covers the downtown core.

FOR MORE INFORMATION

Contact the *Convention and Tourism Bureau of Greater Montréal,* Mart F, Suite 1, Frontenac, Box 889, Place Bonaventure, Montréal H5A 1E6, (514–871–1595).

Or visit the *Montréal Reception Center* of the Department of Tourism, 2 Place Ville Marie, at the corner of University and Cathcart. Or write Tourisme Québec, Case Postale 20,000, Québec, G1K 7X2, Canada.

Accommodations

HOTELS, INNS, AND PENSIONS

Except in such special circumstances such as Expo '67, the Olympics, or the Grey Cup Festival, Montréal offers a wide variety of accommodations to the budget-minded visitor. Double-occupancy

The Metro

NORTH

NORTH-WEST EXTENSION

DU COLLEGE

DE LA SAVANE

NAMUR

PLAMONDON

CÔTE SAINTE-CATHERINE

SNOWDON

VILLA MARIA

VENDOME

ATWATER
ST-HENRI
LIONEL GROULX

CHARLEVOIX
SOUTH-WEST EXTENSION
DE L'ÉGLISE

ANGRIGNON
MONK
JOLICOEUR
VERDUN

LA SALLE

GEORGE VANIER
LUCIEN L'ALLIER
BONAVENTURE
PLACE D'ARMES
VICTORIA

MAISONNEUVE BLVD.
CHAMP-DE-MARS

GUY
PEEL
MCGILL
PLACE DES ARTS
SAINT LAURENT
BERRI DE MONTIGNY

HENRI BOURASSA

SAUVÉ

CRÉMAZIE

JARRY

JEAN TALON

BEAUBIEN

ROSEMONT

LAURIER

MONT-ROYAL

SHERBROOKE

BERRI ST.

EAST-END EXTENSION

BEAUDRY
PAPINEAU
FRONTENAC
PRÉFONTAINE
JOLIETTE
PIE IX
VIAU
L'ASSOMPTION
CADILLAC
LANGELIER
RADISSON
HONORÉ-BEAUGRAND

LONGUEUIL

ILE SAINTE-HÉLÈNE

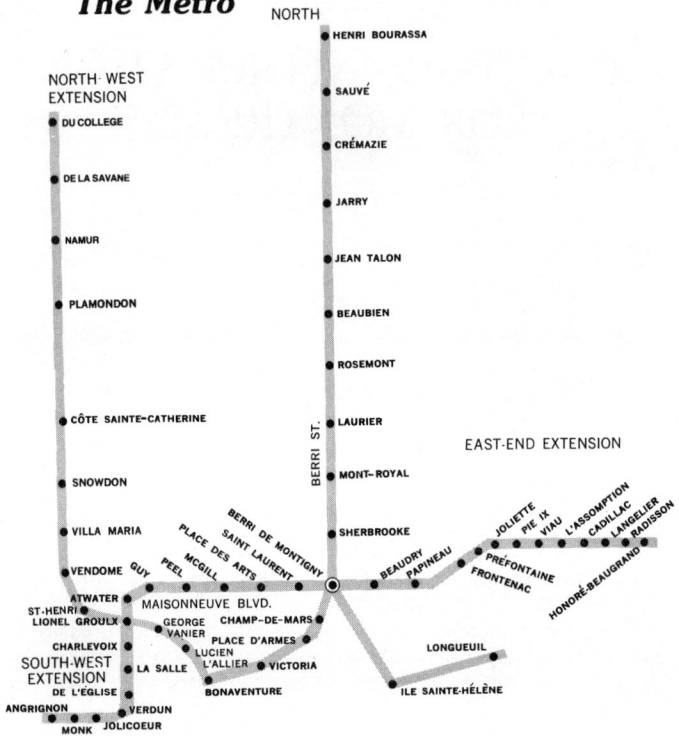

rates are *Inexpensive:* less than $60.00, and *Moderate:* $60.00–$75.00. There are always motels, of which Montréal has quite a few in its outlying areas; but for those wishing to be more at the center of the action, here are some of the best accommodations available:

Inexpensive

Hotel Le Merlion, 1240 Drummond St., in the heart of downtown, 184 rooms. *Hotel de Dorval,* 6600 Côte-de Liesse, near airport, indoor pool, courtesy limo to and from airport. **Le Royal Roussillon,** 1610 St. Hubert St., just east of St. Denis St., 107 rooms.

Moderate

Château Versailles, 1659 Sherbrooke St. W., close to downtown, 79 rooms, free parking, air conditioning, color TV, nicely decorated. **Ramada Inns:** There are three of them: downtown, at 1005 Guy St., in the heart of Montréal, 205 rooms, good service; at 6445 Décarie Blvd., in the northwest section of Montréal, but minutes from downtown by connecting expressway, 104 rooms; and at the Olympic Park, at 5500 Sherbrooke St. E., 240 rooms. **Le Sherbourg,** 475 Sherbrooke St. W., 116 rooms, indoor pool and sauna, indoor parking. Dorval Airport at 6600 Côte-de-Liesse, Saint-Laurent, 220 rooms. **Wandlyn Inn Motel,** 7200 Sherbrooke St. E., in the city's east end near the Olympic Village.

Y'S AND INNS

The **YMCA,** at 1450 Stanley St., Downtown, is $35.50 a night double occupancy; the **YWCA,** at 1355 Dorchester Blvd. W., downtown, from $32.00 to $36.00 double.

Auberge des Glycines, 819 de Maisonneuve Blvd. E., $50.00–$60.00 double; **Alpes Touristes,** 1245 St. André St., $30.00–$45.00 double; and **The Shangri-La,** 157 Sherbrooke St. E.

RESTAURANTS

There are over 3,000 restaurants in Montréal. The choice of food and the variety of prices vary accordingly. From the pizza parlor to the ultra-chic purveyor of French cuisine, from the hot-dog stand to the exotic Greek, Italian, Chinese, German, Indian, or Indonesian restaurant, the visitor is generally assured of good-quality food. Here is a sample of what one can be expected to pay for a full-course meal, exclusive of drinks, tips, and taxes (there is a 10 percent provincial tax on all meals over $3.25): *Inexpensive:* under $10.00 and *Moderate:* $10.00–20.00.

Inexpensive

Ben's Delicatessen, at 990 de Maisonneuve Blvd. W., one of the best of its kind; **Le Mazot** and **Le Saint-Mâlo,** on St. Denis St.; most of the Chinese restaurants, in the Chinatown located next to Old Montréal; most of the Greek restaurants, on Park Ave., Duluth St., and Prince Arthur St.; and all the pubs, brasseries, and taverns (taverns are generally males-only enclaves) where meals are served with beer or wine.

Moderate

There is a very wide choice of restaurants that you can explore at leisure. Most of the restaurants of this type advertise their menus and prices on the outside. To name but a few: **Auberge Chez Henri,** at 3715 St. Lawrence Blvd., French cuisine; **Auberge La Belle Poule,** at 406 St. Sulpice St., French food in a maritime décor and in the heart of Old Montréal; **Bistro St. Joseph,** at 354 St. Joseph Blvd., typical Québec cuisine; **Bianca and Franco,** a good Italian restaurant at 7143 St. Dominique St.; **Delmo's,** a fine seafood place in Old Montréal, 211 Notre Dame St. W.; **La Mancha,** at 5179 Côte des Neiges, serving Spanish food in an appropriate décor; **La Mer à Boire,** at 429 St. Vincent, in Old Montréal, is French, cozy, and warm, with accordian music.

In summer, there are the sidewalk and terrace cafés most of which are either in Center Town, Old Montréal, or on St. Denis St.

Here one can enjoy a slow drink or a light snack while watching the world go by. These places have literally boomed in recent years. They have become an important part in making Montréal the next best place after Paris this side of the Atlantic.

What to Do and See

MUSEUMS

Château Dufresne, at the corner of Pie IX Blvd. and Sherbrooke St. E., in front of the Botanical Garden, offers exhibitions of Canadian handcrafts and decorative art. Thursday to Sunday, noon to 5:00 P.M., adults $2.00, senior citizens $1, students 75 cents, free to children under 12.

Château Ramezay, at 280 Notre Dame St. E., in Old Montréal, displays fine exhibits reminiscent of the military, economic, and social life of the 18th century and the first half of the 19th. Guided tours from Tuesday to Sunday, 10:00 A.M. to 4:30 P.M. Adults $2.00, children, students, and senior citizens $1.00.

Wax Museum of Montréal, at 3715 Queen Mary Road. Open from 9:00 A.M. to 9:00 P.M. every day. Adults $4.50, children $1.75.

Grey Nuns Museum, at 1185 St. Mathieu St., just west of Center Town, has collections dating from the beginning of Colonial Canada and carefully preserved by the Grey Nuns Order, since its foundation in 1737. Open Wednesday to Sunday, from 1:30 P.M. to 4:30 P.M., free admission.

Montréal Museum of Fine Arts, at 1379 Sherbrooke St. W., offers a large collection of master painters as well as Canadian art and special exhibitions all year round. Open from Tuesday to Sunday, adults $2.00, children 12–16, 50 cents.

Museum of Contemporary Art, at Cité-du-Havre, maintains a permanent collection of Canadian and foreign contemporary art, including the largest known collection of works by the famed Québec artist Paul-Émile Borduas. Open Tuesday to Sunday, 10:00 A.M. to 6:00 P.M., free admission.

Canadian Railway Museum, 122A rue Saint-Pierre, in Saint-Constant (south shore), houses a collection of historic railway engines and passenger cars. Open May to September every day from 9:00 A.M. to 5:00 P.M. Adults $3.00; students $2.00; children 5 to 12 $1.50.

St. Joseph's Oratory Museum, at 3800 Queen Mary Rd., part of the huge St. Joseph's Oratory complex, offers exhibits of religious art. Guided tours every day, from 9:00 A.M. to 5:00 P.M., contributions voluntary.

Ste. Helen's Museum on Ste. Helen's Island and easily accessible by the Jacques Cartier Bridge or the Métro. Its large collection of military equipment and Indian artifacts from the Colonial period of 1608 to 1867 is housed in a former armory. In summer it features demonstrations by two regiments, one French, one English, in original dress on its parade grounds. Open every day from May to September, adults $1.50, children $1.00, and from Tuesday to

Sunday between the months of September and May, adults $1.00, children 75 cents.

McCord Museum, at 690 Sherbrooke St. W., in front of McGill University, is an ethnological museum featuring a unique collection of 350,000 photographs of Montréal's life. Friday, Saturday, and Sunday, 11:00 A.M. to 5:00 P.M., adults $1.00, children 50 cents.

Musée Universel de la Chasse et de la Nature at 1260 Remembrance Rd., on top of Mount Royal, features hunting and nature exhibits. Open all year from 10:00 A.M. to 8:00 P.M., closed Monday. Adults $2.00, students and senior citizens $1.00.

Saidye Bronfman Museum, at 5170 St. Catherine Road, on the western slope of Mount Royal, houses collections of national and international contemporary art. In summer, open from Monday to Thursday, 9:00 A.M. to 6:00 P.M., from 9:00 A.M. to 5:00 P.M. on Friday, and from 9:00 A.M. to 12:30 P.M. on Sunday. Free admission.

Sights and Attractions

Churches and parks are numerous in Montréal. Here are a few of these, plus some special attractions which are either free or reasonably priced:

The Botanical Garden, on Pie IX Blvd., corner of Sherbrooke St. E. Open all year from 9:00 A.M. to 6:00 P.M. Adults $2.00, children $1.00. The outdoor gardens are free.

Dow Planetarium, at 1000 St. Jacques St., adults $2.50, children $1.25. Laser shows: adults $4.00, children $2.50.

LaFontaine Park, features a Garden of Wonders (a children's zoo) on Sherbrooke St. E., in front of Notre Dame Hospital.

Notre Dame Basilica, on the Place d'Armes, contains beautiful stained-glass windows and hand-carved woodwork.

Montréal Aquarium, at La Ronde, one of the three islands of the Man and His World complex. Adults $2.00, children and senior citizens $1.00.

Mount Royal Park, on Mount Royal, boasts beautiful trees, promenades, and breath-taking views of the city.

SHOPPING

There are also a number of markets where one can enjoy the sight and taste of a rich variety of farm produce. On the Island of Montréal there are six of them; all operate year-round from Monday to Saturday, generally from 6:00 A.M. to 6:00 P.M., and until 9:00 P.M. on Fridays. They are: the **Atwater Market,** between Atwater, Green and St. Émilie Sts. and the Lachine Canal; the **Marché Central,** at the junction of Crémazie Blvd. and L'Acadie Blvd.; the **Marché de Lachine,** between Norte Dame and Piché Sts. and from 17th to 19th Sts. in Lachine; the **Marché de L'Ouest,** a new one, at the junction of de Salaberry St. and Sources Blvd., in Dollard des Ormeaux; the **Marché de Maisonneuve,** between Ontario and Létourneau Sts., reopened after a 20-year interruption; and the **Marché du Nord,** on Jean Talon St., between Henri Julien and Casgrain Sts., two blocks east of St. Lawrence St.

SPORTS

For spectator *sports,* follow the Montréalers; they go for baseball with the Expos and football with the Concordes—both played at modernistic Olympic Stadium. And in winter Montréalers go mad about hockey when the Canadiens are playing at the Forum on St. Catherine St. As for your personal pleasure, you can enjoy the municipal pools—there are about 20 of them—the bicycle tracks which are fast developing, the open skating rink of Beaver Lake or the easy ski slopes of Mount Royal in winter, or just plain follow the jogger ahead of you.

Entertainment

There is always something going on in Montréal. Its splendid **Place des Arts,** on St. Catherine St., just east of St. Lawrence, features a constant round of events, from world-renowned entertainers and popular singers to more classical music rendered by the famed Montréal Symphony Orchestra under Swiss conductor Charles Dutoit, and the Montréal Opera Company. Check first, then select.

THEATERS play both in French and in English.

The Centaur Theater, at 453 St. François Xavier, in Old Montréal, plays in English only from October to June.

The National Theater School of Canada, at 5030 St. Denis St., plays in English and in French from October to May.

The Saidye Bronfman Center, at 5170 St. Catherine, plays in Yiddish.

For amateurs of French, there are the *Compagnie Jean Duceppe,* at the **Port Royal Theater** in the Place des Arts complex; **Théâtre Denise-Pelletier,** at 4353 St. Catherine St. E.; the **Théâtre d'Aujourd'hui,** at 1297 Papineau St.; the **Théâtre du Nouveau-Monde** (TNM), at 84 St. Catherine St. W.; the **Théâtre Populaire du Québec,** 500 Sauvé St. W.; the **Théâtre de Quat'Sous,** at 100 Pine St. E.; and the **Rideau Vert,** at 4664 St. Denis St.

CINEMAS. Montréal offers the whole range of current films both in French and in English—and the cinemas advertise heavily. Just check the local papers especially on Fridays and Saturdays. (There are three French and one English paper published in Montréal.)

NIGHTLIFE. Bars and discothèques are numerous and range from the popular to the exclusive, from the standard price to the outrageous. **Bars** in the reasonable range are the *Déjà Vu,* 1224 Bishop St.; *Thursday's* (Les Beaux Jeudis), 1449 Crescent St., *L'Express;* 3927 St. Denis St.; *L'Air du Temps,* on St. Paul St. W., in Old Montréal; and *Woody's,* 1238 Bishop St. in Center Town. Most of these bars provide free hors d'oeuvres during the Happy Hour (from 5:00 P.M. to around 7:00 P.M.). As for **discothèques,** your best bets are the hotel discos and the magazines in hotel rooms which list a number of the current ones. By mentioning names the risk is great that this information might be obsolete by the time the guidebook is published!

However, it could be mentioned that the best section to find lively nightlife is in the downtown section around Crescent St., de Maisonneuve Blvd., Bishop St., Mountain and even St. Catherine Sts. Old Montréal and St. Denis Street also have a selection of popular nightclubs and show bars.

Rhapsodie Club, Four Seasons Hotel, Peel and Sherbrooke.

Winnie's, 1455 Crescent St.

Sir Winston Churchill Pub, 1459 Crescent St.

Kicks, 2051 Mountain St.

Le Bijou, 300 Lemoyne St.

AROUND MONTRÉAL

Just one hour by car from the busy center of Montréal are the Laurentian Mountains, vast playground of the North. They offer water bugs, nature lovers, and skiers an endless panorama of beauty and year-round recreation

Access is easy via the high-speed Laurentian Autoroute (toll) and Hwy. 117, which is often called the "main street" of the Laurentians because it passes directly through many of the major resort towns. Along both routes you will see names such as Rosemère, Sainte-Thérèse, Saint-Janvier, Saint-Antoine, Blainville, Saint-Jérôme—all peaceful little towns scattered along the way like gems in a setting of natural beauty.

Your goal, should you choose to take a ride north, should be Mont-Tremblant, currently being developed by the Québec Government into a vast, well-integrated modern leisure complex. The Laurentians are not only a world-renowned winter paradise providing cross-country skiing, snowshoeing, snowmobiling and the most beautiful downhill skiing in Eastern Canada, they also offer a choice of huge lakes skirting the mountain heights and plenty of activities for the outdoor-minded, from fishing to camping to canoeing.

The whole Laurentians region is worth exploring. Whether you decide to stick by the main road or try your luck at map reading, take either Hwy. 125 to Saint-Donat (83 miles from Montréal) or Hwy 344 to Saint-Michel-des-Saints (96 miles). Whatever way you choose, you will be well rewarded by the change of pace and scenery from cosmopolitan Montréal.

On another occasion, a trip along the St. Lawrence River's south shore, from Montréal to Sorel (40 miles), will lead you to the Richelieu River, a modern-day haven for sailing and yachting. From Sorel, Hwy. 133 skirts the Richelieu River to Saint-Jean and Iberville, covering some 55 miles, a route lined with historical towns and villages dating back to colonial times and events that shaped the nation. Stop at Saint-Ours and have a look at the Manoir Saint-

Ours, built in 1792, one of the most elegant historic mansions in the country and one of the few remaining from feudal times.

Should you choose to go east via the north shore, take Hwy. 138, formerly known as "old Route 2" and, further back, the Chemin du Roy, or King's Rd. Open since 1734, this road dates from the beginning of the colonial years and passes by old seigneuries, manors, and ancient churches and historic landmarks, with the river in view.

At the end of this road is another unforgettable Québec destination: Quebec City.

EXPLORING QUEBEC CITY

Quebec is the capital of the Province of Québec. It also has the distinction of being the most European city on the North American continent. There are many ways to visit the old part of this city, but the most rewarding is a walking tour. All that is really needed is a comfortable pair of walking shoes. But if you are romantically inclined—and have a little money to spare—you can hire a calèche inside the city wall on d'Auteuil Street. For $30, the drivers, switching from French to English, will take you through the most interesting sections of Québec.

The focal point of old uptown Quebec is Place d'Armes and the Château Frontenac. This castle-like hotel dominates the square, and its turrets and towers are visible for miles. Constructed in 1892 and still owned by the Canadian Pacific Railway, it is one of Canada's most beautiful hotels, commanding a matchless view of Quebec City. At its feet, overlooking the St. Lawrence River, is the Dufferin Terrace, where one can see the roofs of the town below. For less than a dollar, a beautiful old lift will take you down the escarpment where a short walk around will offer you an unforgettable sight of well-renovated old houses.

The heart of Old Lower Town Quebec, along the riverfront, is woven with small streets studded with many architectural gems of the 17th and 18th centuries. These streets have names such as Rue Sous—le—Fort and Petit-Champlain. They will lead you to Place Royale and the Notre-Dame-des-Victoires Church, the oldest standing house of worship in North America.

Should you happen to have lunch in one of the many restaurants that offer both good food and atmosphere in this section, take in a little exercise by walking back uptown, either by the Côte-de-la-Montagne or use the stairs that will lead you halfway. From there you will come to Quebec's cathedral and the Latin Quarter where stands the original building of Laval University, founded in 1852.

Back at the Château Frontenac and going west is Rue Saint-Louis, the first street laid out in Quebec. Beautifully restored old houses line both sides, and most of these have been converted into very reasonably priced rooming houses. A ten-minute walk from Place d'Armes will lead you to the Citadel, complete with walls, bastions, ancient guns, barracks, and a museum, which you can tour on an escorted visit for $2.25 for adults, $1.00 for young people. And there you are at Saint-Louis Gate, where the street changes name to Grande-Allée and leads directly to the elegant Parliament buildings. There, between Grande-Allée and the escarpment that overlooks the river, is Battlefields Park, a wide expanse of beautifully groomed landscape which will lead you, at its western limit, to the Québec Museum, housing a large collection of Québec's fine arts and crafts.

PRACTICAL INFORMATION FOR QUEBEC CITY

Transportation

AIR: Quebec City's airport, in the suburb of Sainte-Foy, is served by major airlines.

CAR: From the U.S., northeast, take Québec Hwy. 73. From Montréal, No. 20 is an express route on the south shore; or take No. 40 on the north shore of the St. Lawrence River from Montréal. From Gaspé, take No. 132.

BUS: There is full service from *Greyhound* and *Voyageur Bus Lines.* City bus fares are $1.10.

TRAIN: Both *Canadian National* and *Canadian Pacific Rail* operate into Quebec through their joint passenger service, *ViaRail,* which also offers package tours of the province.

BOAT: From Lévis by ferry; from Montréal by the St. Lawrence.

TAXIS cost $1.20 drop and 70 cents per km.

SIGHTSEEING TOURS are available from Place d'Armes (*Grey Lines*). *Old Quebec Tours Ltd.* also operates an Old Quebec City Tour. Call (418) 872–9226.

FOR MORE INFORMATION

Contact the *Quebec City Region Tourism and Convention Bureau,* 60 Rue d'Auteuil. Or write *Tourisme Québec,* Case Postale 20,000, Quebec, GIK 7X2. Or visit the Department's *Reception Center* at 12 Sainte-Anne Street, tel.: 1–800–361–5405, seven days a week, from 9:00 A.M. to 5:00 P.M.

Accommodations

Quebec City has a happy choice of accommodations for visitors, from the numerous hotels on Boulevard Laurier (coming by car from Montréal) to the charming rooming houses of Grande-Allée and Saint-Louis St. as well as along Rte. 2 which lies on the north side of Québec. Be sure to book reservations in advance.

HOTELS

Prices for double-occupancy are: *Inexpensive* $60.00 and less, and *Moderate* $60.00–$75.00.

Inexpensive

Hôtel Château Laurier, 695 Grande-Allée, 54 rooms, free parking, TV; **Beau Site,** 6 Laporte St., with splendid river view, 8 rooms, free parking; **Château de Pierre,** 17 Ste. Genevieve Ave., charming 15-room guesthouse in Old Quebec; **Le Voyageur Laurentien,** 2250 Sainte-Anne, 62 rooms, free parking, indoor and outdoor pools, TV.

Moderate

Auberge du Tresor, 20 Ste. Anne St, 23 rooms, TV, near Château Frontenac; **Hôtel Universal,** Chemin Sainte-Foy, 133 rooms; **Hôtel Manoir d'Auteuil,** 49 d'Auteuil, 16 rooms, free parking, some air conditioning, TV; **Manoir Ste. Genevieve,** 13 Ste. Genevieve Ave., overlooking Governor's Park, antique inn with modern amenities.

HOSTELS

Centre International de Séjour, on Ste. Ursule St., $6.00 per night, per person, with breakfast, without bedding; with bedding $7.00; **Auberge de la Paix** (open summer only), 31 Rue Couillard (same rate); **YMCA** has no rooms; **YWCA,** 855 Holland, $18.00 per night, per person; two persons, $14.00 each; three persons, $9.00 each.

INNS AND TOURIST HOMES

The *Quebec City Region Tourism and Convention Bureau,* at 60 Rue d'Auteuil, distributes a listing of 30 tourist homes in the Old City and a large choice of hotels and motels, including quality ratings, prices, facilities, addresses, and phone numbers. The free brochure also includes a listing of motels and hotels in Sainte-Foy, Ancienne-Lorette, Beauport and outlying areas. Better write for it well in advance: it is not advised to come into town at the height of the season without reservations.

Restaurants

Quebec City is the home of good French cooking in the Americas. But prices are only slightly lower than those in Montréal. Prices per person for a full-course meal, excluding drinks, tips, and taxes are *Inexpensive:* under $10.00, and *Moderate:* $10.00–$20.00.

Inexpensive

Le Biarritz, 136 Ste–Anne St., French cuisine; **La Boite à Spaghetti,** 22 Côte de la Fabrique, Italian dishes; **Cafe Latin,** 8 Ste–Ursule St., salads and French specialities; **Le Gaulois,** 65 Buade St., Québec cooking and seafood in a pub atmosphere; **Café Buade,** 31 Buade St.

Moderate

Au Chalet Suisse, 32 Ste.–Anne St., fondues; **Au Petit Coin Breton,** 1029 St–Jean St., crepes and salads; **Le Picotin,** 4 Petit Champlain St., French cuisine; **La Potinière,** Hilton Hotel, 3 Place Québec; **Le Saint-Amour,** 48 Ste.-Ursule St., in old Québec.

MUSEUMS

Musée du Québec (free admission), Parc des Champs de Bataille, antiques and modern Canadian Art.

Musée de Cire (Wax Museum), 22 Rue Sainte-Anne ($2.00 adults; $1.00 students; 75 cents children); displays historic figures related to the history of Québec.

Musée du Fort, 10 Rue Sainte-Anne; diorama light and sound ($2.75 adults; $1.25 children).

Musée de l'Hôtel-Dieu (free admission), 32 Charlevoix; treasures of the Augustine Order from the 17th and 18th centuries.

Musée des Ursulines (Centre Marie de l'Incarnation) (adults $1.00; students 50 cents; children 25 cents), 12 rue Donnacona; history since the beginning of the colony.

Parc de L'Artillerie, (free admission), 2 rue d'Auteuil. Exhibits of Quebec military and industrial history, with reconstructed officers' quarters and children's center.

Special Attractions

Quebec City offers special attractions every year which both the Québec people and their visitors can enjoy. In early July go to the **Québec Summer Festival,** 10 days of celebrations commemorating the founding of Quebec City, with musicians, singers, and dancers taking over the streets, squares, and stages. At the end of August there is **Expo-Québec,** an annual agricultural, commercial, and industrial fair. At Carnival time, the famed **Québec Winter Carnival** animates the streets for almost the whole month of February, culminating in the famous canoe race across the frozen waters of the St. Lawrence between Quebec City and Lévis.

Quebec City also offers an **Aquarium,** at 1675 Avenue du Parc, in Sainte-Foy; a **Promenade** along the Saint-Charles River; the **Sainte-Foy Outdoor Recreation Center,** 3030 Rue Laberge, with year-round activities; and a **Zoological Park** in Orsainville, north of the city, home of hundreds of birds and mammals from Canada and around the world.

NIGHTLIFE

N.B. Quebec City is not a swinging city. Discos are few and far between. The hotels are your best bet for finding one. Hôtel le Concorde, disco **"Le Cabaret";** no cover charge. Drinks about $3.50. Hotel Hilton, disco **"L'Eden";** no cover charge, drinks around $3.50. **La Cousinière** (disco), Place Laurier; no cover charge, drinks about $3.50.

AROUND QUEBEC CITY

Quebec City is the starting point for delightful excursions into some of the province's most colorful and picturesque tourist regions. There is the Beaupré Coast, on the north shore of the St. Lawrence and going west, which will lead you to the fantastic Montmorency Falls (higher than Niagara) and the charming Orléans Island, connected to the mainland by a modern bridge. A short distance from there is Sainte-Anne-de-Beaupré's Shrine, a place of worship that attracts visitors by the thousands year after year.

On the south shore, either crossing the St. Lawrence River by the Québec bridge or taking the ferry across to Lévis, Rte. 132 will lead you east along the Lower St. Lawrence, with its historic towns and villages, to Sainte-Flavie where the Gaspé tour begins.

North of Quebec City lies the Lake Beauport region with its beautiful lakes and forests, and east of Quebec City the Mont Sainte-Anne Park, one of the most prestigious ski centers in Eastern Canada. This park has now been turned into an all-season recreation complex, with a golf course and cycling trails.

EXPLORING THE PROVINCE OF QUÉBEC

Recently the Province of Québec was divided into 18 tourist regions. Each features a good information service through a permanent Regional Touristic Association and offers a number of budget-minded, all-inclusive tours. The system is coordinated through a central government agency, **Information Tourisme Québec.** Information is available by phone (no charge) at 1–800–361–5405, or by writing to Tourisme Québec, Case postale 20 000, Québec G1K 7X2, Canada.

Below is a general description of each tourist region along with an address to write to for specific information. Although we have not made hotel and restaurant recommendations, we would like to point out the latest development in the Québec tourist industry, the bed-and-breakfasts establishments. A guide to rural homes that offer such accommodations has been compiled by the Ministère du Loisir, de la Chasse et de la Pêche (Leisure, Hunting, and Fishing Department) in cooperation with the Fédération des agricotours du Québec (Rural Tours Federation).

The guide offers a choice of over forty B&B's throughout the eastern part of Québec, where you can find inexpensive food and shelter in a congenial atmosphere. Rates are uniformly fixed for all the participant homes: $24.00 for two people to a room, breakfast included, $9.00 for children under 12. Some of the homes even offer laundry service.

Additional information and reservations: *Fédération des agricotours du Québec,* 1415 Jarry St. E., Montréal, Québec H2E 2Z7 (514) 374–4700.

Îles-de-la-Madeleine (Magdalen Islands)

Geographically located in the middle of the St. Lawrence Gulf, the Magdalen Islands are a paradise for the nature lover. Life is slow and simple, and nobody minds when the fog stops all activity at the airport. Life centers around two villages, Havre-aux-Maisons and Cap-aux-Meules. Tours leaving either from Quebec City or from Dorval Airport offer transportation by boat or by air and accommodations at the Bellevue or Boudreau motels.

For more information: *Association touristique régionale des Îles–de–la–Madeleine,* Case Postale 1028, Cap-Aux-Meules. Îles-de-la-Madeleine, Québec G0B 1L0, (418) 986–5462.

Gaspésie (the Gaspé Peninsula)

A long-time favorite of the Québec visitor, the Gaspé Peninsula offers an ever-changing panorama of life along a seacoast. An excellent road allows for a complete circuit, first going down the St. Lawrence River to Gaspé Point, then coming back by the Matapedia Valley. All along there are good, moderately priced inns and pensions and ample seafood such as delicate Matane shrimps, fresh cod tongues, clams, and the celebrated lobster. The Gaspé tour is mostly done by car, but there are organized tours, from one to four nights, leaving from Quebec City and Montréal.

For more information: *Association touristique régionale de la Gaspésie,* Case postale 810, Carleton, Québec G0C 1J0, 1–800–463–0829.

Bas Saint-Laurent (Lower St. Lawrence)

This region on the South Shore of the St. Lawrence River stretches from Lévis (in front of Quebec City) to the Gaspé region. Populated by three-hundred-year-old villages with names such as Kamouraska, Témiscouata, Rmouski, Cacouna, it offers a variety of sights and interests. There are a lot of open-air activities as in the nature center of Pohénégamook, where two-night weekend stays are available.

For more information: *Association touristique régionale du Bas Saint-Laurent,* 506 Rue Lafontaine, Rivière-du-Loup, Québec G5R 3C4, 1–800–463–1318.

Région de Québec (Quebec City Region)

This interesting centuries-old region is described in greater detail in the chapter on Quebec City, But note that there are special tours leaving from Montréal, including a four-night trout fishing excurison (price on request) or a six-night "Romantic Rendezvous" at Mont Sainte-Anne, where you can stay in a deluxe apartment or private lodge with open fire and have the use of a car for 7 days (1,500 kms. free). If you're feeling particularly extravagant, add to your stay a "millionaire's day" complete with a chauffeured limousine for shopping or touring and a gastronomic dinner with dancing in a discothèque at the end of the day.

For more information: *Office du Tourisme de Québec,* 53 rue D'Auteuil, Quebec City, Québec G1R 4C2, (418–692–2503).

Charlevoix

Charlevoix is that mountainous region which stands immediately east of the Québec region and on the north shore of the St. Lawrence. It offers a mixture of sea and sharply rising mountains dented into a series of awe-inspiring capes, and features the famed Île-aux-Coudres, an island celebrated both by painters and nature lovers. The region is easily accessible by car from Quebec City—the ride itself is worth the trip. There are also tours leaving from Montréal or Quebec City.

For more information: *Association touristique régionale de Charlevoix,* 136 Boulevard de Comporté, La Malbaie, Québec G0T 1J0, 1–800–463–3368.

Pays de l'Érable (Maple Country)

This scenic region of beautiful forests and quiet villages forms a triangle between the Appalachians, Beauce County, and the St. Lawrence River. An easy ride from Quebec City, it offers pleasures in all seasons: summer visits to such places as St. Jean-Port-Joli, where the most famous Québec sculptors reside; rich colors and small-game hunting in the autumn; cross-country skiing and snowmobile trails in winter; and in the spring, of course, all the delicious products of the maple tree. All year round there is a two-day weekend tour leaving Quebec City.

For more information: *Association touristique régionale du Pays de l'Érable,* 800 Autoroute 20, Bernières, Québec G0S 1C0, 1–800–463–3381.

Mauricie, Bois-Francs, Centre du Québec

This region spreads along the St. Maurice Valley, midway between Montréal and Quebec City. Also known as "the Heart of Québec," it boasts Trois-Rivières as its capital. This region features a number of annual events that attract visitors by the thousands: the St. Maurice canoe race, the Trois-Rivières Auto Grand Prix, and the duck hunting season. There is also the famed Notre-Dame-du-Cap sanctuary in Cap-de-la-Madeleine, right across Trois-Rivières. A two-night tour leaving from Montréal or Quebec City in the summer months will help you discover most of the charms of this region.

For more information: *Association touristique régionale du Coeur du Québec,* 197 rue Bonaventure, Trois-Rivières, Québec G9A 5M4, 1–800–567–8646.

Estrie

Estrie is the Québec name for the Eastern Townships, bordering the United States. They also house the most important concentration of popular arts in Québec. Song, music, and popular festivals are held all year long in Bromont, Mount Orford, and numerous other localities. Estrie's main city is Sherbrooke. Summer and winter sports are plentiful. A one-hour ride from Montréal or Quebec City will get you there. So will a number of one- or two-night tours leaving from either city.

For more information: *Association touristique régionale de l'Estrie,* 2883 rue King, Sherbrooke, Québec J1L 1C6, 1–800–567–6076.

Richelieu/Rive Sud

Rich in history, this region lies north of the American border and spreads out on both sides of the Richelieu Valley. The scene of memorable battles, its glorious past remains alive through old manors, forts, and monuments well preserved. The north end of this region borders the St. Lawrence River and includes the Sorel Islands, a compact group of islands particularly well suited for boating and hunting. Recommended is an auto ride along Rte. 132, between Contrecoeur and Valleyfield. Main events of the year are the International Regatta at Valleyfield, the Apple Festival at Rougemont, and the summer plays on the theater-boat anchored at Saint-Marc. Also to see are the Safari Park in Hemmingford and the craftsmen's village in Sainte-Martine. One- or two-night tours are available from Montréal or Quebec City.

For more information: *Association touristique régionale Richelieu/Rive Sud,* 1564 rue Bourgogne, Chambly, Québec J3L 1Y7, 1–800–361–3614.

De Lanaudiére

The name comes from Marie-Charlotte de Lanaudière, wife of Barthélemy Joliette, a member of the family of the famed explorer. Barthélemy himself founded the city of Joliette, capital of this region. De Lanaudière begins at the east end of Montréal island and spreads northwest. A region famed for its natural beauties, it features such resort places as Rawdon, Saint-Michel-des-Saints, and Saint-Charles de Mandeville, and countless falls created by the swift rivers that abound. Six- and nine-night canoe-camping safaris are available from Saint-Michel-des-Saints. Transport from Montréal can be arranged.

For more information: *Association touristique régionale de Lanaudière,* 3467 Rue Queen, Rawdon, Québec J0K 1S0, 1–800–363–2788.

Laurentides (Laurentians)

This region encompasses the mountainous north of Montréal and its features are outlined in the Montréal section.

For more information: *Maison de tourisme des Laurentides,* 142 rue de la Chapelle, Saint-Jérôme, Québec J7Z 5T4, 1–800–363–2573.

Montréal

See *Exploring Montréal* section.

Outaouais Québécois

This region covers the Québec part of the Ottawa Valley, A hunting and fishing paradise, it offers 20,000 lakes, 24 rivers, and more than a hundred purveyors centers. The Gatineau Park is rapidly developing its skiing facilities, but remains at all times a favorite destination for a car ride. Then there are the cities of Hull (in Québec) and Ottawa (in Ontario), the nation's capital, with its Parliament buildings and its beautiful Rideau Park. Ottawa is only 200 kms. (120 miles) from Montréal. Tours of Ottawa and of Gatineau Park are available from Montréal or Quebec City, with prices on request depending on the accommodation required.

For more information: *Association touristique régionale de l'Outaouais,* Case Postale 2000, Succursale B, Hull, Québec J8X 3Z2, 1–800–567–9651.

Abitibi-Temiscamingue

Bordering Ontario and stretching in a north-south direction west of Montréal, this region is an ideal destination for outdoor types. Fishing, hunting, canoe-camping excursions—some lasting as much as 800 kms. (500 miles)—await the visitor who has no taste for big city crowds. There is also a fairly wide selection of camping grounds for those who want to explore on their own. Two four-night tours are available from Montréal.

For more information: *Association touristique régionale Abitibi-Témiscamingue,* 212 Avenue du Lac, Rouyn, Québec J9X 4N7, (819) 762–6633.

Saguenay/Lac Saint-Jean/Chibougamau

This is the land of the powerful Saguenay River, a land of early explorers and pioneers. It offers both nature and industry and endless discoveries, from the cities of Jonquière, Tadoussac, Chicoutimi, Dolbeau, and Alma to the vast expanse of Lac Saint-Jean and the close forests of the tundra. One of the top events that draws visitors here is the Lac Saint-Jean swim. This is also the home of the Saint-Félicien zoo, one of the most interesting in Canada, and of ghost town Val Jalbert. A number of tours, from one to five nights, leave from Montréal or Quebec City and can appeal to a wide range of interests.

For more information: *Association touristique régionale Saguenay/Lac Saint-Jean/Chibougamau,* 198 est Rue Racine, Bureau 200, Chicoutimi, Québec G7H 1R9, 1–800–463–9561.

Manicouagan (Côte Nord)

Manicouagan, the western part of the North Shore tourist region, is a country of giants: gigantic hydroelectric developments, giant rivers, giant forests. The region runs down the powerful St. Lawrence River from Tadoussac to the salmon breeding grounds of Baie-Trinité. The road along the river passes through charming, historic villages such as Les Escoumins, Sault-au-Mouton, and Forestville (named for its rich forest industry). Then there are the industrial cities of Baie Comeau and Hauterive and, between the two, "Energy road," the 200-km. way to the gigantic Daniel Johnson Barrage, whose main vault would lodge the entire Place Ville Marie complex in Montréal.

For more information: *Association touristique régionale Manicouagan,* 872 rue Payjalon, Baie Comeau, Québec G5C 2T1 1–800–463–8531.

Duplessis (Côte Nord)

This is the eastern part of the North Shore, extending from Baie-Trinité to Labrador and the Atlantic Ocean. Although a country for the adventurous, everything is accessible by car, by rail, by boat, by plane. It features beautiful Anticosti Island where salmon and deer thrive, and the Mingan Islands. It boasts small but powerful little cities such as Havre-Saint-Pierre, Port-Cartier and Sept-Îles, cradles of the iron ore mining developments. And it offers unsurpassed hunting, fishing, and canoeing. Tours covering either part of the North Shore are offered from Montréal or Quebec City, from two to five nights, the last one covering from Sept-Îles to Labrador City and a visit to Mount Wright.

For more information: *Association touristique régionale de Duplessis,* 1005 Boulevard Laure, Sept-Îles, Québec G4R 4K3, 1–800–463–1755.

Nouveau Québec/Baie James (New Quebec and James Bay)

This is the last—and largest—of the tourist regions of Québec, with 51 percent of the whole Québec territory to itself. It is the land of the Cree and the Inuit, of the Midnight sun, tundra, the Northern lights, of 15-pound Arctic chars, and of over 250,000 caribou. This northern frontier is also the site of the gigantic hydroelectric project of James Bay. Airplane is the only way to get there, but once there the great North opens. There is a choice of tours, from one-day visits to the James Bay project to four-night fishing or hunting trips to glorious fifteen- or nineteen-night trekking and canoeing trips across the Baffin Land or along the white-water George River.

For more information: *Développement touristique Baie James /* Nouveau Québec, Ministère de l'industrie, du commerce et du tourisme, 710 Place d'Youville, 3e étage, Quebec, Québec G1R 4Y4, (418) 643–5872.

New Brunswick

As a vacation spot, New Brunswick has long been overshadowed by comparisons to its neighbors: it doesn't have as much coast and history as Nova Scotia, or as much gentle beach and landscape as Prince Edward Island, and its northern half is French but not as intensely French as Quebec. Yet New Brunswick has variety—it has all that and more. The Fundy Isles near the Maine—New Brunswick international boundary are worth a vacation in themselves, especially the largest of them—Grand Manan Island. The Bay of Fundy, with the world's highest tides, is more vacation-worthy on the New Brunswick than on the Nova Scotia side, especially at Fundy National Park. The Acadian French have their own unique culture distinct from Quebec along the beach-rimmed shores of the Gulf of St. Lawrence. And the St. John River Valley is as pretty an agricultural valley as you'll see anywhere. In addition, historic villages, craft centers, restorations, and other attractions have been developed for the benefit of visitors to the province.

For the tourist on budget, New Brunswick has the advantage of being closer than its neighboring Atlantic provinces. It is only a few hundred miles from most of the northeastern U.S., and the Fundy Isles, for example, are actually closer to the coast of Maine than they are to mainland New Brunswick. The province also has some unique features—among them its covered bridges and a number of free ferries that operate during the summer.

EXPLORING FREDERICTON

Although only New Brunswick's third largest city (after Saint John and Moncton), Fredericton (population 45,000) is the most interesting and pleasant. It was established as the capital of the colony in 1785 and its role was consolidated in 1825 with the establishment of British military quarters. The Military Compound, now restored, is in center town and is a national historic site. It includes one of New Brunswick's principal museums in its officers' quarters. A couple of blocks from the Compound along tree-lined Queen St. are The Playhouse, housing Theatre New Brunswick with year-round live theater, and the Beaverbrook Art Gallery with an impressive array of works from top European and Canadian artists (Gainsborough, Dali, Reynolds, Turner, Hogarth, and the Group of Seven). Nearby

is the Legislative Assembly, seat of the New Brunswick government, which has guided tours when it is not in session. Christ Church Cathedral, one of the best examples of decorated Gothic architecture in North America, is a block from the Legislature, also on Queen St. At the end of University Ave., about 20 minutes' walk from downtown, is the University of New Brunswick, a genteel old institution with a Victorian flavor to some of its buildings. It's on a hill overlooking the city, and the view is worth the walk.

Many people stay in Fredericton and take day-trips to other popular areas of southern New Brunswick. Kings Landing Historical Settlement, an elaborately reconstructed working village of the last century, is 23 miles upriver on the Trans-Canada Hwy., while Saint John is 65 miles southeast, and St. Andrews-by-the-Sea is about 80 miles south.

PRACTICAL INFORMATION FOR FREDERICTON

Transportation

It's $4.00 into town from the airport by bus. Free parking is not difficult to find on residential streets if you don't mind walking ten minutes or so back downtown.

PUBLIC TRANSIT. *Fredericton Transit* buses travel the main thoroughfares and go across the river to nearby communities. Fare 75 cents (exact change needed for mall buses only).

TAXIS. Many taxis don't have meters and often you share a ride with other passengers. Fares start at about $1.20; about $5.00 crosstown.

FOR MORE INFORMATION

The provincial government has summer tourist information offices (June to mid-Sept.) on the Trans Canada Highway just outside the city. Call (506) 455–3092 or (506) 453–2377. Toll free from Canada and the U.S., (800) 561–0123; from within New Brunswick; (800) 442–4442. For handy accommodations guide and other literature write: *Tourism New Brunswick,* Box 12345, Fredericton, N.B., Canada E3B 5C3.

Accommodations

Hotels and motels in the Fredericton area are mostly serviceable and friendly. Prices are generally low to moderate. Only the Lord Beaverbrook Hotel downtown—somewhat of a city institution—tries to be classy and expensive. Rates based on double occupancy:

Inexpensive, under $26.00; *Moderate,* $26.00–$34.00. A 11 percent provincial tax will be added to your bill.

Inexpensive

Hildebrand Bed & Breakfast, 81 Hildebrand Crescent (506) 472–7532. **Back Porch Bed & Breakfast,** 266 Northumberland St. (506) 454–6875. **Fredericton Skyline Motel,** 502 Forest Hill Rd. 40 units, licensed dining room. **Norfolk Motel** on Rte. 2 just out of town. 20 units, a quiet and friendly place. **The University of New Brunswick,** at the end of University Ave., has 50 residence rooms when classes are out. Common bath, coffeeshop, and indoor pool.

Moderate

Country Host Motel, Rte. 2 on the outskirts. 7 units. Restaurant and coffee shop. **Roadside Motel** also on Rte. 2. 29 units, 20 with housekeeping facilities. **Fort Nashwaak Motel Ltd.,** 15 Riverside Dr. 58 units; licensed dining room, bar and pool.

RESTAURANTS AND TAVERNS

Many moderately priced restaurants in Fredericton are in motels on the outskirts, although there are some downtown too. Plain fare at reasonable cost. There are the usual fast-food outlets, a few cafeterias with substantial lunches, and a few taverns where lunch at least can be had cheaply. Price categories (drinks, tips, and tax excluded; 11 percent provincial tax on meals): *Inexpensive,* under $7.00, and *Moderate,* $7.00–$11.00.

Inexpensive

Bar B Q Barn, 540 Queen St. Ribs, fish and chips, and fried scallops. A family spot. **Grandma Lee's Bakery & Eating Place,** 459 King St. **William's Seafood,** Exhibition Grounds, Smythe St., generous servings, fish and chips, etc. **Greenhouse,** Kings Place, King St., salads, etc.

Moderate

Ming's, corner Prospect and Smythe, good family restaurant. **Mei's,** 74 Regent, excellent food. **The Acadian Room,** Wandlyn Motel, 58 W. Prospect St., luncheon specialties, good and low priced.

What to See and Do

New Brunswick has built up a reputation for **crafts,** especially pewter and other metalwork. Fredericton has several studios and artisans' sales rooms. *Aitken's Pewter,* Regent St. is one of the premier pewter studios in the country. The *Boyce Country Market* on George St. operates every Saturday morning with handcrafts, baked goods, and a range of other items for sale. *Shades of Light,* 288 Regent St., sells a variety of quality crafts.

Parks and recreation. A good place to take kids is *Odell Park* off Wagoner's La. It has 200 acres of wooded land—including nature trails, picnic tables, play equipment, duck pond and deer enclosure. *Wilmot Park* of Woodstock Rd. has wading pool and playground and free tennis courts. About 12 miles west of Fredericton on the Trans-Canada Hwy. is *Mactaquac Park,* an extensive provincial park with nature interpretation tours, hiking, an excellent beach, trout fishing, and low-priced Balkan restaurant nearby.

ENTERTAINMENT

The River Room at the Lord Beaverbrook Hotel features folksingers; visit the **Cosmo,** 546 King St., for disco and piano bar, and **The Chestnut Inn,** York St., for folk singing and dancing. The **Poacher's Lounge** at the Diplomat Motel is a popular spot for a quiet drink; the younger set gathers at the **Hilltop Pub** on Prospect St. which features rock bands; **The Rolling Keg,** King St., is a tavern with rock and steak, popular with the young crowd. Prices tend to be moderate at most of these places.

For live theater there is **Theatre New Brunswick** at the Playhouse. **The Comedy Asylum,** dinner theatre at the Wandlyn Motel, Prospect St.

EXPLORING THE SAINT JOHN RIVER VALLEY

The Saint John River Valley is 250 miles of lovely scenery in potato-growing country. From the Québec border the population is French-speaking for about 40 miles up to Grand Falls. Edmundston is a lively French Canadian logging town that's worth a stop. The Trans-Canada along the valley is noted for its scenery. At Hartland there's the world's longest covered bridge (1,282 feet), one of some 90 such bridges in the province. Woodstock has some quaint old buildings in a quite setting. Some 23 miles above Fredericton is King's Landing Historical Settlement—60 buildings, including store, sawmill, homes, church, forge, and working farm. The furniture constitutes one of the best antique collections in Canada. Entry fee is about $4.50 per adult; children over 6, $2.00; family rate about $10.00.

Between Fredericton and Saint John the scenic road is Rte. 102 along the river. There are a number of free ferries worth taking for their sightseeing value in this area.

Saint John

Saint John's recent facelift and new harborfront development (Market Square) changed its image dramatically from grungy to colorful. Bright sidewalk cafés front restored red brick warehouses in which there is a lovely, modern mall. An old tugboat has been refurbished as a bar, a restored Barbour's General Store (1867) and a little red schoolhouse (1876) occupy one corner of Market Slip where the Loyalists first landed in 1784. On Princess St. nearby is a curious building. In 1878, George Chubb had unflattering likenesses of city councilors carved on it as a result of a dispute with the council. The Old Courthouse (1830) has a noteworthy spiral staircase. A short way up Charlotte St. is Trinity Church, rebuilt after the great fire of 1877 that destroyed most of the city.

The New Brunswick Museum deals with the city's ancient traditions and also has an art gallery. It's on Douglas Ave.—rather a long walk from downtown. Visible from the scenic park on which the museum stands is the Martello Tower across the harbor, built in 1812 as a precaution against American attack, and also the Reversing Falls—the mouth of the St. John River, where the rapids reverse twice a day with the tide. A bit marred by industrial effluent, though.

The city also has a small zoo at Rockwood Park—its main amusement area which has swimming, camping, and other facilities as well.

The Fundy Isles/The Fundy Trail

One of New Brunswick's nicer marine drives is the Fundy Trail between Saint John and St. Stephen on the Maine border. St.-Andrews-by-the-Sea is a summer resort and fishing village with an old English charm. There are ruined and restored fortifications, seaside parks, and at the Huntsman Marine Aquarium (attached to government research facilities) playful seals and other marine life that children in particular love.

Off St. Andrews are the Fundy Isles. Deer Island and Campobello Island (the latter known as the summer retreat of President Franklin Roosevelt) with historic buildings, parks, and other facilities.

Grand Manan

But it's the farthest of them, Grand Manan, which is particularly enchanting. Seven miles wide by 15 miles long, it is a paradise for seabird and marine life and for anyone who loves the sea and wants to get away from it all. It has parks, camping, motels, restaurants, and other amenities, but not enough to taint its rough charm. A two-hour ferry ride from Black's Harbour costs $9.00 for a car, $3.00 per foot passenger, $1.50 for children.

Moncton

Between Saint John and Moncton there's Fundy National Park— 80 square miles of seaside playground by the world's highest tides. The provincial park at Hopewell Cape features the "giant flowerpot," an enormous overhanging rock formation with its base eroded by the tides. If you're coming in from Nova Scotia, Fort Beausejour is a national historic site—it was of enormous significance during the French-English wars.

Moncton itself, although mainly English-speaking, is the center of French Acadian culture. At the University of Moncton you'll find the Acadian Museum and Archives, a portrayal of the troubled early history of this people (of which one branch are the "Cajuns" of Louisiana). There's also the Moncton Civic Museum featuring steam engine momentos (Moncton is an important railway junction).

The Acadian Shore

The Acadian shore is on the Gulf of St. Lawrence. Lively human activity is combined with sandy beaches, gentle shores, and abundant seafood. From Moncton, Shediac is the first town you'll come to, home of the Shediac Lobster Festival every July. You'll reach places like Cocagne and Richibucto—all lobster and oyster country. Starting at Richibucto is the new Kouchibougouac National Park— 15 miles of oceanside park with fine beaches. After that are Chatham and Newcastle—the latter has good campgrounds. But the shore road after that takes you to the Acadian towns of Tracadie, Shippagan, and Caraquet in an area reminiscent of the Brittany coast of France. There are several museums of Acadian life in the area, many festivals throughout the summer and just outside Caraquet is the province's reconstructed Acadian village—30 buildings depicting pioneer Acadian ways and crafts, a farm, and other attractions. It is the French alter-ego of King's Landing in the south. Entry fees are $4.00 per adult, $1.50 per child over 6, or $9.00 per family.

If you're traveling by car you may want to cut back to Fredericton via Rte. 8 through the center of the province along the scenic Miramichi River, home to some of the world's finest salmon fishing. There's an interesting Salmon Museum at Doaktown and an excellent Woodman's Museum in Boiestown.

PRACTICAL INFORMATION FOR NEW BRUNSWICK

Transportation

BUS. *SMT* bus lines connects the cities and most medium-sized towns as well as points in-between, especially in southern New Brunswick where train service is poor. Connects with bus lines in Québec, Nova Scotia, and Maine.

TRAIN. *Via Rail* has transcontinental service daily from Nova Scotia to Montréal through Moncton and a half dozen towns in northern New Brunswick. Also service from Moncton to St. John and Fredericton daily.

AIR. *Air Canada* and *Eastern Provincial Airways* fly to Moncton, St. John, and Fredericton from other Canadian points.

FERRY. *CN Marine* operates ferries to Digby, Nova Scotia, from St. John and to Borden, P.E.I., from Cape Tormentine. Reservations at any CN office in Canada or in Bar Harbor, Maine.

FOR MORE INFORMATION

For tourist information call, toll free, 800–561–0123 from Canada and the U.S.; 800–442–4442 from within New Brunswick. Address is: *Tourism New Brunswick,* P.O. Box 12345, Fredericton, N.B., Canada E3P 5C3. Many towns have their own tourist offices. The provincial ones are at Aulac, Edmundston, Lutes' Mountain, Penobsquis, St. Leonard, Fredericton, and Moncton—all on the Trans-Canada Hwy. Also at Bathurst, Campbellton, Campobello, Chatham, Newcastle, Reversing Falls in St. John, and St. Stephen and Waweig. The province's accommodation guide is a useful publication. It contains a complete list of inexpensive places to stay including bed & breakfasts, farm vacations, and campgrounds. So is Colleen Thompson's *New Brunswick Inside Out.*

Accommodations and Restaurants

Motels, especially country and small-town ones, are cheaper on the average than in neighboring provinces. You may get a cabin, for instance, for as low as $14.00 a night in some places. However, New Brunswick is not as well stocked with low-cost tourist homes, bed-and-breakfast places, or motels with housekeeping units as its neighbors. It does have a farm vacation program where you live with a farm family on a weekly basis, and campgrounds are plentiful.

Restaurants aren't plentiful, but most of your average-looking places will provide something sustaining at reasonable prices and usually with friendly service. Truck stops are usually good that way. Look for fish dishes along the coasts.

Price categories for accommodations based on double-occupancy: *Inexpensive,* $24.00 or less, and *Moderate,* $24.00–$31.00. A 11 percent provincial tax will be added to your bill. Restaurants (drinks, tips, and tax excluded; 11 percent provincial tax on all meals): *Inexpensive* (I), under $6.00, and *Moderate* (M), $6.00–$9.00.

BATHURST. *Gloucester Motor Hotel* (M), 100 Main St. 43 units, all with housekeeping. *Danny's Restaurant* (M). Good food plainly served in friendly surroundings. *Ron's Motel* (M), 1958 St. Peters Ave. 28 units. Fine restaurant, bar. *Carleton Hotel,* 300 King St.

CAMPOBELLO. *Ponderosa Motel and Restaurant* (M). Beach nearby; a lovely spot.

CARAQUET. *Hotel Paulin* (I). Quaint old hotel, former trainstop. Bathrooms in common. Good, dining room (M) with delicious seafood and great steak.

DEER ISLAND. *The 45th Parallel Motel and Tourist Home* (I). Restaurant (M) open summer only, good restaurant on premises.

EDMUNDSTON. *Praga Hotel Ltd.* (I), 127 Victoria St. Downtown hotel with licensed dining room. Not elegant but passable. *Gib's Tourist Home* (I), 255 rue de Pouvoir. Six housekeeping rooms.

MONCTON. *Woodland Cabins and Motel* (I-M) in River Glade on the outskirts. 26 rooms, 16 with housekeeping. Licensed restaurant (M) and bar. *Lutes Tourist Home* (I), 2166 Mountain Road. *Hotel Canadiana* (M), 46 Archibald St. 20 rooms.
Restaurant: *Ming Garden Restaurant* (M). Interesting Chinese-Cantonese food.

SHEDIAC. *Shediac Hotel* (I), Main St., 30 units. *Chez Françoise,* (I), Main St., rooms in old mansion, fine restaurant (M).
Restaurants: *Fred's Restaurant* (I), Cap-Pelé, best fried clams in N.B. *Fisherman's Paradise Restaurant* (M).

SAINT JOHN. *Hillcrest Motel,* (I) 1315 Manawagonish Rd. 15 rooms. *Fairport Motel and Restaurant* (M), 1360 Manawagonish Rd. *Johnson's Tourist Home, Watt's Tourist Home,* and *Fundy View Guests* all have a few rooms and are all near each other on Manawagonish Rd. All are inexpensive. The *YMCA* (I), 19–25 Hazen Ave., has 30 rooms for men. Common bathrooms, use Y facilities.
Restaurants. *Diana Restaurant* (I), 51 Charlotte St., *Napoleon Restaurant* (I), 13 Waterloo, and *Reggie's* (I), 26 Germain, are all plain-food restaurants. For lots of good, inexpensive food outlets your best bet is Market Square. *The Continental* (I to M), Market Square offers good food and nice décor. *House of Chan* (M but can run higher) has noon buffets and is one of the area's better Chinese/Canadian restaurants.

Some Principal Sights and Attractions

King's Landing Historic Village, 23 miles from Fredericton, is one of Canada's most ambitious historic village reconstructions. **The Acadian Village** near Caraquet in northern New Brunswick is the French Acadian counterpart of King's Landing in this bilingual province. The **New Brunswick Museum** near the Reversing Falls and some historical points in Saint John are worth a visit. The **Magnetic Hill** near Moncton, where your car appears to coast uphill, is a spot popular with tourists; so is **Hopewell Cape,** where massive rock formations, their base eroded by the tides, appear to teeter in the air.

Prince Edward Island

Canada's smallest province is also its most peaceful and serene. Prince Edward Island simply overflows with a gentleness of nature and spirit that makes it more than just a relaxing experience for anyone wanting to leave the anxieties of the big city behind. Its shores are mostly shallow beach. The water is warm for swimming—you'll have to go south as far as the Carolinas to find water that warm along the Atlantic coast—although summer temperatures are moderate. Its cliffs, like its soil, are a deep and almost mystical red, making a striking color contrast with the green of the vegetation. The land is one of gentle hills streaked yellow and green with grain and potato crops that undulate in the constant breeze.

The island is small—about 100 miles in length—with the sea nowhere more than 15 miles away. The entire island can be explored without excessive driving. Indeed, you can cross its width from the Gulf of St. Lawrence to Northumberland Strait with a few hours' walk in some places. Its quiet country roads are particularly nice to explore by bicycle, and its tidal estuaries invite the canoeist.

P.E.I.'s population is only 125,000, and the capital, Charlottetown, is really only a town of 16,000. Despite its small population, the Island is not short of human activity—there are local festivals, exhibitions, lobster suppers, historic villages, small museums, in almost every corner. And Charlottetown, smalltown or not, has a certain urbanity that few towns that size possess. It also has its share of history—it is here that Canada was conceived in 1864 at a conference that let to nationhood in 1867.

The hotels and motels, especially the big ones around Charlottetown, are no cheaper than anywhere else. But the Island is better endowed with bed-and-breakfast places—mostly called tourist homes here—than its sister Maritime Provinces. Prices are half the commercial rate, you can get home-cooked meals in most of these places, and you can stay a day, a week, or all summer. There is also a considerable number of cottages and motel units with "housekeeping" facilities—a small kitchen where you can cook your own food and save a lot of money. Many cottages have multiple bedrooms for families. The Island being the size it is, one place can serve as your base to explore it all.

EXPLORING
CHARLOTTETOWN

Charlottetown's downtown and environs are pretty well all accessible by foot, and even a random walk will produce an eyeful of Victorian gingerbread and brick architecture plus a general sense of unhurried gentility. If you're going to do it in an organized manner, the place to start is the handsome and modern Confederation Center of the Arts, which was opened on the centennial of the 1864 meeting that led to the creation of Canada. It is the country's national memorial to the Fathers of the Confederation and houses an art gallery, art workshops, a museum library, a children's theater, a memorial hall, and the 1,000-seat Charlottetown Theatre, which offers theatrical fare year-round and is the site of the nationally renowned Charlottetown Festival during July and August.

Across the street from the Center is the old Hughes Drug Store, Canada's first drugstore and a national historic site. Two nearby churches are worth a visit. St. Paul's Anglican Church, just east of Province House (the provincial legislature), is the oldest (1747) Protestant church in the province. Its baptismal register includes the name of Margaret Gordon, sweetheart of author Thomas Carlyle and heroine of his masterpiece, *Sartor Resartus.* St. James Presbyterian Church, better known as "the kirk," has relics from the island of Iona, one of the earliest sites of Christianity in the British Isles, and some impressive stained-glass windows.

Victoria Park at the southernmost tip of the city (yet only some five blocks from Confederation Center) overlooks the harbor and has within its stunning stand of white birches some noteworthy buildings. Government House, built in 1835 as an official residence for the province's lieutenant-governors, is there along with Beaconsfield, a fine example of Victorian architecture which now houses the Prince Edward Island Museum and Heritage Foundation. It is open to the public. Island artifacts are on display. Directly across the harbor is Fort Amherst, a national historic site and park and one of a number of ruined fortifications along the harbor. A mile or so east of Fort Amherst on Rte. 19 is the Micmac Village, a reconstructed Indian village of ancient times. A small ferry crosses the harbor from downtown Charlottetown regularly, giving a short but scenic trip to the Fort Amherst area.

PRACTICAL INFORMATION FOR CHARLOTTETOWN

Transportation

The airport is close to town; $4.00 by taxi. Parking is tight downtown during business hours, but downtown is small. You can find unmetered parking a 15 minutes' walk away. There are no city buses, but points on the outskirts of Charlottetown and beyond can be reached by regularly scheduled *Island Transit Ltd.* buses that serve the province, fanning out from Charlottetown. Call (902) 892–6167 for information.

TAXIS charge a basic $1.75 within certain zones and add a quarter when crossing zones. No meters. Hard to hail. Call or get one at a taxi stand.

TOURS. Double-decker London-style buses tour the city and its outskirts daily, leaving from the Confederation Center. Operated by *Abegweit Tours* (902–894–9966). Fare: adults about $3.75, children $1.00.

FOR MORE INFORMATION

Write *Visitor Services Division,* P.O. Box 940, Charlottetown, P.E.I., Canada, C1A 7M5. The *Charlottetown Visitor Information Center* is at the Royalty Mall on University Ave. Call (902) 892–2457.

There is a reservations and information system that you can dial toll-free from Nova Scotia or New Brunswick, making reservations en route. The number is 1–800–565–7421. You can get information, make reservations, even book theater tickets in advance. Once on the island, counsellors at tourist information centers give you assistance with reservations and other day-by-day needs.

The tourism department has some very good publications: a tour guide of the province, a things to see/things to do publication, a magazine of color photos, and, perhaps most useful of all, a comprehensive guide called *Visitor's Guide.* All are free.

Accommodations

For its size, Charlottetown is very well endowed with accommodations. The large hotels and motels are expensive, mostly in the range of $45.00 to $65.00 a night, double-occupancy. At the other extreme there are many "tourist homes" in town, usually with one to four rooms (although some have more) and in a $14.00 to $22.00 price range, some with breakfast included. In between there are some small motels and cottage units, usually on the outskirts, that fall in the median price range. Many of them have "housekeeping" units with kitchenettes, and some have multiple rooms for groups or families. Price categories, based on double-occupancy: *Inexpensive,* $25.00 or less, and *Moderate,* $25.00–$35.00.

Inexpensive

Most tourist homes (about 60 in Charlottetown). **Ida May's Tourist Home,** 18 Prince St. Five units, communal bath. Nice older home close to downtown. **Doucette Tourist Home,** 36 Cedar Ave. Four units in a quiet residential area near the airport. **Canadian Hostelling Association,** 151 Mount Edward Rd. 65 beds. Showers, kitchen privileges available. Members $5.00, non-members $7.00. Open year round.

Moderate

Duchess of Kent Inn, 218 Kent St. Six rooms with 1870's period furniture. Separate kitchen and living room for guests. **Zakem's Rosebank Cottages** on Hillsborough River three miles from town. Five housekeeping units. **Sherwood Motel** on Rte. 15, 3 miles north of town opposite airport; 17 units, 10 of them housekeeping. **Southport Motel & Cottages** on Rte. 1A 1½ miles from town; 40 units. Some cottages without bath, but inexpensive.

Restaurants

Plain home-style cooking in an informal atmosphere is the most common fare in Charlottetown as on the rest of the island, although Charlottetown has a few quality restaurants. Prices based on full-course dinner. Drinks, tips, and tax excluded. Tax is 10 percent on meals over $2.00. *Inexpensive,* under $7.00, and *Moderate,* $7.00–$10.00.

Inexpensive

Canton Café. Chinese and Canadian food. **Parkdale Homestyle Restaurant.** Solid and homey. **Bernie's Diner** and **Smitty's Family Restaurant** pride themselves on their wholesome, family-style fare. **The Showboat Dining Room.** Home-style cooking and can run into our moderate price range. **The Tower's Restaurant.** Family dining.

Moderate

Aunt Hattie's. In the Royalty Mall. Accent on old-style cooking; homemade baking. **The Dispensary.** Located in historic building, early Canadian atmosphere. **Gentleman Jim's Steak House.** Steak and seafood. **The Claddagh Room.** Seafood and homemade soup are specialties.

What to See and Do

The **Confederation Center Art Gallery and Museum** is one of Canada's leading art museums. Also at the Center are the provincial library and archives. Admission all free. The *Charlottetown Festival,* also at the Center, is one of Canada's summer theatrical highlights. Two full-scale musicals plus the perennial favorite *Anne of Green Gables.* The festival is on six nights a week, June to Sept. **Beaconsfield House** at Victoria Park has displays on island history.

ENTERTAINMENT

There are a number of **bars and lounges** in town (a lounge in P.E.I. is a bar with live entertainment). Prices tend to be moderate and cover charges the exception. *The Tudor Lounge,* Charlottetown Hotel, is quiet, but popular Friday nights. *The Smuggler's Jug,* at the Confederation Inn, has rustic beams, quiet background music. *Prince Edward Lounge* and *JR's Place* feature the better local entertainers.

EXPLORING PRINCE EDWARD ISLAND

The province's main attraction is the Prince Edward Island National Park, some 12 miles from Charlottetown on the north shore. It is 25 miles of beach with campgrounds, resorts, and other attractions. Most of the island's renowned lobster suppers, served nightly in church or community halls, are in the park's vicinity and so is Green Gables House, setting for Lucy Maude Montgomery's beloved novel *Anne of Green Gables.* The park can be crowded during the peak of summer. If you seek true solitude, the province has plenty more beach, much of it accessible at 36 provincial parks around the island.

The national park is in the center of the province, which is divided in three parts. The King's Byway at the eastern end takes you past, among other things, a historical agricultural village and museum at Orwell's Corner and the Lord Selkirk Settlement at Eldon, a memorial to early Scottish settlers. On the Lady Slipper Drive on the western end there's the Acadian Museum at Miscouche depicting the history of the island's French-speaking inhabitants and at Mount Carmel the Acadian Pioneer Village.

PRACTICAL INFORMATION FOR P.E.I.

Transportation

FERRY. *Car ferries* from Borden to Cape Tormentine, N.B., and Wood Islands to Caribou, N.S., cross several times a day. Reservations recommended on Borden ferry, operated by *CN Marine.* Call (902) 855–2030 for ferry information.

BUS. *Via Rail,* which normally operates passenger trains, has bus service from Charlottetown and Summerside to Amherst, N.S., linking with the transcontinental trains. *Island Transit Cooperative* (902 –892–6167) has daily service from Charlottetown to Souris at the eastern end of P.E.I. ($6.00 one way) and to Tignish at the western end (except Wednesday and Sunday, $10.00 one way).

AIR. Direct flights from Halifax and Ottawa via *Air Canada* and *Eastern Provincial Airways* to Charlottetown; stopovers required from other points.

TOURS. *Abegweit Tours* has a bus from Charlottetown to the P.E.I. National Park every day. Leaves 10:30 A.M. and returns in the evening giving you a day on the beach; $6.00 one way, $8.00 return. All-day, 100-mile tours to the south and north shores cost $15.00 per adult, $7.50 per child.

BICYCLES. With its compact size and its network of quiet country roads, P.E.I. is a natural for the cyclist. Bicycles can be rented at *MacQueen's Bicycle Shop,* 430 Queen St., Charlottetown (902– 892–9843), or at *Summerside Advance Rental,* 60 Harvard St., Summerside (902–436–5001). Roughly $12.00 daily, $30.00 weekly, and $30.00 deposit at both places. *Canoeing* is also nice on P.E.I.'s sheltered tidal estuaries. Tourist bureaus can tell you where to rent canoes.

FOR MORE INFORMATION

There are visitor information centers at Wilmot, the Borden and Wood Islands ferry landings, Brackley, Aulac, Cavendish, Kensington, Souris, Stanhope, and Pooles Corner in addition to Charlottetown. Tourism Services address, phone, and advance reservations information same as in *Charlottetown* section.

Accommodations and Restaurants

Several hundred places on the island offer one to four or so rooms or cottages—they may be bed-and-breakfast places, farm-vacation homes, tourist homes, or whatnot. They may or may not have meals (usually cheap) provided or housekeeping facilities, but generally all constitute inexpensive lodging. Camping fees run from $7.00 to $10.00 daily at private campgrounds; at provincial parks it's $7.00 to $9.00 a day depending on services.

Restaurants aren't all that plentiful in rural P.E.I., but this is compensated for by the many lodgings that have housekeeping services or serve meals.

Price categories for accommodations based on double-occupancy: *Inexpensive,* $24.00 or less, and *Moderate,* $24.00–$33.00. Restaurants (drinks, tips, and tax excluded; tax is 10 percent on meals over $2.00): *Inexpensive,* under $7.00, and *Moderate,* $7.00–$10.00.

BRACKLEY BEACH. *Blue Waters Tourist Home*(I), eight units on Rte. 15, 1 km. from national park. On an active farm. Kitchen for use of guests.

CAVENDISH. *Fiddles and Vittles Restaurant*(M). Fresh shellfish, chowder, and steak. Cavendish, at the national park, has several good restaurants but accommodations are expensive.

MONTAGUE. *Hillside Inn* (I), five overnight units in a quiet, friendly setting. Communal showers, bath. Near the ocean.

SOURIS. *Souris West Motel & Cottages* (I), 11 units, 6 with housekeeping. Nice quiet motel. Baths only, no showers. *Bluefin Restaurant* (M). Plain food in unpretentious surroundings.

SUMMERSIDE. *Cairn's Motel*(I-M) on Rte. 1A, 1½ miles from town. 12 units. *Inland Motel*(M) on Rte. 107, 7 km. outside of town in a country setting. 16 units—eight of them housekeeping—with children's playground and picnic area nearby. *Summerside Motel and Cottages* (M), Rte. 1A, 2 miles from town. 36 units, 11 with housekeeping.

Other restaurants: *Brothers Two* (M). Steaks and seafood. Also features "Governor's Feast" June 27–August 31, 6:00–9:00 P.M. daily—island seafood served by cast of performers who also sing and dance. *Island House* (I) specializes in seafood and chicken.

Lobster Suppers

An island tradition, usually served in church or community halls. Mostly from mid-June to various times in the fall, served from 4:00 or 5:00 P.M. daily. Average price around $15. At: *Court Yard Restau-*

rant, Confederation Center, Charlottetown; also at North Rustico, French River, New Glasgow, New London, Rosebank, St. Ann's, Stanhope Beach, and Cardigan.

Some Principal Sights and Attractions

The Lord Selkirk Settlement at **Eldon** is a reproduction of settlers' cabins. The *Log Cabin Museum* at **Murray Harbour** depicts the province's 19th-century heritage. *The Acadian Museum* at **Miscouche** shows the ancient ways of the French Acadian community. P.E.I. has two interesting car museums, the *Spoke Wheel Car Museum* at **Dunstaffnage** and the *Car Life Museum* at **Bonshaw.** There are also two botanical gardens, *Jewell's Garden and Pioneer Village* at **York** (with an antique glass museum nearby) and *Malpeque Gardens,* **Malpeque.** Expect an entry charge of between 75 cents and $2.00 per adult at all these places.

P.E.I. also has many exhibitions and festivals. They include, in July, the *Orwell Corner Strawberry Fair,* **Orwell Corner;** *Garden of the Gulf Fiddle Festival,* **Montague;** P.E.I. *Potato Blossom Festival,* **O'Leary;** *Summerside Lobster Carnival,* **Summerside.** In August there's the *Harvest of the Sea Fair,* **Basinhead,** and *Tyne Valley Oyster Festival,* **Tyne Valley.**

Nova Scotia

The special lures of Nova Scotia are its seacoast and Cape Breton highlands—grand clifftop views in places, waves breaking on rocky sweeps in others, and in still others beaches, marshes and peaceful spruce-topped islands. And just here and there a wharf, a fishing village, a coastal town. Although rugged in places, the coastline is accessible in most areas. Inland, the landscape and vegetation are gentle and intimate and like the coast, infinitely varied.

Nova Scotia, site of some of the earliest permanent European settlements in North America, is also full of history. Whether in town or country, the place is dotted with museums, restored historic houses, mills, historic villages, and so on. Halifax, the capital city, is particularly rich in historical ambience.

The best, in short, is free or nearly so—coast, landscape, history (there may be a small charge at some museums). Food, lodging, and travel are the problems, but there are alternatives, and bargains for the wise traveler. The bed-and-breakfast and farm-vacation places in the country offer real bargains, campsites in provincial parks are cheap, and motels and restaurants off the beaten track can provide savings.

The Halifax-Dartmouth metropolitan area, the province's major destination, is not cheap, but there too the tourist on budget can experience the essentials and remain solvent.

EXPLORING HALIFAX/DARTMOUTH

Halifax and Dartmouth are two cities on either side of Halifax Harbour, linked by two toll bridges and two ferries. Most of the action is in Halifax, which features as good a mix of tradition and modernity as any North American city. Most of the attractions are downtown, which is fairly compact, and the best way by far to savor it all is by walking.

Two "musts" are the Citadel and Historic Properties. The Citadel, a 17th-century hilltop fortress that dominates the city center, is a good place from which to take your bearings. It overlooks downtown and gives a panoramic view of the entire city and beyond. It has acres of grass for strolling or resting and inside has military and pioneer museums harking back to the founding of the city in 1749.

Stroll down past the old town clock, the very symbol of Halifax, and onto George St. You'll pass through Grand Parade, a civic park with city hall at one end and ancient St. Paul's Church at the other. A few more blocks down and you're at Historic Properties—a reconstruction in stained wooden shingle of dockside buildings originally erected in the early 1800's. It now contains a variety of specialty shops and restaurants, a tourist center, serves as the place of departure for water and bus tours, and a town crier yells out a welcome to tourists at regular intervals. Also part of Historic Properties is a block of North American Renaissance buildings on Granville St., considered one of the finest pieces of preserved urban heritage in the country.

Next to Historic Properties along the harbor is a new waterfront development and the ferry terminal. A trip to Dartmouth on the ferry (35 cents) is highly recommended. Primarily it gives a panoramic view of the harbor and both Halifax and Dartmouth. There's a new waterfront development in Dartmouth as well, with plenty of green spaces for a stroll or a rest. A block to the right of the ferry terminal is downtown Portland St., while a half mile to the left is the Dartmouth Heritage Museum attached to the municipal library.

Back in Halifax, the Marine Museum of the Atlantic is handy to the ferry terminal farther south along Water St. The more adventurous may want to walk an extra half-mile to Terminal Rd. and down to the docks where the world's ships tie up.

Now back toward the Citadel. On the inland side of it is the centrally located Public Gardens, a Victorian delight of exotic flora, and an extensive system of parks known as the "Commons." In that vicinity is the province's principal museum, the Maritime Museum, on Summer St.

Away from the city center—in fact at the very tip of the peninsula on which Halifax is located—is Point Pleasant Park. It is surrounded by the sea on three sides, has trails through its woodlands, and has ruins of fortifications. Rather far to walk to from downtown. Best to drive or take a transit bus. The park itself is extensive. Takes a couple of hours to make it worthwhile.

PRACTICAL INFORMATION FOR HALIFAX/DARTMOUTH

Transportation

From the airport, the cheapest way into the city is $7.50 by *airport bus.* If you're driving, parking is tight in downtown Halifax, especially during the business day. If you want to avoid parking fees, a mile or less in most directions will get you to unmetered streets and a 20-minute walk or less will get you back downtown. Information on bicycling available from Bicycle Nova Scotia, Box 3010 South, Halifax, N.S. B3J 3G6.

PUBLIC TRANSIT. The *Metropolitan Transit Commission* (MTC) operates buses in Halifax and Dartmouth with express service to some outer suburbs. The fare is 60 cents. Exact change only.

TAXIS. Fares start at $1.20 and meter up based on time and distance. About $5.50 crosstown, a couple of dollars more over the bridges. Hailing taxis is difficult. Call or pick them up at taxi stands.

FERRIES. Two *ferries* traverse the same route from downtown Halifax to downtown Dartmouth every 15 minutes during rush hours and weekday afternoons. Half-hourly and hourly schedules during slower times. No service Sunday mornings.

TOURS. *Water tours* of the harbor are a Halifax specialty. They leave several times daily from Privateer's Wharf, Historic Properties, and last two hours. Adults $9.00, adolescents (13–18), $6.50; under 13, $3.50. Call (902) 423–7783 or 425–1271. The *Bluenose II* sailing schooner makes similar tours June 26 to August 29 leaving from the same place. Adults, $9.00; $4.00 for under 12's and over 65's. Call (902) 422–2678.

MTC runs charter bus tours for groups of 30 or more at $4.50 per person. Acadian Lines Ltd. has 2½ hour tours leaving major hotels three times a day during peak tourist season—morning, afternoon, and evening. Adults, $6.00; under 12's, $3.00; under 6's free. Call (902) 454–9321.

FOR MORE INFORMATION

The province's main tourist bureau is *The Red Store* at Historic Properties. The City of Dartmouth runs a bureau on Thistle St. Or write: *Nova Scotia Department of Tourism,* P.O. Box 130, Halifax, N.S., Canada B3J 2M7. You can also call toll-free. The following numbers will get you both general information and plug you into the computerized Check-Inns system for booking accommodations across the province. From continental U.S. (except Maine) 1–800–341–6096; Maine 1–800–492–0643; Québec and Newfoundland 1–800–565–7180; Ontario 1–800–565–7140; Prairie Provinces 1–800–565–7166; British Columbia 1–112–800–565–7166. From the Maritime Provinces 1–800–565–7105. In Halifax the number is 424–4247.

Nova Scotia: Where to Stay/What to See/What to Do is a free, comprehensive and most useful publication published annually by the department of tourism.

Accommodations

Halifax is a convention city and there are times when rooms are hard to come by at any price. Best to book ahead. Price categories based on double-occupancy. *Inexpensive,* $28.00 or less, and *Moderate,* $28.00–$36.00.

Inexpensive

Belmont Hotel, 7 Octerloney St., Dartmouth. Good spot near the ferries. 44 rooms, some with some without bath and running water. A bit seedy but okay. **Carleton Hotel** (I-M), 1685 Argyle St., in downtown Halifax. 68 (fairly small) rooms, 40 with bath, and some a bit tatty. A lot of nightlife at ground level. **Queen St. Inn,** 1266 Queen St., Halifax. Converted old home with antique furnishings. One of the nicer places to stay in town. **YMCA,** 1565 South Park St., Halifax. 66 rooms for men with use of Y facilities. **YWCA,** 1290 Barrington St., Halifax. 30 rooms for women with use of Y facilities. **Youth Hostels.** There are 10 in the province, the largest at 2445 Brunswick St., Halifax. Write *Canadian Hostelling Association,* P.O. Box 3010 South, Halifax, N.S., B3J 3G6.

Moderate

Most suburban motels are in this category. Public transit is available to most, but it's not always frequent. **Gerrard Hotel,** 1234 Barrington St., 9 rooms. Halifax. **Four Seasons Motor Inn,** Hwy. 7 at Major St., Dartmouth. 33 units with bath. **Stardust Motel,** 1067 Bedford Hwy.; 51 units with bath, 31 with kitchenettes. **Sterling Hotel,** 1266 Barrington St., Halifax.

Restaurants, Pubs, Taverns

Halifax and environs have many low- to moderate-priced fast-food outlets. Many pubs and taverns serve cheap, wholesome food until early evening—usually from a 3- to 4-choice menu—although you have to be over 19 to get in. There are also many plain-food restaurants where bargains can be had. Watch for fish dishes in particular. But if you're determined to eat lobster you'd do best to buy it cooked at a fish store and eat it wherever you may; lobster is pricey in most restaurants. Price categories (drinks, tips, and tax excluded; 10 percent provincial tax on all meals over $3.00): *Inexpensive:* under $7.00, and *Moderate:* $7.00–$11.00.

Inexpensive

Chowder Bowl, 1681 Granville St., downtown Halifax. A bowl of fish chowder is a meal in itself here. **Denlock's Acadian Grill,** a lunch counter at 1718 Granville St., downtown Halifax. **Lower Deck** and **Middle Deck** pubs serve food until early evening. Sandwiches, chowder, and sausage with beer are specials. **Privateer's**

Warehouse, Historic Properties. **Satisfaction-Feast,** 1581 Grafton St., vegetarian restaurant. **Palm Restaurant,** Prince St., according to actor Tony Randall has best Chinese food anywhere.

Moderate

Hogie's Swiss Steak House, 6273 Quinpool Rd. Family place with special menu for children. **Le Quelque Chose Cafe,** next door to Sam's on Hollis St. Great quiches, salads, desserts. **McKelvie's,** 1680 Lower Water St., across from Maritime Museum. Great fish restaurant. **Sanford's the Brewery,** Lower Water St. Natural foods, crêpes, and quiche are specialties. **The Silver Spoon,** 1866 Water St., noted for desserts and snacks.

What to See and Do

Inside the **Citadel** are a military museum and a museum of Nova Scotia history, including audiovisual presentations. The **Nova Scotia Museum** on Summer St. has general human and natural history exhibits. The new **Marine Museum of the Atlantic** on Water St. is the major marine museum on the East Coast. The **Dartmouth Heritage Museum and Art Gallery** on Wyse Rd. depicts early life in Dartmouth. **Province House,** the seat of the Nova Scotia government, is the oldest legislative building in Canada. The **Public Archives of Nova Scotia** and the **Art Gallery of Nova Scotia** are both on the Dalhousie University campus. Entrance to all of these is free. All are open evenings during summer months, although some close at 5 P.M. weekends. Check at (902) 424–4247 for details.

The **Halifax Commons,** in center town, has a children's playground, wading pool, playing fields and lots of grassy area. Dartmouth is known as the "City of Lakes"—it has 22 of them with many small parks, beaches, and picnic areas. June to mid-August there are **band concerts** at the Public Gardens in Halifax every Sunday at 2:00 P.M. In late September there's the metropolitan area's largest party, the week-long **Joseph Howe festival.**

ENTERTAINMENT

Halifax has a fair array of nightlife. Lots of places for a quiet drink, or a loud one, for just the price of the drink. If you want entertainment, it will cost somewhat more either in variable cover charges or the price of drinks. Cover charges are generally around $3.00; some spots only charge on weekends.

The **Privateer's Wharf** in Historic Properties is one of the most popular night spots for young professionals. **The Jury Room** in the Carleton Hotel is a popular and jam-packed bar with no entertainment. **The Victory Lounge** at the Lord Nelson Hotel is the city's best-known spot for a quiet drink. The **Lobster Trap Cabaret** in the Trade Mart Building on Brunswick St. is loud and noisy with exotic dancers and stage revues. **My Apartment,** 1740 Argyle St., is a popular bar, with free hamburgers at 4:30 P.M.

The **Rebecca Cohn Auditorium** at Dalhousie University is the city's center for live concerts and other musical presentations. Call (902) 424–2298. Larger productions take place at the **Metro Center,** a sports and cultural complex downtown. From early July to mid-August there's the Summer Festival of Live Theater at Neptune Theater.

EXPLORING CAPE BRETON

With its rugged highlands and sweeping seascapes, its residual Gaelic culture and intimate villages, Cape Breton is a very popular tourist destination. Of particular note is the Cabot Trail, a 184-mile coastal (and mostly cliffside) drive of spellbinding views. Cape Breton also has one of the most advanced bed-and-breakfast programs in the Maritimes, making a budget vacation a real possibility.

There are two other major attractions in Cape Breton apart from the Cabot Trail. One is a complex of coal mining museums, complete with underground tours and other attractions, at Glace Bay, about 10 miles from Sydney, the major city. The other is the massive Fortress Louisbourg, a reconstructed 18th-century French fortress and village 22 miles from Sydney. There are day bus tours from Sydney—but take a lunch, the restaurants are expensive at the site. If all that doesn't suffice, the rest of Cape Breton is peppered with museums and other attractions linked to its rich mix of culture: Scottish, Irish, Acadian French, Indian, and others. Of particular note are the Nova Scotia Highland Village at Iona on Rte. 233, a reconstructed early Scottish settlement, and the Gaelic College at St. Ann's where you'll find pipers and costumes.

EXPLORING MAINLAND
NOVA SCOTIA

The "Mainland" is the entire province excluding Cape Breton and, for our purposes, Halifax/Dartmouth as well. Although not a specific tourist area there are points of interest throughout. If you're traveling other than by air, you'll be passing through much of it anyway on your way to Halifax or Cape Breton. In some cases you will have a choice of route—seashore or inland—with radically different environments.

If you arrive at Yarmouth by ferry from Maine—a major tourist entry point—the South Shore and the "Valley" route both beckon. The South Shore has some of the province's most interesting coastline, but you must follow the old trunk highways known as the "lighthouse route." For a classic old-style fishing town, drop down to Lunenburg. It has the province's fishery museum and is a bit of a living museum itself. The inland "Valley" way will take you through the pleasantly agricultural Annapolis Valley. A short side trip will take you to Port Royal, site of the first permanent European settlement in Canada in 1605. The sea—the Bay of Fundy with the highest tides in the world—is never far away, but requires little side trips to get to. Back of Kentville, the Cape Blomidon Provincial Park is worth visiting—it gives a panoramic view of Minas Basin and the agricultural lands from a high vantage point. If you're on foot and headed for Halifax from Yarmouth, the Via Rail train through the Valley gives better scenery than the South Shore bus which follows the superhighways mostly, although it does dip down to Lunenburg.

From Halifax to Cape Breton the Eastern Shore (Hwy. 7) is a winding and quiet coastal drive that takes you past Sherbrooke Village, the province's principal historic village. The alternative is the Trans-Canada Hwy. on the other side of the province—faster but less interesting.

PRACTICAL INFORMATION FOR NOVA SCOTIA

Transportation

BUS. Service is nonchalant at times, but buses provide low-cost transportation. They serve most small towns and any stops in-between. *Acadian Lines Ltd.* is the biggest bus company. Most companies also have buses for charter as well as tours.

TRAIN. The train from Yarmouth to Halifax through the Annapolis Valley provides a scenic ride. Trains also link Halifax with Truro and Amherst (and on to the rest of Canada) as well as with Sydney, but they aren't always on convenient schedules. *Via Rail* runs all the trains.

AIR. *Air Canada, CP Air,* and *Eastern Provincial Airways* (EPA) link Canada and the world with Halifax International Airport. Air Canada and EPA serve Sydney from various points while Air Canada flies Boston-Yarmouth daily. EPA flies mostly within the Atlantic Provinces with flights to Montréal and Toronto.

FERRY. Ferries link Yarmouth with Bar Harbor and Portland, Me.; Digby with Saint John, N.B.; Caribou with Wood Islands, P.E.I.; and North Sydney with Port-aux-Basques and Argentia, Nfld. *CN Marine* operates all except Yarmouth-Portland [Prince of Fundy Cruises —(207) 775–5611 in Portland] and Caribou to P.E.I. (no reservations needed). CN Marine reservations can be made at any CN ticket office in Canada or toll-free 1–800–341–7981 in mid- and northeastern United States, 1–800–432–7344 in Maine.

FOR MORE INFORMATION

Tourist information desks are located on all ferries to Nova Scotia with the exception of the Bar Harbor and Portland ferries where the desks are located on the American side of the terminals. There are full tourist bureaus at Yarmouth, Digby, Amherst, Pictou, and at Historic Properties, Halifax. For the address of the Nova Scotia Department of Tourism, and toll-free numbers for information and accommodations, check the Halifax/Dartmouth section.

Accommodations and Restaurants

In the towns look for out-of-the-way motels a mile or more from downtown and away from major traffic arteries. Prices will be lower and service adequate. Avoid the fancy motels along the expressways. Many are overpriced and service is only average. Most towns also have a few guest homes with three or four rooms, a common bath, and prices under $20.00 per night. In the country there are the bed-and-breakfast places—private homes that will take overnight guests at $12.00 to $20.00 a night. Longer-term visitors may opt for the highly recommended farm and country vacations (costs range from $90 to $130 per person per week; half that for children; includes three meals a day and you live as part of the family). Campgrounds are plentiful and range between $4.00 and $7.00 a night for a spot.

Most population centers have fast-food outlets—fried chicken, fish-and-chips, and so on. Modest-looking restaurants, in country or in town, often provide good home cooking at reasonable cost, although sometimes not. You may have to take potluck. Service is always friendly and informal.

Price categories for accommodations based on double-occupancy: *Inexpensive* (I) $24.00 or less, and *Moderate* (M), $24.00–$32.00. Restaurants (drinks, tips, and tax excluded; 10 percent provincial tax on all meals over $3.00): *Inexpensive* (I) under $6.00, and *Moderate* (M) $6.00–$10.00.

AMHERST. *Brown's Guest Homes* (I–M), 158 Victoria St. 3 rooms. *Fisher Motel* (I–M), 17 Copp Ave. 34 units. *Tantramar Motel* (I–M), Hwy. 2 and 6 one mile north of Amherst. 16 units. Licensed restaurant (I–M).

ANNAPOLIS ROYAL. The *Cheshire Cat* (I-M), Upper Clements. Bed and breakfast. Dinner by arrangement. *Fundy View House and Cabins* (I), Goanville Ferry. Fireplace in some units.

ANTIGONISH. *The Bonnie Brea Inn* (I), 95 College St. 28 rooms, 16 with bath. Restaurant (M) attached. *The Lobster Treat Restaurant* (M but can run higher) on the Trans-Canada Hwy. Drab outside, smart inside.

DIGBY. *Basinview Motel* (I), 5 miles east of Digby on Hwy. 1. 12

units, not all with bath. *Harbourview Inn* (M) at Smith's Cove on the outskirts of Digby. Licensed restaurant (M), featuring local foods. Ocean nearby, playgrounds. Friendly place to stay.

Peggy's Cove. Sou'wester Rest. (I), fresh fish.

LUNENBURG. *Bluenose Lodge* (I), 10 Falkland St. 9 rooms with dining room (I-M). *Ranch-O Motel,* 2.2 km. from town overlooking ocean at Mason's Beach. *Lover's Lane Inn,* 2.4 km. northwest of Peggy's Cove on Route 333. 6 cottages and 7 bedrooms.

SYDNEY. *Athenry Manor* (M), 259 Kings Road. 19 rooms. *Cliefden House Ltd.* (I), 106 Bentick St. 16 rooms, not all with bath and some without running water. *Paul's Hotel* (I), Pitt St. and Esplanade. 15 rooms, some without bath. Working class hotel.

Most motels in Sydney have moderately priced restaurants. *Jasper's* (M), downtown, is open around-the-clock with plain, tasty foods.

YARMOUTH. *El Rancho Motel,* (I-M), Lakeside Drive. 16 units. Boating, fishing, swimming. Restaurant— *Captain Kelly's Kitchen* (M), 577 Main St. *Ferry Inn and Motel Ltd.* 216 Main St. Hotel-motel complex. Hotel rooms cheap (not all have running water), motel moderate. *Midtown Motel* (M), 13 Parade St. 20 units. Complimentary Continental breakfast. *Harris' Quick 'n Tasty* (M), a couple of miles out of town on Hwy. 1, is a popular seafood restaurant—one of the best in the province in fact—frequented by locals. *Harris Seafood Restaurant* (M), just across the highway is run by the same people, is more expensive but noted for its seafood.

Some Principal Sights and Attractions

CAPE BRETON

The *Cabot Trail,* as gripping a seaside drive as you'll find anywhere, is Cape Breton's most popular attraction. It runs through *Cape Breton Highlands National Park* which has camping facilities and is itself spectacular. *Fortress Louisbourg* on the opposite shore is one of the most extensive restorations ever undertaken in Canada; includes both the fortress and nearby 18th-century village. At Glace Bay is the *Miner's Museum, Miner's Village* and tours of the coalmines. In Baddeck the *Alexander Graham Bell Museum* has displays of the works of the inventor of the telephone who spent his summers here. *Bute Arran,* (I) Baddeck, B&B, across from Bell Estate, $15, maple syrup for breakfast. At Iona, the *Nova Scotia Highland Village,* a replica of an early Scottish settlement. At Margaree, the *Museum of Cape Breton Heritage.* At Cheticamp, the *Acadian Museum* offers handicraft demonstrations and delicious, low-cost Acadian food.

MAINLAND NOVA SCOTIA

Museums, historic buildings, and attractions fairly abound in Nova Scotia, and it's a good idea to get a complete listing (available at any tourist bureau). The major sites are the following. The *"Habitation"* at Annapolis Royal, site of Samuel de Champlain's settlement in 1605—the first permanent white settlement north of the Gulf of Mexico. *Sherbrooke Village* at Sherbrooke is a restored, functioning 19th-century village. *Kejimkujik National Park* in the center of the province is a good spot to soak up some nature; so is *Blomidon Provincial Park* 15 miles north of Kentville, which has a spectacular high view of the Bay of Fundy.

Newfoundland

Newfoundland is a craggy northern experience, not at all like the gentle Maritime Provinces to the south. It is a land of great peninsulas jutting far out at sea, of rocky islands, fjords, and a jagged coast where icebergs may float by even in summer. It is a land of rugged outports with an Old World flavor jammed at the foot of rocky cliffs, and exuding a culture unique in English-speaking North America. And it is a land of history: the nations of Europe fished here from before Columbian times and at L'Anse-aux-Meadows, on the northern tip of the province, is the reconstructed site of the first known European presence in the Western Hemisphere, a Viking settlement of A.D. 1000.

The attraction is there, and Newfoundland is worth it even if it's only a once-in-a-lifetime experience. That said, however, it must be added that Newfoundland is not cheap. Getting there is an expense to begin with and hotel prices in St. John's, the capital, have spiraled upward since the discovery of oil offshore.

Yet there are ways of avoiding the worst. Accommodations in communities surrounding St. John's are more reasonable, and Newfoundland is developing a program of "hospitality homes"— equivalent to the bed-and-breakfast and farm-vacation homes of the mainland, except that these offer seashore vacations, some in isolated outports. Or you need not go to St. John's at all, which is on the eastern extremity of the island. The ferry from Nova Scotia will deposit you and your car at Port-aux-Basques on the western side; from there you can explore the 400-mile-long western shore which contains the eerily beautiful Gros Morne National Park, the most spectacular mountain environment east of the Rocky Mountains (and a vacation in itself for outdoors types). The road continues up an equally spectacular coast to the aforementioned Viking settlement near St. Anthony. On your way up you may want to take a ferry to Labrador. Or you could turn east at Gros Morne and explore the north shore of the province instead—less coast but more communities.

Newfoundland is also a province of ferries. Many outports have no roads (the province's south coast has none at all) and ferries serve as the lifeline. They make wonderful sightseeing tours and are not very expensive, although they're not always on convenient schedules.

While you're in Newfoundland, you may want to sample screech, the local brew. Once a popular working man's drink, screech was

made by steaming or washing out Jamaica rum barrels with boiling
water. The residual liquor was particularly potent. Screech, a name
coined by U.S. servicemen stationed in Newfoundland during World
War II, refers to the reaction of those who drank too much of it.
Since that time, the process has been refined, and screech is now
prepared from legitimate Caribbean rum and bottled by the Newfoundland Liquor Corporation.

EXPLORING ST. JOHN'S

Although you may not want to stay in St. John's very long if
you're on budget, the city is very worthwhile. Its history goes back
to the very beginning of the white man's presence in the Americas
and it has a deep charm. Signal Hill National Historic Park, the last
landfall before Europe and the place where Marconi received the
first transatlantic wireless signal, is somewhat a symbol of the city
and gives a panoramic view of it.

For a walking tour, start with a general ramble along Water St.,
the architecturally fascinating old heart of the city and the place
where Basque sailors bought and sold as long as 500 years ago.
Take your bearings at the War Memorial, near the landing of Sir
Humphrey Gilbert in 1583. A short walk west on Duckworth St.
leads to the Newfoundland Museum, where the tragic story of the
Beothuk Indians—Newfoundland's aboriginal people—is told. The
race became extinct in 1829. Nearby, Church Hill offers a wealth
of church history and architecture: the provinces main Roman Cath-
olic, Anglican, and United Church cathedrals are there. A few
hundred yards more takes you to the storied Colonial Building, seat
of government when Newfoundland was a dominion of Great Britain (it joined Canada in 1949) and now home of the Newfoundland
archives. Nearby is the equally storied Government House, home
of Newfoundland governors since 1829. Next to that are historic
buildings dating to the 1600's. Top it off with a stroll through
Gower St., a row of Victorian houses restored under the city's
heritage program.

PRACTICAL INFORMATION
FOR ST. JOHN'S

Transportation

Downtown from the airport costs $3.50 by taxi. Generally taxi
fares start at about $1.50, up to $2.40 for the first mile and 90
cents per mile thereafter. St. John's (population 84,000) is not that
big, however, and most destinations can be walked.

PUBLIC TRANSIT. The *Metrobus* operates in the city and outlying areas; 60 cents is the basic fare, 80 cents for longer distances; exact change needed. A number of small bus operators serve other regions of the Avalon Peninsula. Tourist bureaus have further information.

FOR MORE INFORMATION

There are tourist information bureaus at the Tourist Châlet, Trans-Canada Hwy. (709–368–5900); City Hall, New Gower St. (709–722–7080); Colonial Building, Military Rd. (709–753–9380); and Newfoundland Museum, Duckworth St. (709–576–2461). Write: *Department of Development and Tourism,* P.O. Box 2016, St. John's, Newfoundland, Canada, A1C 5R8. Phone (709–576–2830).

Accommodations

St. John's has become an expensive city as a result of oil exploration, and sometimes accommodations are hard to come by at any price. It's wise to book ahead. There are quite a few housekeeping motel units, though, and campgrounds right on the outskirts ranging from $5.00 to $9.00 per night. Motel prices come down as you get away from the city—places like Carbonear, Harbour Grace, Dunville, and Whitbourne which are up to 50 miles away but have bus service to the city. Rate categories based on double-occupancy: *Inexpensive* under $30.00, and *Moderate* $30.00–$42.00. (*Note: A 12 percent provincial tax will be added to the total bill.*)

Inexpensive

The Old Inn, 157 LeMarchant Rd. 14 rooms not far from center-town; plain but engaging. **Sea Flow Tourist Home,** 53–55 William St. Functional accommodations near downtown. Kitchen facilities available.

Moderate

Parkview Inn, 118 Military Rd. Dining room. Nice parkside spot near downtown. **Greenwood Lodge and Motel,** at Mount Pearl, just out of town. Includes 5 housekeeping units. **Skyline Motel,** 337 Kenmount Rd. 31 units. Lounge and dining room.

Restaurants

Meals in the average restaurant aren't all that expensive, especially if the meal is fish. Fish, prepared in the traditional manner—nourishing but not exciting—is abundant and generally cheap. Other foods have to be brought in a long way and are more expensive. Full-course meals (drinks, tips, and tax excluded—12 percent tax on meals over $3.00) categorized as follows: *Inexpensive* under $6.00, and *Moderate* $6.00–$10.00.

Inexpensive

Captain's Cabin. Cafeteria in Bowring's Department Store, with full meals and good view of the harbor. **Ches's,** 9 Freshwater St. Boasts the best fish and chips in Canada. **King Cod,** 122 Duckworth St. Unique fish and chip spot.

Moderate

Colonial Inn, in suburban Topsail, Hwy. 3. Menu limited, but good. Cozy surroundings. Reservations recommended. **The Pink Poodle Restaurant,** 675 Topsail Rd. A quaint place that specializes in Newfoundland dishes.

What to See and Do

The **Newfoundland Museum** on Duckworth St., with the story of the vanished Beothuk Indians, artifacts from famous shipwrecks, and other aspects of Newfoundland's long history is among Canada's more interesting museums. **Signal Hill National Park,** full of history and offering a stunning panoramic view, is a must, and it's close to downtown. The city has many parks. The largest is *C.A. Pippy Park* with botanical garden, animal enclosure, playground, hiking trails and campgrounds. **Bowring Park** in the city's west end is also popular, while the large **Quidi Vidi Lake** in the west end has park all around. Seabird nesting grounds can be seen some 30 miles to the south of the city.

ENTERTAINMENT

Newfoundlanders are a very outgoing people and put a lot of energy into their entertainment. Most St. John's cocktail lounges, bars, and "clubs" (taverns) are lively places, most with a somewhat Irish touch. Prices, however, have been creeping up as in other aspects of city life; cover charges, where they exist, vary.

Rob Roy Pub, 6 George St. is a Scottish pub with live entertainment. **Sundance Saloon** is at the corner of George and Adelaide. **Just Valerie's** is an Old English pub and restaurant at 391 Duckworth.

The **Arts and Culture Center** on the Confederation Pkwy. has a year-round program of performing arts presentations.

EXPLORING NEWFOUNDLAND

The West Coast

From the ferry terminal at Port-aux-Basques, some 125 miles of interesting mountain drive brings you to the logging town of Corner Brook. From there it's another 60 miles to the prime attraction of the coast, Gros Morne National Park—700 square miles of gripping mountain and coastal views with hiking trails, campgrounds, a nature interpretation program, fishing, and more. From the park there's 200 more miles of relentless coastal drive, up to St. Anthony and the reconstructed Viking settlement of A.D. 1000. At St. Barbe you may want to take the ferry across the Strait of Belle Isle to Labrador. A 60-mile drive up the Labrador coast and the road gives out: you're up against one of the last frontiers. Along that road is the Pinware River Provincial Park, with some fine fishing.

Central Newfoundland

Instead of following the coast north to St. Anthony, you may wish to turn back at Gros Morne and travel east to central Newfoundland and its north coast. Here you'll follow the Trans-Canada Hwy. The roads off it generally run to the outports of the highly indented coast. A destination of Twillingate or Fogo Island with more ocean, coast, fishing outports, and deep-grained Newfoundland character makes for an adventuresome holiday. Grand Falls, a paper mill town and retail center, is the largest community along this strip. It contains the Mary March Museum with displays of natural history in the region. Mary March was the Christian name of Shanawdithit, last of the Beothuks, who died in 1829.

PRACTICAL INFORMATION FOR NEWFOUNDLAND

Transportation

AIR. *Air Canada* serves St. John's and Stephenville from other Canadian points. *Eastern Provincial Airways* serves St. John's and most towns in the province from Toronto and the Maritime Provinces.

FERRY. Car ferries cross several times a day from North Sydney, N.S., to Port-aux-Basques. Rates are cheaper early in the day and weekdays. A six-hour crossing. Reservations required. Also from North Sydney to Argentia some 50 miles from St. John's—an 18-hour crossing. Newfoundland's numerous coastal ferries also make great sightseeing. For information on all ferries, contact *CN Marine* or any *Via Rail* ticket office in Canada; in the U.S. call toll-free 1–800–432–7344 in Maine and 1–800–341–7981 in other Northeastern states.

BUS. *Terra Transport* operates the Newfoundland bus system. Known as "road cruisers," the buses reach most island communities, although they can be slow.

FOR MORE INFORMATION

For information, write *Department of Development and Tourism,* P.O. Box 2016, St. John's, Newfoundland, A1C 5R8. Tel.: (709–576–2830). There are tourist desks on the ferries from Nova Scotia, and offices at Port-aux-Basques (709–695–2262), Stephenville, Corner Brook (709–639–9792), Deer Lake (709–635–2202), Springdale (709–673–3110), Grand Falls (709–489–6332), Gander (709–256–8370), Clarenville (709–466–3100), Marystown (709–279–3830), and Dunville (709–227–5602). The province's accommodations guide is useful.

Accommodations and Restaurants

Seek out the rural motels. Prices are usually quite low and service very friendly. Center town accommodations in places like Corner Brook, Gander, Stephenville, and others tend to be expensive. Also there are quite a few low-cost tourist homes as well as housekeeping units. Specify if you want room with bath in some of the cheaper motels. Camping fees in the province are between $5.00 and $9.00 per night, depending on services, and Newfoundland has many interesting provincial parks. Price categories for accommodations based on double-occupancy (a 12 percent provincial tax will be added to your bill): *Inexpensive* under $28.00, and *Moderate* $28.00–$40.00.

Most motels, even small rural ones, have restaurants. Fish and salt-meat dishes—traditional Newfoundland fare—provide the best bargains. Price categories (drinks, tips, and tax excluded; tax is 12 percent on meals over $3.00): *Inexpensive* under $6.00, and *Moderate* $6.00–$9.00.

CORNER BROOK. *Bridge Way Motel* (M), Riverside Dr. 10 housekeeping units on the outskirts. *Power's Tourist Home* (I), 33 Main St. Two rooms in nice private home. Restaurants: *ABC Restaurant*(I), 4 Caribou St., and *Country Restaurant*(I) provide plain fare at reasonable cost.

DUNVILLE. *Northeast Arm Motel*(M). 8 rooms in a quiet setting by the sea. Restaurant (also M) on the premises.

GANDER. *Airport Inn* (M) on Trans-Canada Hwy. (TCH). 65 rooms, 8 housekeeping. Dining room at *Albatroll Motel*(M), Trans-Canada Hwy., is licensed, specializes in seafood.

GRAND FALLS. *Car-Sans Hotel*(M), 8 rooms. Dining room and lounge. *Town & Country Inn* (I). 9 rooms. Dining room (I-M).

LEWISPORTE. *Brittany Inn* (M), at Notre Dame Bay. 34 rooms. Dining room (I-M). *Chaulk's Tourist Home* (I). 6 rooms, communal bath. Near the ocean.

MARYSTOWN. *Marystown Motel* (M), 10 rooms, lounge.

ST. ANTHONY. *St. Anthony Motel* (M). 23 rooms, with restaurant. A friendly spot. *Howell's Hospitality Home* (I). 9 units. Restaurant (I-M).

TWILLINGATE. *Anchor In Motel* (M). 14 rooms by the sea. Dining room.

Some Principal Sights and Attractions

At *L'Anse-aux-Meadows,* near **St. Anthony,** is the reconstructed Viking settlement of A.D. 1000—a site on the World Heritage List of the United Nations. The *Port-aux-Choix National Historic Site,* with an interpretive center, is at an important Maritime Archaic Indian (and later Dorset Eskimo) burial ground dating back 4,500 years. It's halfway between Gros Morne National Park and St. Anthony. At **Grand Falls** there's the *Mary March Regional Museum* —natural history, history of logging, and the story of the extinct Beothuk Indians. At **Gander,** an important air junction before jet travel, there's the *Gander Airport Aviation Exhibit* showing the history of transatlantic travel in particular.

Manitoba

Manitoba has a rich cosmopolitan flavor that is lacking in some other Canadian regions.

While most provinces have assimilated their newcomers, Manitobans have been encouraged to preserve the cultures, languages, and traditions of their original homelands. Because of the emphasis on maintaining ethnic ties, the province's 1,042,500 citizens shun the melting pot and speak with pride about the "Manitoba mosaic." They also celebrate their heritages each year at a series of major festivals at various locations throughout the province.

The biggest of these is Folklorama, which takes place every August in Winnipeg, Manitoba's capital city. Approximately 40 different ethnic groups operate pavilions for the 10 days of the festival, tempting the public with the food and entertainment of their native lands. Other large multi-cultural happenings include the Ukrainian Festival in Dauphin during the August 1 long weekend; the Icelandic Festival at Gimli on the same weekend; and the Festival du Voyageur, which attracts thousands to Winnipeg's French-speaking suburb of St. Boniface in February.

Actually, Indians were the first residents of the 251,000-square-mile territory that was to become Manitoba. As early as 1600, four distinct Indian tribes were making their homes in different parts of the territory.

In the north, the Chipewyans were camped on the rugged Tundra around Hudson's Bay; the Cree and Salteaux roamed the great forests of the Canadian shield in the center; and the Assiniboines hunted the broad southern plains along the present Canada–U.S. border.

By 1612, European explorers were arriving, discovering a land with an abundance of animals and game. This led to the development of a lucrative fur trade, reaching its zenith in 1670 when King Charles of England granted exclusive possession of lands draining into the Hudson's Bay to an English fur-trading syndicate, the Hudson's Bay Co. Faced with ever-increasing food import costs, officials of the company decided in 1811 to establish a permanent agricultural settlement at the junction of the Red and Assiniboine in the southern half of the company's territory.

Originally known as the Red River Colony, the settlement eventually became Winnipeg—a city that today has a population of 600,000. In the 1860's, the first waves of white European settlers flowed into the colony, swelling the number of citizens from 2,500 to 12,000. Soon, a bitter struggle for supremacy erupted between the farmers and fur traders, requiring strong policing efforts by the fledgling North West Mounted Police. The dissension continued until 1870 when Manitoba entered Canada after the Hudson's Bay Co. relinquished control of all its western Canadian land for a payment of 300,000 pounds sterling from the three-year-old Canadian government.

Before the transfer was completed, the Métis (half-Indian, mostly French-speaking) fur traders, led by 25-year-old Louis Riel, vigorously fought the takeover in a series of battles that became known as the Red River Rebellion. The rebellion, one of the few major uprisings in Western Canada's otherwise placid history, was put down by Canadian authorities and Riel was hanged. Once a villain, Riel is today regarded as a hero. He is honored by a statue on the Manitoba Legislature grounds, and his tomb is one of the main tourist attractions at St. Boniface Cathedral in suburban Winnipeg.

When Manitoba joined Canada in 1870, it was known as the "postage stamp" province because its area included only the settled section around Winnipeg. Completion of the transcontinental railway in 1885 made Winnipeg the grain market and financial and wholesale distribution center for all of Western Canada. However, its role has slipped somewhat since the 1920's, as the Panama Canal's completion provided an alternative means of shipping goods to the west.

Today, half of Manitoba's population lives in Winnipeg and the other half in rural areas. The only other major urban centers are Brandon, 38,000; Portage La Prairie, 13,000; and Thompson, 14,-000. The first two communities are agricultural distribution centers in western and central Manitoba respectively; while Thompson is the northern Manitoba headquarters of INCO Ltd., which operates several nickel and zinc mines in the area.

Manitoba has had a slow rate of growth in recent years, depending on its large agricultural and manufacturing sectors to maintain a reasonable level of prosperity.

The province has been governed since November 1981 by Premier Howard Pawley's New Democratic (Socialist) government.

EXPLORING WINNIPEG

There are many interesting sites to see on a walking tour through Winnipeg's various districts.

Try starting at Portage Ave. and Main St., the main downtown intersection in the heart of the city. Known as the windiest corner in North America, Portage and Main is dominated by the modern skyscrapers of the grain companies and financial institutions that have always been the foundation of Winnipeg's economic life.

The 32-story Winnipeg Commodities Tower, on the southwest corner, houses the computerized trading floor of the 300-member

Winnipeg Commodity Exchange. The exchange operates Canada's only futures markets for grain, gold, and silver, with excitement reaching a peak at the closing at 1:15 P.M. daily. Tours can be arranged by phoning (204) 949–0495.

Diagonally opposite, on the northeast corner, is the 34-story Richardson Building, which is the head office of James Richardson and Sons Ltd., an international grain and securities firm that was founded by Winnipeg's most prominent establishment family. Built in 1970, the Richardson building was the catalyst for a downtown building boom that a decade ago brought many new structures to the core.

Also in the Portage and Main district are the head offices of the Canadian Wheat Board, the Canadian Grain Commission, and the Canadian International Grain Institute, all federal agencies that look after different aspects of Canada's important export grain trade.

If you walk five blocks north on Main St. from Portage Ave., you will eventually come to Winnipeg's City Hall and the Centennial Concert Hall across the street. The concert hall, which regularly hosts performances by major touring artists, is the center of a cultural complex that includes the Manitoba Museum of Man and Nature and an adjacent planetarium, the Manitoba Theatre Center, the Playhouse Theater, and the Warehouse Theater.

Winnipeg itself is the home of many professional arts groups who present regular seasons of performances from fall to spring. Among these groups are the Royal Winnipeg Ballet, the Contemporary Dancers, the Manitoba Theatre Center, and the Winnipeg Symphony Orchestra. In summer, Broadway musicals are featured at Rainbow Stage in Kildonan Park in north Winnipeg.

Other points of interest in the downtown district include the Winnipeg Art Gallery, at Portage Ave. and Memorial Blvd., the main public library, at Donald St. and Smith Ave., and the Winnipeg Convention Center, at Carlton St. and St. Mary's Ave. All these edifices may be visited at little or no cost. Outside the core, the most inexpensive fun is to be found in the city's major parks.

Assiniboine Park in the south end is the site of the city's zoo and a tropical garden; Kildonan in the north has a golf course and a swimming pool; Sargent in the west-central area has tennis courts, a pool, and an athletic complex; Bird's Hill in the northeast has a beach and camping areas; and St. Vital in the southeast has picnic areas, a pond, and a toboggan slide.

No visit to Winnipeg would be complete without a visit to St. Boniface, a French-speaking suburb just across the river from the city's downtown district. It is the largest Francophone community in Western Canada and has lots to interest visitors, including the tomb of Métis Leader Louis Riel, the ancient St. Boniface Cathedral, the Franco-Manitobaine Cultural Center, St. Boniface College, and two excellent French restaurants, La Vieille Gare and La Grenouillere.

A definite "must" is the St. Boniface Museum, 494 Tache St., which is the oldest building in Winnipeg and the largest structure of oak-log construction in North America. Before becoming a museum in 1967, the building had served since 1846 as the main western Canadian convent of the Sisters of Charity of Montréal, better known as the Grey Nuns. Today, it houses a wide variety of exhibits depicting the early days of the Red River Colony. The museum is open year-round and admission is free, but donations are gratefully accepted.

Finally, visitors should make an effort to see Manitoba's Legislative Building on Broadway Ave., which is one of the finest neoclassical structures in the world. It was begun in 1913, but a shortage of labor and materials during the First World War delayed completion until 1920. Arrangements for tours may be made through the security guards on the main floor, tel. (204) 945–3700.

Outside Winnipeg, Manitoba is a haven for those who like outdoor recreation. In summer, both tourists and residents flock to the beaches on Lake Winnipeg and in the Whiteshell. Northern Manitoba, meanwhile, offers many excellent areas for fishing, hunting, canoeing, and hiking. The province's major parks—to be found in all corners of Manitoba—are open year-round, but campground and picnic areas have a limited season from mid-May until the end of September.

PRACTICAL INFORMATION FOR WINNIPEG

Transportation

AIR. Winnipeg is the transportation hub of Western Canada. The Winnipeg International Airport is accessible from every major center in the world. The principal airlines operating from Winnipeg include *Air Canada, CP Air, Pacific Western, Nordair, Wardair, Northwest Orient, Frontier,* and *Perimeter.*

CAR. Three major highways connect with the perimeter highway, which circles the city to relieve crosstown traffic. The Trans-Canada Hwy. (# 1) runs east-west. Hwy. 75 S. connects with U.S. Interstate 29 and Minnesota 95 (entry point—Emerson, open 24 hours per day). Hwy. 59 connects with Minnesota 59 (entry point—Tolstoi open from 8:00 A.M. to 10:00 P.M. daily).

Within the city, a combination of integrated freeways, suburban beltways, and bridges keep public transit and private vehicles moving. Major routes are numbered, odd numbered going east/west and even numbered north/south.

BUS. Public transit is all by bus. Fare is 80 cents for adults and 35 cents for children, 5 to 17 years old. Children under 5 travel free when accompanied by an adult. Bus stops are clearly marked. Exact fare is necessary. If transferring to a different bus en route to your destination, request a transfer for each fare paid at the time the fare is paid. Depending on the route, buses generally start running around 6:00 A.M. You can usually catch the last bus of the day around midnight Sunday or 1:30 A.M. any other day. Free bus service between downtown locations along the marked Blue & Gold Dash routes, Monday to Friday, 11:00 A.M. to 3:30 P.M. Round-the-clock transit information at (204) 284-7190.

One major bus route runs between downtown and the Winnipeg International Airport. That bus arrives at the airport every 13 minutes during peak periods and every 23 minutes other times. Limousine service is also available between airport and major downtown hotels. This service operates coincidentally with major flight arrivals and costs $4.00 per person.

TRAIN. Winnipeg is also accessible by rail—primarily *VIA Rail* from Canadian destinations. A downtown bus depot handles bus passengers from all over North America.

TAXIS are found at numerous taxi stands downtown and at the airport. If a stand is not readily visible, the easiest way to get a taxi is to phone one of the numerous taxicab companies listed in the telephone directory Yellow Pages. Direct lines to major cab companies are found in hotels, downtown building lobbies, the airport, railway stations, shopping centers, the bus depot, and in any location where frequent taxi pickups are necessary.

Taxi fare starts at $1.35 the minute you step into the cab and increases by $1.10 per mile of traveling and 10 cents for every 30 seconds of waiting time. Average fare from the airport to the center of the city is usually between $7.00 and $8.00.

PARKING. Like all large cities, Winnipeg's roads are busy and parking space near the city center is limited. Parking meters, when available, take 5-cent, 10-cent and 25-cent coins. The space costs 5 cents for 6 minutes. Most metered spaces and many free parking spaces have time limits posted. These limits range from ½ hour to 2 hours. Also take note of restrictions during rush hours.

After 6:00 P.M. parking space is free at almost all metered spots Monday to Friday. In the city-owned and metered lots on Stradbrook and Osborne, and on Alexander and Main, parking is free only after midnight. Similarly, parking around the main Post Office is free only after 10:00 P.M. You don't have to "feed the meter" on Sunday.

All the large suburban shopping centers offer free parking. St. Vital, Unicity, Garden City, and Polo Park Shopping Centers are among the largest and are within half an hour driving distance from downtown during normal conditions.

During the winter months, at the discretion of the mayor, overnight parking on the streets is limited to only a few hours. If you come to Winnipeg and there's snow on the ground, it is best to check with the police or tourist department as to parking restrictions because they are not always posted.

Studded tires are allowed on Winnipeg streets from October 1 to April 30. Devices to free the windows of frost are mandatory. Block heaters are a necessity during Winnipeg's winter. Plugs are usually provided in public parking garages and should be used.

TOURS. Sightseeing tours of Winnipeg and the surrounding countryside are readily available and vary seasonally.

The *Prairie Dog Central* is a turn-of-the-century vintage steam train that operates every Sunday from June to September, taking passengers from Winnipeg to Grosse Isle, a 36-mile excursion. The Vintage Locomotive Society Inc. at Box 217, St. James P.O., Winnipeg, Manitoba, R3J 3R4 (phone 204–284–2690) offers information on this tour.

Also seasonal are riverboat tours, which generally run daily from May to October, as long as the two Winnipeg rivers, the Red and the Assiniboine, remain free of ice and are navigable. Prices for these excursions range from $3.00 per person to $11.00 per person, depending on the time of day and the destination. Information about these sternwheel boats can be obtained from the two companies that operate them (phone 204–339–1696 or 204–669–2824).

Comprehensive bus tours of the city are offered by the same companies that run the riverboat cruises and information can be obtained from those offices. In some cases double-decker London buses chauffeur the tours. A double-decker bus tour also operates in conjunction with Via Rail during the train's Winnipeg stopover. Information can be obtained from Tour Office, 2285 Main Street in Winnipeg.

FOR MORE INFORMATION

Travel Manitoba operates Tourist Information Centers at numerous convenient locations throughout the province.

From mid-May to early September, daily from 8:00 A.M. to 9:00 P.M., free literature and personalized travel counseling is available at the following locations: Canada/U.S. Border—Hwy. 75; Canada/U.S. Border—Hwy. 10; Manitoba/Ontario Boundary—Hwy. 1; Manitoba/Saskatchewan Boundary—Hwy. 1; Winnipeg East—Hwy. 1 East near Bypass; Winnipeg West—Hwy. 1 West near Bypass; Downtown Winnipeg—Legislative Building. Watch for the "?" symbol and the Travel Information Trailer at various festivals and community events.

In addition, you can obtain personalized travel counseling by telephoning the toll-free number 1–800–665–0040. In Winnipeg call 945–3777. There is a 24-hour recorded message at (204) 942–2335 (long-distance charges applicable) that provides current information on attractions, events, park vacancy rates, and ski conditions.

Transit information is (204) 284–7190. Write for free literature and information to: Travel Manitoba, 7th floor - 155 Carlton Street, Winnipeg, Manitoba R3C 3H8.

Accommodations

For hotels and motels, bed-and-breakfast, hostels and apartment hotels, reservations generally should be made in advance. Rates are higher in hotels close to downtown and the airport. Many of the hotels listed are in the suburbs and within easy access of transit. Rates, based on double-occupancy, are *Inexpensive:* $35.00 and less, and *Moderate:* $35.00–$50.00

Bed-and-breakfast was introduced in Manitoba in 1980. Twenty-two Winnipeg homes offered the service that summer, and guests appeared to be more than satisfied. A wide range of homes are registered, from modest bungalow to river-front mansion. The price ranges between $20.00 and $30.00 a night per room, double-occupancy, including breakfast. Hosts are often conversant in several languages. Brandon began B&B service in 1983. Anyone interested can contact Tillman Burgess at B&B, 35 Pontiac Bay, Winnipeg, Manitoba, R3K 0S6; Wilf Organ at B&B, P.O. Box 5, Petersfield, Manitoba, R3K 0S6; or Department 1135, Travel Manitoba, Winnipeg, Manitoba, R3C 0V8.

HOTELS AND MOTELS

Inexpensive

Aberdeen Hotel, 230 Carlton St., R3C 1P5. Good downtown location. Rooms with or without bath. Poor service but very inexpensive. **Lincoln Motor Hotel,** 1030 McPhillips St., R2X 2K7. Pleasant hotel on the northern outskirts but an easy transit ride downtown. **Osborne Village Motor Inn,** 160 Osborne St., R3L 1Y6. Located in a quaint remodeled shopping and restaurant area and within walking distance of downtown. **Westminster Motor Hotel,** 685 Westminster Ave., R3C 0Z4. Pleasant bustling atmosphere. Outdoor pool.

Moderate

Assiniboine Gordon Inn *on the Park,* 1975 Portage Ave., R3J 0J9. Friendly service on the western outskirts of Winnipeg. Easy transit ride downtown. **Balmoral Motor Hotel,** Balmoral and Notre Dame, R3B 2R4. Pleasant but noisy. Close to Health Sciences Centre. **Charleswood Motor Hotel,** 3425 Roblin Blvd, R3R 0C5. Friendly facilities in the southwestern part of Winnipeg. **Dakota Village Motor Hotel,** 1105 St. Mary's Rd., R2M 3T6. Congenial but noisy. **Friendship Airport Hotel,** 1800 Ellice Ave., R3H 0B7. Good airport location. **Golden Oak Inn,** 826 Regent Ave. W., R2C 3A8. Comfortable surroundings in Eastern Winnipeg. **Norlander Inn Motor Hotel,** 1792 Pembina Hwy., R3T 2G2. Located on Hwy. 75 at the southern end of the city.

APARTMENT HOTELS

Bachelor apartments that rent for about $290 per week are located in several convenient downtown spots. **Colony Square Apt. Hotel,** 555 St. Mary's Ave., R3C 3X4, has an outdoor swimming pool and sauna. **Holiday Towers Apt. Hotel,** 170 Hargrave St., R3C 3H4, has airport limousine service, more restaurant facilities, an indoor and outdoor pool and sauna. **Place Louis Riel Hotel,** 190 Smith St., R3C 1J8, also has an indoor pool and a sauna.

HOSTELS

Knappen House Youth Hostel, 210 Maryland St., R3G 1L6. A quiet residential area close to downtown. Operates year-round from 5:00 P.M. to 10:00 A.M. Closed Christmas and New Year's. Resident hotel manager. Rates are $7.00 to $9.00 per night and include washroom facilities, showers, blankets, pillows, and kitchen facilities. Guests must share in daily cleaning chores. No bookings will be guaranteed without a non-refundable deposit of $2.00 per person.

YMCA, 301 Vaughan St., R3B 2N7. Coed accommodation right downtown. $16.00 per night or $80 per week for single room including indoor pool and sauna. **YWCA,** 447 Webb Pl., R3R 2P2. Ladies' residence, downtown. $22.00 to $25.00 per night includes pool and sauna. Rooms are air-conditioned. All accommodations are subject to a 6% sales tax except those rented by the month.

Restaurants

Winnipeg's population traces its origins to countries and cultures throughout the world. Because Winnipegers have clung so lovingly to their ethnic origins, Winnipeg's restaurants reflect the finest ethnic cuisine. Truly the best bargains in European and Asian delicacies are found in the various ethnic locales of the city. For the best Italian food, try Corydon Ave. near the junction of Pembina Hwy. The best in Jewish and Ukrainian delicatessen is in the city's famed North End. Of course the best in French cuisine is in St. Boniface. There is no sales tax on orders of $6.00 or less. Sales tax is 6 percent on orders of $6.00 or more.

Liquor laws in Manitoba are rather complex. Specific terms are used to describe premises serving alcoholic beverages to the public.

A beverage room serves beer, spirits, and wine for no longer than 14 hours per day between the hours of 9:00 A.M. and 1:00 A.M., Monday through Saturday. Entertainment may be provided.

A restaurant with a wine license serves wine with meals between 11:00 A.M. and 1:00 A.M. daily. Some restaurants have a wine and beer license that allows them to serve beer as well. Entertainment may be provided.

Fully licensed dining rooms serve spirits, beer, and wine with meals between 11:30 A.M. and 1:00 A.M., Monday to Saturday. Entertainment may be provided.

As a general rule, the more complete the liquor license, the higher the food prices tend to be. Restaurants also tend to raise prices for the dinner menu. "Luncheon Specials" in better Winnipeg restaurants usually come directly off the dinner menu—only the price is changed. A couple can eat a complete lunch (appetizer or soup, entree, dessert) in a Winnipeg restaurant for $20.00, but $25.00 is the minimum you can usually expect to pay at dinner. However, at some of our listed restaurants, a dinner for two is still less than twenty dollars.

The following list can only be a limited selection of the eating and drinking establishments in Winnipeg. The major food chains such as McDonald's and Burger King have been omitted because they are typical of the American outlets, but they are represented in Winnipeg and do have inexpensive fast-food meals.

Inexpensive

No list of inexpensive restaurants would be complete without mentioning the numerous pizza restaurants. Winnipeg boasts of having more pizza restaurants than any city in Western Canada. You'll find the pizza restaurants listed in the Yellow Pages of the Winnipeg telephone directory under "RESTAURANTS—Pizza."

Alycia's, 559 Cathedral Ave. Ukrainian specialties, licensed. **D'8 Schtove,** 1531 Pembina. Hearty Mennonite food. **Good Old Days,** 143 Sherbrooke. Pleasant tearoom with copious Friday-night buffet. **Harman's Drug Store,** Portage Ave. at Sherbrooke St. Good service and great food at this friendly lunch counter. **Kelekis,** 1100 Main St. A family restaurant specializing in great hamburgers, hot dogs, and fries. A Winnipeg fixture for more than 50 years. **Mr. Greenjeans,** Eaton Place. Loud piped-in music, but quiche, ribs and tuna sandwiches are good. **Oasis Delicatessen and Fruit Ltd.,** 906 Main St. Counter service only. Featuring Jewish and Ukrainian deli sandwiches, herring platters, and homemade pie. Open from 9:00 A.M. to 5:30 P.M. only. **Salisbury House,** locations throughout Winnipeg. Winnipeg's version of fast food. Try the wafer pie. **YMHA Restaurant,** 370 Hargrave St. The only real Kosher deli in Winnipeg. Open odd hours, so phone (204) 943–7624 if you plan to go.

Moderate

Acropolis, 172 Sherbrooke St. Greek dining in style. Some American-style steak and seafood as well. Full liquor license. **Bistro Dansk,** 63 Sherbrooke St. Danish dishes such as roast chicken with apricot and walnut stuffing on the dinner menu. Lunch is soups, salads, and open-faced Danish sandwiches. Wine licence. **Bombay Restaurant,** 598 Ellice. Supposedly the most authentic East Indian food. **Old Market Cafe,** Albert St. at Arthur. Italian and Greek entrees. Superb Italian ice cream. Open 21 hours a day. **Haynes Chicken Shack,** 257 Lulu St. Famous for its mouth-watering Southern fried chicken and spareribs. Full license. **Mehra's India Gardens,** 765 McDermot. Authentic East Indian dishes including spicy curries, vegetarian dishes, and an excellent *gulab jaman* dessert.

Full license. **Homer's,** 520 Ellice. Greek and North American menu. Licensed. **Samovar,** 1199 Fife St. Homemade Ukrainian food and soups. Wine license. **Slava,** 666 Broadway. Modest premises with hearty Russian dishes. **Teepee,** 236 Edmonton St. Winnipeg's only Native Indian restaurant featuring appetizing game dishes. **Tokyo Joe's,** 132 Pioneer. Korean/Japanese dishes cooked by master chef Tokyo Joe himself.

This section cannot close without mentioning Winnipeg's famous Chinese restaurants. Good prices are pretty standard from one to another. Traditionally people go in groups and order several different dishes. These are served in the center of the table and everyone helps themselves to a little bit of everything. It can make for a fun evening at a reasonably inexpensive price.

What to See and Do

MUSEUMS AND ART GALLERIES

Aquatic Hall of Fame and Museum of Canada, 25 Poseidon Bay. Contains ancient history on aquatics including the Cutty Sark Club collection of ship models. Open daily throughout the year, 9:00 A.M. to 10:00 P.M. Admission free.

Archives of the Conference of Mennonites in Canada, 600 Shaftesbury Blvd. Western Canadian, Russian, and Prussian Mennonite documents, manuscripts, photos, and detailed genealogies. Large display area and art gallery. Open Monday to Friday, 8:30 A.M. to 5:00 P.M. Admission free.

Dalnavert-MacDonald House, 61 Carlton St. Restored Victorian home of Sir Hugh John MacDonald, former Premier of Manitoba and son of the first Prime Minister of Canada. Open for guided tours, with the last tour ½ hour before closing. Admission: adults $1.50, students and Senior Citizens $1.00, children 12 and under 50 cents. For information call (204) 943–2835.

The Fort Garry Horse Museum, McGregor Armoury, McGregor St. at Machray Ave. Depicts the Cavalry of Western Canada and the Tankers of Manitoba. Open Tuesday evenings and Sunday afternoons.

Fort Whyte Nature Centre, 2205 McGillivary Blvd. Built around several man-made lakes, a refuge for wildlife native to the area. Admission to the center is free. Lectures and workshops on Sunday afternoons and evenings on seasonal topics. Hours vary seasonally. For more information, call (204) 895–7001.

Grant's Old Mill, Portage Ave. at Booth Dr. A reconstruction of an original watermill, believed to be the first west of the Great Lakes and the first instance of hydro power in Manitoba. Grist ground daily in summer and sold in souvenir bags. Open daily May 1 to September 1 and weekends September 1 to October 31. Admission: adults 50 cents, children 25 cents.

Historical Museum of St. James-Assiniboia and 1857 Red River Log Style House, 3180 Portage Ave. Pioneer displays and artifacts—vintage dental equipment, 1894 buggy, cutter, etc.

Open September to May by appointment. May 15 to September 1 daily. Admission: adults 50 cents, children 25 cents.

Living Prairie Museum, 2795 Ness Ave. A 40-acre Tall Prairie Grass nature park. Nature center contains displays and slide program. Guided tours available during summer months. Nature center hours: June 29 to September 7, 10:00 A.M. to 8:00 P.M. Remainder of the year: weekdays 9:00 A.M. to 4:30 P.M. Open weekends in fall and spring from noon to 5:00 P.M. Admission free.

Manitoba Legislative Building, Broadway Ave. at Osborne St. One of the first neoclassical structures in the world. Home of the famed 23-karat Golden Boy, perched high atop the central tower. Guided tours arranged by phoning (204) 944–3700 between 9:00 A.M. and 5:00 P.M. Admission and tours free.

Manitoba Museum of Man and Nature, 190 Rupert Ave. An ongoing exhibit program dealing with the natural world and people's relationship to their environment. Permanent galleries and traveling exhibits. Open: May 15 to September 15, Monday to Saturday and holidays, 10:00 A.M. to 9:00 P.M. Sunday noon to 9:00 P.M. September 16 to May 14, Monday to Saturday, 10:00 A.M. to 5:00 P.M.; Sunday and holidays, noon to 6:00 P.M. Admission: adults $1.50, family $5 maximum, Senior Citizens and children under 6 (with adult) free.

Le Musée de St. Boniface, 494 Ave. Tache. Housed in the oldest building in the City of Winnipeg. Displays depict life of the Métis and the French Canadians of the Prairies. Open year-round. Donations accepted.

Riel House, 330 River Rd. (One block south of Bishop Grandin Blvd. in St. Vital.) A national historic site depicting the cultural, social, and economic lives of the Riel and Lagimodière families in the Red River Settlement of the 1880's. Telephone (204) 257–1783 or 233–4888.

Seven Oaks House Museum, Rupertsland Ave. East, 1½ blocks from Main St. in West Kildonan. The oldest habitable home in Manitoba. Open: mid-May to mid-June weekends, 10:00 A.M. to 5:00 P.M.; mid-June to Labor Day, daily 10:00 A.M. to 5:00 P.M. Admission: Adults 75 cents, students up to 18 years, 25 cents, children under 6 free.

Ukrainian Museum of Canada, Manitoba Branch, 1175 Main St. Ukrainian folk arts and crafts brought by the original pioneers. Open: June 15 to September 15, Monday to Friday, 10:00 A.M. to 12:00 A.M. and 1:00 P.M. to 4:00 P.M. Donations accepted.

Western Canadian Aviation Museum, 11 Lily St. (Directly behind the Manitoba Museum of Man and Nature.) Displays of vintage aircraft and related memorabilia. Open: Wednesday to Friday from 10:00 A.M. to 4:00 P.M. Donations accepted.

Winnipeg Art Gallery, 300 Memorial Blvd. The gallery hangs between 25 and 30 exhibitions annually which include early and contemporary Canadian works, Inuit art, and traveling international exhibits. Closed Mondays. Open Tuesday to Saturday, 11:00 A.M. to 5:00 P.M., and Sundays, noon to 5:00 P.M. Admission free. Telephone for tour information at (204) 786–6641, extension 53.

Winnipeg Mint, Trans-Canada Hwy. at Lagimodière Blvd. A branch of the Canadian Mint displaying Canadian and foreign coins. From the tour gallery visitors can see coins being made. Admission free. For tour information and hours call (204) 257–3359.

ENTERTAINMENT

Winnipeg has 19 theater companies, two dance companies, eight ethnic theaters, and three orchestras—the Winnipeg Symphony, the Manitoba Chamber Orchestra, and the Royal Winnipeg Ballet orchestra. In season, their performances are held in the **Centennial Concert Hall,** the **Winnipeg Art Gallery,** the **Playhouse Theater,** and throughout large auditoriums in the city.

SPORTS. There is a professional Canadian Football League team, the Winnipeg Blue Bombers, a professional National Hockey League team, the Winnipeg Jets and various junior sports teams.

There is year-round thoroughbred and harness horse racing at *Assiniboia Downs.* During summer months, professional auto racing flourishes at the *Winnipeg Speedway,* and the outdoor theater is held at *Rainbow Stage* in Kildonan Park. There are four public golf courses and three indoor public swimming pools in Winnipeg.

PARKS. Winnipeg has 920 public **parks.** The largest park, *Assiniboine Park,* has a magnificent zoo, a horticultural conservatory, a duck pond, beautiful formal floral gardens and in winter, a skating rink and toboggan slide.

Hours, performance dates, and times, places, etc., are easily obtained from the Travel Manitoba Office; phone (204) 944–3777 for personalized information or (204) 942–2535 for recorded information.

FESTIVALS AND SPECIAL EVENTS. The third week of June is the annual *Red River Exhibition* and parade. In August, there is *Folklarama,* a Festival of Nations, which turns the city into a mini world's fair. A passport, for under $10.00, gains you admission to pavilions throughout the city where you can enjoy ethnic cuisine, exhibitions, and top-notch entertainment.

NIGHTLIFE. Cabarets and Discothèques are allowed to serve spirits and wine between 5:00 P.M. and 1:00 A.M. Monday to Saturday. Live entertainment is provided. Unless there's a cover charge, your only cost is drinks.

Dayton's Nite Club, 329 Portage Ave., Live music. 5:00 P.M.–2:00 A.M., Monday through Saturday.

The Big A Disco Tavern in the Assiniboine Hotel on Portage Ave. at Albany St. Cover Charge Thursday to Saturday. Hours: 8:00 P.M. to 1:00 A.M., Monday to Saturday.

Brandy's, 109 Princess St., is a licensed dining room with disco music after 8:30 P.M. Opens at 11:30 A.M. daily, Monday to Friday. Opens at 6:00 P.M. Saturday. Disco to 1:00 A.M. No cover charge.

Broadways, 222 Broadway in the Hotel Fort Garry. Live music with popular groups; stand-up bar. Monday through Thursday, 7:00 P.M.–1:00 A.M.; Friday and Saturday, 7:00 P.M.–2:00 A.M.

Georgie's, Kirkfield Park, 3321 Portage Ave. Western music and dancing. No cover charge. Monday to Saturday, 7:30 P.M. to 1:00 A.M.

Hollow Mug, International Inn, 1808 Wellington Ave. Licensed dining room with dancing nightly from 7:45 P.M., except during shows. Stage shows usually excerpts from Broadway musicals. No cover charge.

Marty's Food & Beverage Company, 167 Bannatyne Ave. Reasonably priced entrees and generously sized drinks. Large dance floor. New favorite of the disco-rock crowd. 11:30 A.M. to 1:00 A.M. Monday to Saturday. No cover charge.

Rorie St. Marble Club, 65 Rorie St. Another very popular disco dining room in Winnipeg's theatre district. Live entertainment in the lounge. Giant video screen featuring rock videos on the dance floor. No cover charge. 5:00 P.M. to 2:00 A.M. Monday to Saturday.

Elbows, Holiday Inn, 350 St. Mary's Ave. Open 7:00 P.M. to 2:00 A.M. Monday to Saturday with continuous sound-and-light shows between acts. Good bands from out of town. Live musical entertainment following. Cover charge Friday and Saturday.

Drinks in cabarets and discos run anywhere from $2.50 up. Food in the discos which are also dining rooms tends to be expensive. You should make reservations if planning on eating at any of the cabaret/dining rooms.

Pubs are popular beverage rooms in Winnipeg. Entertainment is usually live. Drinks start around $1.50 for domestic beer and are generally cheaper than drinks in cabarets. It would be impossible to list all the pubs in Winnipeg, most of which are located in hotels. This list is just a few of the more popular ones, especially those who specialize in a certain form of music.

Bottles, 177 Lombard East. Stand-up comedians one week per month. One of Winnipeg's newest night spots.

Norwood Hotel, 112 Marion St., features top-20 high-energy entertainers. The *Americana Pub* of the Marlborough Inn, 331 Smith St., features live entertainment. Middle-of-the-road entertainers perform in the Oval Room of the Fort Garry Hotel, 222 Broadway Ave., and the *Pan Am Lounge* of the International Inn, 1808 Wellington Ave.

Popular Western pubs include: the *Airport Hotel,* 1800 Ellice Ave.; *Continental Hotel,* 550 McPhillips St.; *Downs Motor Inn,* 3740 Portage Ave.; *Sneaky Pete's,* 451 Portage Ave.; *St. Boniface Hotel,* 171 Dumoulin and the *Westbrook Inn,* Keewatin at Pacific Ave.

Outdoor **folk entertainment** without liquor is an annual event in Bird's Hill Park for one July weekend every summer at the *Winnipeg Folk Festival.* Entertainers from throughout North America converge to entertain huge crowds. Tickets to this event usually sell for around $35.00 for the weekend, $15.00 for a day. *Children's Festival* is a mini-version held in June.

Tickets to most city events can be purchased at the Attractions

Ticket Office in any Eaton's Department Store and at the University of Manitoba, or at the Bay Ticket Office in any Bay Department Store.

Free events are common all summer in most city parks. Information can be obtained by phoning (204) 885–1500.

PRACTICAL INFORMATION FOR RURAL MANITOBA

TRANSPORTATION. The main method of transportation in the province is by road. Circle Tours Ltd., 301 Burnell St., Winnipeg, Manitoba R3G 2A6 and Fehr-Way Tours Ltd., 1110 Henderson Hwy., Winnipeg, Manitoba, R2G 1L1, operate bus tours of the province. These vary in length from one day to seven days and usually encompass a theme such as "historic" or "agricultural" tour.

The intricate river and lake system of the province is perfect for canoe tours. Routes and guide information can be obtained from Manitoba Travel (see Winnipeg section).

Fly-in hunting lodges exist in the North but the cost is usually prohibitive.

MUSEUMS. Almost every town in Manitoba has a small museum. Morden has a research station. Winkler has its *Thresherman's Museum.* A list of Manitoba Museums is available from Travel Manitoba.

WHAT TO DO. The natural geographic areas of Manitoba each offer unique naturalist activities. You can rock hound in Souris, Manitoba (which has the longest free-swinging suspension bridge in Canada), tour a natural desert in Carberry, or relax in the wooded hills of *Riding Mountain National Park.*

U-Pick Berry farms throughout Southern Manitoba allow you to pick your own strawberries in season.

Manitoba's hunting and fishing are among the best in North America. Information and guides are available from Travel Manitoba. In addition, Manitoba communities hold festivals and fairs year round. Travel Manitoba can provide a yearly Calendar of Events describing these. Some of the more popular ones include the *Trapper's Festival* in the Pas, the *Morden Corn Apple Festival,* the *Flin Flon Trout Derby,* and *Altona Sunflower Festival.* There's always something to do in sunny Manitoba!

ACCOMMODATIONS. The Hostelling Association of Manitoba has four hostels that provide economical accommodation for visitors traveling through the province. In Winnipeg, there is **Knappen House,** 210 Maryland St., which opens daily at 5:00 P.M. and closes at 10:00 A.M.; overnight charges are $8.00 and $10.00. **Brandon's**

Youth Hostel is on hospital grounds on Hwy. 1A half a mile south of the Trans-Canada Hwy., opening at 5:00 P.M. and closing at 9:00 A.M. with overnight charges of $8.00 and $10.00. The same hours and charges apply at Glenboro's hostel, the **Hiwin-Glen Farm,** two miles west of the Glenboro Esso station on Hwy. 2. In addition, the **Lilac Motel,** 25 miles east of Winnipeg on Hwy. 1 near the junction of Hwy. 12, offers hostel facilities, as well as providing camping and a dug-out swimming pool.

Manitoba Farm Vacations are inexpensive. The cost of a farm holiday is $30.00 per day for adults and $15.00 per day for children under 12 accompanied by an adult. All meals are included.

The 57 farms involved in the program vary from small dairy operations to enormous grain-growing businesses. Each farm offers a variety of facilities such as riding, golf, fishing, boating, and swimming. The association also pre-arranges hunting trips on private farmlands.

Three different types of accommodation are available: full-room and board, cottages where guests have their own meal-preparation facilities, and trailer/tenting areas.

For further information, contact: Manitoba Farm Vacations Association, Box 2580, Winnipeg, Manitoba, R3C 4B3. Phone: (204–943–8361).

BRANDON

Transportation

Brandon, on the east-west Trans-Canada Hwy., is served by *Greyhound* Buslines and *Via Rail. Perimeter Airlines* offers air passenger service from Winnipeg.

Accommodations

Price ranges are $25.00 to $35.00 for *Inexpensive,* and $35.00 to $45.00 for *Moderate.*

Hillcrest Motel (I), 1st St. N., Hwy. 1A, Box 91, Brandon, Manitoba, R7A 5Y6. Provides guides, fishing and hunting licenses and bait. **North Hill Inn** (I), Box 265 Brandon, Manitoba, R7A 5Y8. A modern motel with a good restaurant and an adjoining golf course. Pleasant view overlooking the city. **Western Motel** (I), 1148–11th St. R7A 5C2. Just plain friendly service with no expensive frills.

Canadian Inn (M), Box 484, Brandon, R7A 5Z4. Reasonably priced luxury accommodation. Indoor pool.

Colonial Inn (M), 1978 Queens Ave., Brandon, Manitoba, R7B 0T1. An indoor swimming pool in this modern motel. **Mid-Way Friendship Inn** (M), Hwy. 1A, 1st St. N., Box 451, Brandon, Manitoba. Clean comfortable hotel.

HOSTELS. Brandon Youth Hostel, 500 feet from Trans-Canada Hwy. off 1A. About 2½ miles from downtown Brandon. Transit bus stops directly in front every half hour and goes downtown. Rides cost 40 cents, exact change. There are communal dorms (male, female, and coed) with adjacent washroom facilities. Kitchen facilities are free. Laundry facilities available at nominal charge. Sheet sleeping blankets are free. No pillows. Hostel hours are 5:00 P.M. to 9:00 A.M. Fees per night range from $8.00 to $10.00. The **YWCA,** 148–11th St., Brandon, Manitoba R7A 4J4. A double room is $12.00 for the night.

Things to See and Do

Brandon has three public golf courses, two heated indoor pools and two outdoor pools. The **Canada Games Sportplex** offers racquetball, swimming, tennis, and track and field activities. Racquetball equipment may be rented. There is a charge for facility use.

The **Provincial Exhibition of Manitoba** is held in the city in mid-June with stage shows, a casino, a parade, agricultural exhibits, band competitions, and a midway.

Several Brandon motels have pubs and dining rooms. Regulations are the same as those in Winnipeg.

Museums

B. J. Hales Museum of Natural History, A. E. McKenzie Bldg., Brandon University. Mounted specimens of birds and mammals, bird eggs, insect and geology displays, and Indian artifacts. Information on hours available from (204) 728–4029 or (204) 728–9520, extension 407. Admission free.

Brandon Allied Arts Centre, 1036 Louise Ave. Classes and workshops throughout the year. Programs in performing arts. Open: September to June 9:00 A.M. to noon and 1:00 P.M. to 5:00 P.M., Monday through Saturday. 2:00 P.M. to 5:00 P.M., July and August. Admission free.

Brandon Museum Inc., 122–18th St. Home of the first mayor of Brandon. Artifacts and miniature city council chamber. Open: Tuesday to Sunday, 2:00 P.M. to 4:00 P.M. Admission: adults 50 cents, students and children 25 cents.

PORTAGE LA PRAIRIE

Transportation

Portage la Prairie, 50 miles west of Winnipeg on the Trans-Canada Hwy., is served daily by *Greyhound Bus Lines* and *Via Rail.*

Accommodations

Mayfair Motel (I), 66 Royal Rd. S., Portage la Prairie, Manitoba, R1N 1T5. Clean, quiet, and quaint.

Sunset Motel (M), Box 34, Portage la Prairie, Manitoba, R1N 3B2. Quiet and convenient accommodation.

Museums

Fort la Reine Museum, Pioneer Village, and **International Tourist Bureau,** 1 mile east of Portage on Hwy. 1A. Native and pioneer artifacts depicting life in the 1700's. Free picnic grounds, washrooms, and information. Open daily all summer from 2:00 P.M. to 5:00 P.M. Admission free.

THOMPSON

Transportation

Thompson in North Manitoba, 600 miles north of Winnipeg, is linked by jet passenger aircraft with Winnipeg. The city is serviced by rail and by *Grey Goose Bus.* By road, motorists from Southern Manitoba have a choice of two routes, one through the Pas, Manitoba, and a more direct route via Grand Rapids.

Accommodations

Hotels in Thompson are all within the same price range, $30.00 to $50.00 per day. **Burntwood Motor Hotel,** Selkirk Ave. and Cree Rd., and **Mystery Lake Motor Hotel** on the same corner are the most popular of the four Thompson hotels.

Entertainment and Dining

Thompson has several excellent dining establishments and night life is colorful at the city's clubs.

The Community's *Nickel Days* summer festival and *Winter Carnival* provide frolic and entertainment.

Throughout the year, nearly 10,000 people tour the Inco Metals Co.'s surface plant facilities. The tours are for persons 16 years old and over. Wear sturdy footwear and dress for the weather. Tours available by reservation Tuesday to Saturday at 10:30 A.M. and 1:30 P.M., from June to the end of August, and Thursdays at 1:30 P.M. from September to the end of May. Contact: Inco Metals Co., Thompson, Manitoba.

Saskatchewan

Saskatchewan, in the center of the three prairie provinces, is Canada's largest producer of grain and is nicknamed "the Wheat Province." This is because 60 percent of the country's wheat, plus most other major crops, are grown each year on 873 million acres of Saskatchewan farmland. The province's first settlers were attracted in the 1880's by soil, topography, and weather conditions that were just right for agricultural production. Subsequently, Saskatchewan was officially incorporated in 1905, launching the province on the road to urbanization and increasing industrial diversification. However, agriculture still ranks as the largest individual source of income for Saskatchewan residents, producing almost $4 billion annually.

But Saskatchewan's 251,700 square miles of territory is more than farmland. It is, in fact, rich in contrast—ranging from the rugged rocky north to parkland in the center and to prairie in the southcentral and southeast areas.

The scenic, hilly Qu'Appelle Valley runs through part of the southern prairie district. And in the southwest, there is dry ranchland with badlands and some of the highest hills east of the Rockies.

Geographically, Saskatchewan is bordered by Manitoba on the east, Alberta on the west, the Northwest Territories on the north, and Montana and North Dakota on the south. Roughly the shape of a rectangle, the province extends for 761 miles from north to south and has an average width of 335 miles. The varied landscape provides excellent opportunities for recreation. Fishing, canoeing, camping, and hunting are superb in the north and good everywhere else.

A trip through the province will take the visitor from the badlands of the southeast or Cypress Hills in the southwest through flat grain lands to the pre-Cambrian country of lakes and forests in the north. Along the way, the traveler can stop at more than 300 campgrounds, 17 provincial parks, 91 regional parks, and the Prince Albert National Park. In winter, Saskatchewan also caters to the outdoor enthusiast, with many cross-country ski locations and 16 sites for downhill schussing.

The province's population of approximately 980,000 is almost equally split between urban and rural dwellers. There are eleven cities in Saskatchewan, but most of the action takes place in the two biggest—Regina, the capital, and Saskatoon, both of which have populations of about 160,000. These two cities offer restaurants, entertainment, and historical attractions comparable to any in North America, but because of their compact size, the visitor can get around with much more ease than in most major metropolises.

Finally, Saskatchewan has become an economic power in the past decade because of the increasing development of its minerals and natural resources. The province is the world's largest source of high-grade potash, as well as being Canada's leading uranium producer. There are also substantial deposits of heavy oil, coal, and sodium sulphate, all of which raise millions of dollars for the provincial treasury every year.

EXPLORING REGINA

As the capital city of one of Canada's fastest-developing provinces, Regina offers an abundance of attractions to visitors, many of them moderately priced. Originally named "Pile O' Bones," Regina was re-christened in honor of Queen Victoria when it was incorporated in 1903.

The city was established in 1882 as a divisional point on the Canadian Pacific Railway, and its prime role for years was to serve as an agricultural distribution and service center for southern Saskatchewan. More recently, Regina has added a manufacturing base to its economy, being the home, for example, of Interprovincial Steel and Pipe Corp. Ltd. (IPSCO), the largest steel mill in Western Canada. But even today, agriculture is of prime importance to the city, as 150 trucking companies that haul grain and farm machinery make their headquarters in this rapidly-expanding community.

Regina is also a "government" city. Besides having an impressive new multistory city hall that was built in recent years, it is also the seat of the provincial legislature which is ruled by the Conservative Party led by Premier Grant Devine. The Conservatives ousted the New Democratic (Socialist) Party in early 1982, ending a reign which had lasted nearly forty years. The NDP had established 20 crown corporations to handle everything from mining ventures to hydro development to car insurance. The office towers of these government corporations are a main feature of Regina's skyline. And equally imposing is the Provincial Legislative Building, erected in the early 1900's, which sits on the western edge of Wascana Center, a 2,300-acre park, lake and recreational paradise in the heart of Regina.

Wascana Center

No visit to Regina is complete without a visit to Wascana Center, the main outdoor playground in the city. The center dates back to 1883 when Wascana Creek—a small winding marshy waterway— was dammed to create a reservoir to provide a permanent supply of water for wildlife. Since then, flocks of the famous Canada geese have made their home in the center—and are still a common sight today. Development of parkland around the Wascana reservoir has been especially rapid since the formation of the Wascana Center Authority in 1962. The authority, which is responsible for the park's administration and growth, is an independent body composed of representatives from the Saskatchewan government, the city of Regina, and the University of Regina.

Under the authority's direction, the Wascana Park has become a showplace of imported trees, colorful floral gardens, and green lawns—a triumph of planning comparable to anything in North America.

On the eastern edge of the park is a $500,000 marina that is a focal point of year-round activities. In summer, the marina offers rentals of boats, roller skates, and tandem bicycles. Then, when cold weather arrives, the rental office switches over to cross-country skiis and skates. Food and refreshments are available at the marina's restaurant for all tired "sportsmen," including passing walkers and joggers.

Other popular attractions at Wascana Center are a museum of natural history, Willow Island for picnics, and a 360-acre marsh and bird sanctuary that is extensively used by migratory wildfowl. On a historical note, the center has on display the boyhood home of former Canadian Prime Minister John Diefenbaker, which was opened for tours after being moved to Wascana from Borden, Saskatchewan, in 1967. Also on the grounds is the Louis Riel statue, commemorating the Métis leader whose band fought against the transfer of the Red River Colony to Canada in 1869–70.

A pamphlet describing four different walking tours of the Wascana park may be obtained from the center's information office. In addition, a 70-passenger London double-decker bus makes its way through the center on a regular summer schedule of tours.

Other Attractions

There are lots of other things to see and do in Regina at reasonable cost. For example, the city has close to 300 restaurants in every price range, a phenomenal number for a city of 165,000 people.

As far as history is concerned, Government House on Dewdney Ave. W. has been renovated and refurbished in the style of earlier days. It was the seat of the North West Territories government from 1891 to 1905 and the Saskatchewan government from 1905 to 1945. Each summer, Government House is the scene of a play— *The Trial of Louis Riel*—which is a dramatic re-creation of Riel's trial in 1885. Admission to the play is $3.00, while there is no charge to inspect Government House.

Regina is also the home of the Royal Canadian Mounted Police, Canada's national police force, and the R.C.M.P. Centennial Museum, with its crime and historical exhibits, is a "must" on every visitor's agenda. Other spots drawing the history lover—all free of charge—are the Plains Historical Museum, 1801 Scarth St., the

Museum of Natural History, Albert St. and College Ave., and the Saskatchewan Sports Hall of Fame, 2205 Victoria Ave.

In summer, a major tourist attraction is Regina's Buffalo Days, which runs for 12 days in July–August. The city's citizens are even friendlier than usual—and everybody dresses up in Western outfits. Men grow beards, waitresses become saloon girls; and stores, banks, hotels and night spots deck themselves out in Buffalo Days décor.

The annual Regina Exhibition—with a midway and name entertainment—is an integral part of the Buffalo Days' celebration. In addition, Saskatchewan talent is featured daily on an outdoor stage in downtown Victoria Park.

As befits an agricultural center, Regina is the venue for two major farm shows each year—the Western Canada Farm Progress Show in the spring and the Canadian Western Agribition in the fall. The latter is Canada's largest livestock exhibition and offers four nights of professional rodeo and three nights of equestrian events.

A further point of interest in Regina is the $125 million Cornwall Center office and shopping plaza. Built to revitalize the downtown core, the center houses an Eaton's department store, 90 other retail outlets, a four-theater cinema and twin office towers. The city is also the home of the University of Regina which has 7,000 students and two campuses—one on the Wascana Pkwy. and the other on College Ave.

PRACTICAL INFORMATION FOR REGINA

Transportation

AIR. Regina is served by four major airlines—*Air Canada,* Canada's national airline, *Frontier Airlines* of Denver, *Pacific Western,* and *Norcanair* which serves in-province destinations.

Norcanair's scheduled and charter flights are more expensive but quicker. The fare to Saskatoon is $64.50 single, $129 return. The airline also flies to Prince Albert, La Ronge, and other northern points. There is no city bus service between the airport and downtown, but limousine service is available.

TRAIN. It is also a stopping point for *Via Rail,* Canada's national rail passenger service. Eastbound and westbound trains leave daily.

BUS. For the economy-minded, *Saskatchewan Transportation,* the province's largest bus company, offers transportation virtually everywhere in Saskatchewan. The fare from Regina to Saskatoon, the province's second largest city, is $15.10 one-way. If you travel return in midweek, the price is 25 percent off. *Greyhound Buslines* and *Moose Mountain Lines* connect Regina with destinations throughout North America.

Public transit in Regina is by bus. Exact fare is required. Adult fare is 65 cents. Buses operate from around 6:00 A.M. to about midnight. Transit information: 569–7777.

TOURS. Saskatchewan Transportation also offers summer one-day and multi-day tours for senior citizens. Some of the destinations are Big Muddy Badlands, Cannington Manor Historic Park, Yorkton's Western Development Museum, Cypress Hills, Duck Mountain, and the Batoche battleground.

Prices, based on room sharing, are $270 single, $214 double, $196 triple, and $185 quadruple, usually for four days. Reservations can be made at bus depots in all Saskatchewan cities.

USEFUL ADDRESSES

Tourism Saskatchewan, 2103 - 11th Ave., Regina, S4P 3V7, is the best source of travel information for all of Saskatchewan. In Regina call 787–2300. Phone them toll-free from anywhere else in the province at 1–800–667–3674; from any other Canadian location at 1–800–667–5822.

Accommodations

Regina has more than its share of first-class hotels and motels, but there are also a number of moderately priced establishments for the budget-conscious traveler. Try these for size (prices quoted are based on double-occupancy):

Inexpensive: under $35.00; and *Moderate:* $36.00–$48.00.

Inexpensive

Georgia Hotel, 1927 Hamilton St. Clean, comfortable rooms. Shopping and theatre nearby. **LaSalle Hotel,** 1840 Hamilton St. Budget restaurant on premises. **North Star Motel,** Hwy. 1 E. Modern air-conditioned rooms. **Plains Motor Hotel,** Albert St. and Victoria Ave. Comfortable rooms and a good restaurant.

Moderate

Coachman Inn Motel, 835 Victoria Ave. (Some rooms also I.) **Intowner Motel,** 1015 Albert St. Satellite T.V. and queen-size beds. **Relax Inn,** 1110 Victoria Ave. E., S4P 0N7. Probably the best bargain in semi-luxury accommodation. Clean pool and whirlpool indoors.

HOSTELS

Turgeon International Hostel, 2310 McIntyre St. Restored Heritage House near downtown and walking distance to Wascana Park. Dormitory style rooms with meals available. Laundromat. Canoe rentals. $5.00 to $8.00 per night, year-round.

There is also a YMCA at 2400–13th Ave., tel. (306) 757–6661, and a YWCA at 1900 MacIntyre St., tel. (306) 525–2141. Rates are $17 to $20 per night, $75 per week.

For more information about Regina accommodation contact: *Regina Tourist and Convention Bureau,* 2145 Albert St., open Monday to Friday, 8:45 A.M.–5:00 P.M. (306) 757–6631.

Restaurants

To get value for your food dollar in Regina, you must know the names of restaurants that charge reasonable prices but still maintain a pleasant atmosphere. Prices at all establishments listed range from $5.00 to $15.00 per meal.

Bartleby's Dining Emporium, 1920 Broad St. Antique décor and tops in atmosphere. Full beverage menu. No reservations necessary.

Bonzzini's, 4634 Albert St. Italian cuisine featuring pasta, veal and chicken.

The Brother's Theatre Restaurant, 1867 Hamilton St. Features live dinner music and European and Chinese cuisine.

The Empringham Room, 686 Pasqua St. Known for its good food, specializing in prime rib and smorgasbord.

Chinese Palace, 4355 Albert St. Full beverage selection, with take-out and delivery service available.

Geno's, in the Gordon Rd. shopping center. Offers fine Italian food.

Grandma Lee's. Albert St. and Seventh Ave. Soup and sandwiches, home-baked breads and pastries.

Plains Flag Inn, 1965 Albert St. Dining room features noon smorgasbord, evening buffet, and full menu.

Ruby Tuesday's, 1515 Albert St. A '60's atmosphere of rock music and great food.

Westwater Inn, 1717 Victoria Ave. Pioneer kitchen reflects Saskatchewan's agricultural heritage with a varied menu.

Waldo's, 3970 Albert St. Steak, seafood, salad bar, family-priced with a children's menu.

What to See and Do

The Devonian Pathway is Regina's latest relaxation addition. It's an eight kilometre meandering bike path. Bike rentals are available at reasonable rates from Youth Unlimited at 525–2148.

Regina is also the home of a number of first-class art galleries and museums, most of which are free. For example, the budget-conscious visitor should make an effort to see the **Norman Mackenzie Art Gallery,** College Ave. at Scarth St., which has a collection of 600 permanent works, focusing on Saskatchewan and Canadian artists. Similarly, the **Dunlop Art Gallery,** in the Regina Public Library, 12th Ave. and Lorne St., features the work of local artists and some exhibits on loan from the National Gallery, while the **Gallery on the Roof** atop the Saskatechewan Power Building,

2025 Victoria Ave., exists exclusively to promote Saskatchewan art and artists.

MUSEUMS. Most of Regina's museums are free. Heading the list are *Teleroma,* 2121 Saskatchewan Drive, dedicated to telephone and telecommunications history; the *Museum of Natural History,* Albert St. and College Ave.; and the *Plains Historical Museum,* 1801 Scarth St., featuring artifacts of the pioneer west. Also "must sees" are the *Saskatchewan Sports Hall of Fame,* 2205 Victoria Ave.; *Government House,* Dewdeney Ave. W.; and the *RCMP Centennial Museum* near Pasqua Street at 11th Ave.

SPORTS. In summer and fall, Regina offers Canadian professional **football** at Taylor Field, with *Saskatchewan Roughriders* taking on teams from across the nation. The city is also home of *Regina Rams* who have won seven Canadian junior football championships since 1954, and *Regina Pats,* a top junior **hockey** team which plays in the 5,500-seat Agridome. **Thoroughbred racing** takes place at the Regina Exhibition track during a 43-day season that lasts from August to October.

ENTERTAINMENT. Regina has an abundance of theater, dance, symphony and popular music concerts. Here's a rundown:

Globe Theatre, Regina's popular professional theater troup, presents a season of six mainstage productions from fall to spring. Tickets for the plays—staged in the old city hall in the Scarth Street Mall—are $8.00 Fridays and Saturdays, $7.00 weekdays.

The Regina Modern Dance Works, 1923 Osler St., mounts about eight performances a season, featuring both the resident dance troup and touring performers. Phone (306) 527-0656 for further information.

The Regina Symphony Orchestra presents a season of concerts with guest soloists in the magnificent Saskatchewan Center of the Arts standing on the south shore of Wascana Lake. Built 11 years ago, the center—a tourist attraction in itself—is also kept busy with conventions and performances by touring artists and theater groups.

Actually, the center is a combination of three superb facilities— the 2,029-seat *Centennial Theatre,* the smaller *Jubilee Theatre,* which can be used for theater-in-the-round or proscenium performances, and *Hanbridge Hall,* the venue for conventions which can serve 1,000 diners or seat 1,600 people for meetings.

NIGHTLIFE. Regina offers a wide variety of night spots catering to all musical tastes at relatively modest prices. Almost every inn and motel has a pub featuring sound systems with or without disc jockeys. Summer sees a prolific growth of outdoor pubs and eateries. **The Heartland Club,** in the Sandman Inn, 4025 Albert St., appeals to middle-of-the-road audiences. Rock'n'roll fans can catch local entertainment at **The Paddock,** 4223 Dewdney Ave. **The Pump,** 641 Victoria Ave. E. is a country-western bar featuring live entertainment. **Shooter's,** 2075 Broad St., is a cowboy bar offering live country music. Locals recommend the pubs at the **Vagabond Motor Inn,** 4177 Albert St., and the **Seven Oaks Motor Inn,** 777 Albert St.

EXPLORING SASKATOON

Straddling the South Saskatchewan River, Saskatoon, the second-largest center in the province with 155,000 people, is a city of bridges and gorgeous riverbank views. It has excellent shopping, fine restaurants and hotels, and a variety of cultural attractions.

The city's history dates back to 1882 when John Lake, leader of the Temperance Colonization Society, set up a settlement for his followers on the banks of the beautiful South Saskatchewan River. Originally, he had decided to call the spot "Minnetonka," but changed his mind when he was presented with a tasty batch of berries called "Saskatoons." From that day—August 20, 1882— the city was named Saskatoon, which is derived from a Cree Indian name for the berries.

Today, Saskatoon is the fastest growing large city in Saskatchewan. Building permits have reached $250 million a year as Saskatoon rapidly expands its role as principal distribution center for the province's potash, uranium, and heavy-oil industries.

The city is also the home of the province's largest university, the University of Saskatchewan, which offers tours to the public, tel. (306) 343–3389. A highlight on campus is the John G. Diefenbaker Centre, which displays mementos of the career of the Saskatchewan-based former Canadian prime minister.

PRACTICAL INFORMATION FOR SASKATOON

Transportation

AIR. Saskatoon is served by four airlines: *Air Canada,* which serves national destinations; *CP Air; Norcanair,* supplying in-province service; *Frontier,* linking with the U.S., and *Pacific Western,* flying right across the prairie region. A limousine service operates from the airport to major downtown hotels. Cost is $3.50 per person. Taxi fare for the same trip is about $7.00.

TRAIN. *Via Rail* has re-instituted its famous Northern East-West daily train service through Saskatoon. Much more scenic than the already beautiful southern trip through Regina, the train departs daily westbound at 10:59 P.M. or eastbound at 6:30 A.M.

BUS. *Saskatchewan Transportation Co.* (STC) offers bus service throughout the province. *Greyhound,* meanwhile, looks after national and international bus traffic. *Heritage Bus Tours* of Saskatoon's architectural history are booked through the Chamber of Commerce at (306) 242–6681. Local transit buses require exact fare of 60 cents for adults and 30 cents for children. Transit information is 664–9100.

CAR. Access by car is by the Trans-Canada Hwy. and the Yellowhead Hwy. from the east and west and by Hwys. 6 and 11 from the south. There is also a Saskatchewan city bus service, plus sightseeing tours arranged by several companies. Downtown parking restrictions vary from 15 minutes to two hours, so watch signs. Meters cost five cents for 7½ minutes. Parking is free on Sunday at all meters.

Accommodations

Prices based for a double room are categorized: *Inexpensive:* $30.00 and below, and *Moderate:* $30.00–$58.00.

Inexpensive

Patricia Hotel, 345–2nd Ave. N. Downtown location. Quiet, friendly and modern. **Y.W.C.A.,** 220–24th St. E. Accommodations from $4.00 per day. Meeting rooms and indoor pool.

Moderate

Confederation Flag Inn, 3330 Fairlight Dr. Close to ViaRail Train Station, airport, and shopping. **Holiday House Motor Hotel,** 2901 8th St. E. Modern rooms with a wide range of facilities including indoor and outdoor pools. **Idylwyld Motel,** 1171 8th St. E. A fully modern hotel featuring a variety of accommodations. Near airport. **King George Hotel,** 157 2nd Ave. N. Full service hotel with conference rooms and cable T.V. **Relax Inn,** 102 Cardinal Cresc. Indoor pool and sauna. Close to airport.

Restaurants

Artful Dodger, 119–4th Ave. S., is an old English pub with traditional "pub" foods at reasonable prices; **The Commodore,** 108–2nd Ave. N., specializes in prime rib; **Tiffany's,** 1015 8th St. E., is a place for Italian cuisine, especially pizza; and **Nino's Pizza,** at three locations in Saskatoon, is another "must" for those who like Italian food.

What to See and Do

ENTERTAINMENT. *Persephone Theatre* is the latest addition to Saskatoon's professional theater scene. The *Twenty-Fifth Street House,* Saskatoon's other **professional theater** company, presents a season of mainstage productions each winter. For **sports** fans, the *Saskatoon Blades* of the Western Canadian Junior Hockey League and the University of Saskatchewan football and hockey teams play regularly during their respective seasons.

Night spots with reasonable prices include: *Foxy's,* 2901 8th St. E. with rock videos; *Hugh's,* 90 22nd St. E., with live disc jockey rock shows; The *Bar K Ranch House,* 2115–22nd St. W.; *Pubbin's,* 701 20th St. W., also home to D.J. rock entertainment; and the *Texas T,* 3331 8th St. E. which features live country and western talent.

Northcote River Cruises also offer **cruises** on the Saskatchewan River in summer, boarding from behind the bandstand south of the Bessborough Hotel. Adults $4.00, children $1.00.

MUSEUMS AND GALLERIES. Saskatoon's *Mendel Art Gallery,* near the South Saskatchewan River, is a must to visit, featuring an outstanding permanent collection and a year-round conservatory. Other points of interest include the *Western Development Museum,* 2610 Lorne Ave. S., which is an authentic replica of a typical Saskatchewan community in 1910, and the *Ukrainian Museum of Canada,* 910 Spading Cres. E., which depicts the history of Canadians of Ukrainian heritage. Visitors should also try to see the *Shoestring Gallery,* a Saskatchewan artists' co-operative at 813B Broadway.

FOR CHILDREN. There is the *Kinsmen Park* at 25th St. and Spadina Cres., just across from the Mendel Gallery. It offers a merry-go-round, train, and ferris wheel, plus a concession with ice cream, soft drinks, and hot dogs.

Your family may also wish to spend its leisure time enjoying the *Forestry Farm Park and Zoo,* just east of Saskatoon. The park is open daily from 7.00 A.M. to 9.00 P.M., while the zoo—with all the animals outside—is open from 10.00 A.M. to 8.00 P.M. For further information, phone (306) 373–0494.

USEFUL ADDRESSES

Saskatoon Tourist and Convention Bureau, 308 24th St. E., S7K 4RQ, (306) 242–1206; *United Cabs,* (306) 652–2222; *Radio Cabs,* (306) 242–1221; the *Centennial Auditorium,* (306) 653–3722; and *Saskatoon City Hospital,* Queen St., (306) 242–6681.

EXPLORING RURAL SASKATCHEWAN

The countryside of Saskatchewan is rich in contrasts. It ranges from the flat, unending prairie farmland of the south to the rugged rocky north—a paradise for hunting and fishing.

It is also a province of parks. There are 99 regional parks, 17 provincial parks, and one major national park. The provincial parks, for example, offer camping, boating, swimming, nature interpretation programs, hiking trails, and horseback riding.

But perhaps the "jewel" is Prince Albert National Park, 40 miles northwest of Prince Albert, a 6,250-acre wilderness area that combines beautiful scenery with a wide variety of recreational facilities.

There are also festivals in virtually every Saskatchewan community each summer. And if you are looking for an economical holiday, many Saskatchewan farms offer accommodation to tourists.

PRACTICAL INFORMATION FOR RURAL SASKATCHEWAN

Transportation

Saskatoon and Regina, the province's major cities, are served by *Air Canada, Frontier,* and *Pacific Western* airlines. *Greyhound* bus lines brings in visitors from across the country; while *Via Rail,* the nation's rail passenger service, serves Regina and Saskatoon every day.

CAR. East-west access to southern Saskatchewan is provided by the Trans-Canada Hwy., which passes through such major cities as Regina, Moose Jaw, and Swift Current.

In the north, the Yellowhead Hwy., which starts in Manitoba, runs through Saskatoon on its way to Edmonton and other Alberta centers. Altogether, there are 13 ports of entry between Saskatchewan and the United States, with a major route being Hwy. 6 linking Regina with Montana.

USEFUL ADDRESSES

SaskTravel, 2103 - 11th Ave., Regina, S4P 3V7, can supply up-to-date information on just about everything in Saskatchewan. Call 306–787–2300 year-round during regular office hours. In summer (June to Labor Day), there are toll-free lines for in-province calls: 1–800–667–3674 from Saskatchewan cities and 1–800–5822 from other Canadian locations.

Accommodations

Some of the best bargains in rural hotels in Saskatchewan are: the **Beefeater Inn** in Estevan, the **Park Lodge Motor Hotel** in Moose Jaw, the **Beaver Motor Hotel** and the **Towne House Motel** in North Battleford, the **Coronet Motor Hotel** in Prince

Albert, the **Corona Motor Hotel** in Yorkton, and the **Imperial 400 Motel,** the **Rodeway Inn,** and the **Travelodge** in Swift Current. In all cases, the prices are moderate, averaging $35.00–$40.00 (double) per night.

FARM VACATIONS. Farm vacations provide an opportunity for urban dwellers to enjoy country life by spending a holiday with a Saskatchewan farm family. More than 25 Saskatchewan farms offer this type of vacation. Contact: Mrs. Irene Lightbody, secretary, *Saskatchewan Farm Vacations Association,* Box 24, Bateman, Sask., SoH-oEo. Tel: (306) 648–3530. Rates may vary at each farm, but usually run around $30.00 per day for adults and $20.00 for children under 12, meals included.

CAMPING. There are more than 400 campgrounds in Saskatchewan. About half are privately owned and fees vary greatly among them. The other half are located in the more than 400 parks, Provincial, National and Regional, found throughout the province. Entrance to the parks is $2.00 to $3.00 per day per car or $6.00 per season, with the pass being good at all regional parks. Camping fees are $4.00 to $5.00 for serviced sites and $2.00 to $3.00 for non-serviced.

Fees at Saskatchewan's 17 provincial parks are $4.00 per vehicle per day or $15.00 for the season, with the pass being good at all provincial parks. Camping fees are $7.00 for serviced sites, $6.00 for non-serviced and $5.00 for overflow. Four provincial parks— *Cypress Hills, Duck Mountain, Moose Mountain,* and *Greenwater* —have deluxe lodges or winterized log cabins for rent at prices ranging from $43.00 to $51.00 per night for groups of four people.

Trans-Canada Campgrounds on Hwy. 1 are located at Maple Creek, Besant, McLean and Moosomin, with fees being the same as at provincial parks. Meanwhile, at *Prince Albert National Park,* fees are $2.00 for park entry for four days, $1.00 for one day and $10.00 for a season pass, while camping fees are $4.00 to $5.00 for serviced sites and $2.00 to $3.00 for nonserviced.

For more information about camping contact SaskTravel, 2103 - 11th Ave., Regina, S4P 3V7. In summer call 787–2300 from Regina, or the toll-free 1–800–667–3674 from other points in Saskatchewan, or 1–800–667–5822 from anywhere else in Canada.

What to See and Do

MUSEUMS, PARKS, HISTORIC SITES. The province has a chain of four *Western Development Museums,* each of which depicts a different Saskatchewan historical theme through extensive exhibits. The various museums and their themes are: Moose Jaw, the story of transportation, Hwys. 1 and 2; North Battleford, the story of agriculture, Hwys. 16 and 40; Saskatoon, the integrated story of western development; 2610 Lorne Ave. S., and Yorkton, the story of the people, Hwy. 16 W. Admission: adults $1.50; Senior Citizens $1.00; under 16, 50 cents; preschoolers free; family rate, $4.00.

Another place to see is the *Moose Jaw Wild Animal Park* in the City of Moose Jaw, 25 miles west of Regina. The park has exotic and native-to-Saskatchewan animals, plus a picnic area. Admission: $1.00 for adults; 50 cents for those 12–17 years; 25 cents for those 6–12 years; free for senior citizens and children under 6. A seasonal vehicle pass is available for $10.00. An interesting spot is the *Batoche National Historic Site* northeast of Saskatoon. It was the scene of the Riel Rebellion of 1885 when Métis insurrectionists formed a provisional government to protest their lack of rights. The rebellion was put down by the North West Mounted Police and militia. The church and rectory at Batoche are the original buildings where the last battle took place. Admission is free and there are plenty of other battle sites in the area.

Battleford National Historic Park, at the town of Battleford, is most famous for sheltering settlers during the Riel Rebellion. It was established as a North West Mounted Police Post in 1876 and was used until 1924. Although the post was under siege during the Riel Rebellion, five original buildings remain. Admission free.

Fort Walsh National Historic Park, 70 miles southwest of Maple Creek, is the site of another famous North West Mounted Police post established in 1875. Back in the bad old days, it experienced much Indian unrest, being attacked by thousands of Sioux warriors who fled the U.S.A. after the Battle of Little Big Horn and other confrontations with the cavalry. The post and a nearby trading post have been reconstructed. Admission free.

Many visitors also trek to the *Imhoff Art Gallery* at St. Walburg. More than 200 paintings are on display in the studio of an award-winning German muralist who retreated to Saskatchewan after an exhausting career in the U.S. Admission under $3.00, open May to September.

FESTIVALS. Saskatchewan is also a province of festivals. Here are some of the major ones:

Now 33 years old, the *Kinsmen International Band Festival* attracts 7,000 participants to Moose Jaw each May. Over a hundred amateur bands compete in many categories and participate in a spectacular parade.

Another big event is the *Saskatchewan Handcraft Festival* that takes place each July in Battleford. Craftspeople in Saskatchewan are among the most accomplished in Canada, and the festival gathers them together for a giant show and sale of their work. There's also a Bavarian garden, variety shows, and an old-time jamboree. Battleford is 170 miles northwest of Saskatoon on the Yellowhead Hwy.

Other important Saskatchewan festivals include *Pioneer Days* each July in Saskatoon and *Buffalo Days* in early August in Regina.

Alberta

Actually a giant plateau (ranging from a minimum of 2,000 feet above sea level to well over 12,000 feet at the mountainous summit of the Canadian Rockies that form its western boundary with British Columbia), Alberta contains an astonishing variety of geographical features to enjoy.

Semi-arid prairie, badlands and slow, lazy rivers combine with parklands, hill country, and total alpine milieu, yielding a most enjoyable environment. An abundance of lakes, trout streams, and white-water challenges add interesting recreational possibilities.

Alberta is large—over 200,000 square miles—and of that, nearly 60 percent is public forest lands. There's a great deal of room to explore here. To make things easy, 60 provincial parks, 5 national parks, 10 forest reserves, and 14 tourist zones have been established to aid visitors in planning a vacation best suited to their time, inclination, and budget.

This province is wealthy. Among all the provinces, Alberta's growth rate has been the highest over the last decade. It has become the important western Canadian center for banking, resource industries, commerce, and economic decision-making. Agriculture remains an important component in the economy of the province.

The prices charged for food, lodging, and transportation are significant factors for visitors to consider. Fortunately, in Alberta, there are three strong savings incentives—no sales tax; no accommodation tax; and possibly the lowest price-per-gallon for gasoline in Canada.

Alberta is young in fact and in attitude. It joined Canada in 1905 and its history of buffalo and Indians, the fur trade, Mounties, and whisky forts is strong in the memories of Albertans. Ranching was the first enterprise and, in the Calgary area, a cowboy or "Western" style still prevails. Although the cities contain by far the greater percentage of Alberta's 2.3 million people, those persons are only one full generation removed from a rural situation. Satisfaction, an outgoing friendliness, and a candid manner are the marks of Alberta and its people.

EXPLORING CALGARY

Calgary, once a North West Mounted Police outpost in Blackfoot Indian territory, now is the financial center of Western Canada and a sophisticated, modern city with a population of over 623,000 that is increasing rapidly. It is a community that is and has always been growing and changing.

No matter when you visit, Calgary always appears to have been built just last year and still suffers from the turmoil of construction everywhere you look. It's clean. It's new. It's a paradox! Calgary is over 100 years old and proudly clings to its historical image of "the friendly ol' Cowtown," all the while snapping an impatient finger under the nose of the past and concentrating its surprising energies on making a remote future a firm reality before noon tomorrow.

Very much a city in an incredible hurry to have what any other place has—and then some, Calgary's pride in the past continues to give it personality as well as a spicy interest for visitors. Calgary is a forever "boomtown" that has not fallen to arrogance and pretentiousness, nor has it ever lost its charm or its heart. These qualities are its great appeal.

As in most everything Albertan, Calgary is large—over 300 square miles in area—yet, its downtown section is quite confined. Built in the valley of the Bow River, the major business portion finds itself hemmed-in by the floodplane escarpments; thus, Calgary can easily be explored on foot.

The Calgary Tower is a natural place to begin. Situated nearly in the geographic "bull's-eye" of the city, the tower offers an unchallenged view 75 miles in every direction. It is the second-tallest structure of its kind on the continent and features a revolving dining room, lounge, and observation deck. There is an elevator charge of $2.25.

Besides giving you the opportunity to peer down on the city like some omnipotent eagle, the tower also allows you to orient yourself. Calgary is designed on a grid pattern with streets running north and south and avenues east and west. All are numbered in the downtown area, with the bisectors being the Bow River and Centre St. Once this is understood, finding your way around is a cinch. Remember, if you are searching for an address in a remote area of the city, you must know what quadrant it is in—N.W., N.E., S.W., or S.E.

Directly across from the Calgary Tower, on 9th Ave. S.E., is the Convention Center complex housing the Glenbow Museum. The Glenbow is comprised of three stunning exhibition floors of art, native and Western history, militaria and international artifacts. It carries a modest $2.00 admission charge.

Calgary has adopted the "Plus-15" concept of elevated walkways throughout the downtown core. Immediately adjacent to the

Glenbow (one floor up in the Convention complex) is one of the many Plus-15 gardens. A stroll through is enjoyable and leads to the city's main downtown mall on 8th Ave. This is an outdoor mall and it passes many examples of Calgary of another day.

Sandstone buildings dating back to the early part of the century give insight into an earlier Calgary when automobiles were just beginning to replace horses. Even earlier, cattle drives used this same gentle walkway. At the corner of 8th Ave. and 1st St. S.W., the Alberta Corner once boasted "the longest bar in the West." Diagonally, across the intersection, the Bay (Hudson's Bay Co.) Department store still provides interesting shopping opportunities.

From the third floor of the Bay, visitors may take an internal walkway to the spectacular Devonian Gardens across 2nd St. S.W. The Gardens cover 2.5 acres and consist of more than 20,000 plants and a mile of pathways past waterfalls, fountains, and ponds.

The Devonian Plus-15 system leads to Eaton's Department store and 4th Ave. S.W., where a walk north takes one to Prince's Island in the Bow River. Prince's Island is a quiet oasis featuring spacious lawns, stately poplar trees, outdoor art displays, and a jogging/ trimtrack convenience. Circling back along 5th Ave. eastward, takes one through a steel, glass, and concrete canyon of office towers which house many of Calgary's financial giants—oil companies, developers, and investors. There are over 450 oil companies in this city alone.

The Armengol Sculptures, on the grounds of the Public Education Center at 5th Ave. and 1st St. S.E., are fondly known to Calgarians simply as "the people." Collectively recognized as "The Family of Man," these 18-foot human-form castings originally were designed for the British Pavilion at Expo '67 in Montréal. The trek continues to the birthplace at 9th Ave. and 6th St. S.E. Fort Calgary was built in August of 1875 by a detachment of the then "North West Mounted Police" at the confluence of the Bow and Elbow Rivers. Admission free.

PRACTICAL INFORMATION FOR CALGARY

Transportation

AIR. Calgary's International Airport, serves *Air Canada, American, CP Air, Lufthansa, Pacific Western, United, Western Airlines,* and *Wardair.* The inter-provincial *Time Air* also uses this airport.

BUS. *Greyhound's* head offices are located here and it is the major to/from Calgary carrier. An airport-to-downtown transporter is available at $5.00 per one-way trip, $8.00 return. Within the city, an elaborate system of busses and LRT (light rail transit) provide excellent service. Cost is $1.00; exact change required. Additionally, *Gray Line* offers a number of city tours, some include all necessary admissions to attractions.

TAXIS. The initial cost is $1.50, then $1.00 per mile.

RAIL. Calgary is situated on the main line of the *Canadian Pacific Railway* (C.P.R.). Passenger service is handled by *Via Rail.*

FOR MORE INFORMATION

The *Calgary Tourist and Convention Association* is well able to respond to all enquiries regarding visitation and accommodation. They may be reached by telephone at (403) 263–8510, or by writing *Hospitality Centre,* 237–8th Ave. S.E., Calgary, Alberta T2G 0K8. For the convenience of visitors already in Calgary, this organization maintains year-round booths at the base of the Calgary Tower and Calgary International Airport.

Accommodations

The prices charged at first- and second-class hotels are generally expensive, running upward from $80.00 a night. Still, there are many fine facilities that are more reasonable. During the first two weeks of July, the Calgary Stampede literally sells out the city. As a result, accommodation is at a premium and up in cost approximately 20 percent. Further, many properties require a minimum of 3-day stay. If you intend to take in the Stampede, pre-planning is a necessity. The Calgary Tourist and Convention Association can be of immense help. They will locate accommodations to suit your requirements, and they have perfected a system whereby visitors may stay with Calgarians in their own homes.

Price categories for double-occupancy are: *Inexpensive:* under $40.00, and *Moderate:* $40.00 to $60.00.

Inexpensive

Calgary North TraveLodge, 2304–16th Ave. N.W. T2M 0M5. Air conditioning, coffee, pool, color TV. **Mirage Airport Inn Calgary,** 1808–19th St. N.E. T2E 4Y3. Remote from downtown, but new and clean with air conditioning, color TV, and telephones. **Budget Motor Inn,** 4420–16 Ave. N.W., T3B 0M4. Color TV, kitchens, family rates. **Relax Inn North** and **South,** 2750 Sundridge Blvd. N.E., T1Y 3R2; 9206 Macleod Tr. S. T2J 0P5. Air conditioning, dining, pool, phones, and color TV. **Hotel Regis,** 124–7th Ave. E. T2G 0H5. 96 rooms, half with private bath. Basic.

Moderate

Airliner Inn, 4804 Edmonton Trail. T2E 3V8. Remote with an array of entertainment, lounge, and dining facilities. **Hotel Empress,** 219–6th Ave. S.W. T2P 0R2. Downtown, air conditioning, dining, and lounge. **La Concha Motel,** 2440–16th Ave. N.W. T2M 0M5. Air conditioning, coffee, sauna, TV, and phones. **Plum Tree Inn,** 1947–18 Ave N.E., T2E 7T8. Color TV, free parking, children under 17 free sharing with parents. **Westgate Motor Hotel,** 1111 –33rd St. S.W. T3C 1N9. Dining, dancing, lounge, TV, air conditioning, phones. **York Hotel,** 636 Centre St. S. T2G 2C7. Downtown, dining, dancing, entertainment, TV, and phones. Family plan available.

CAMPGROUNDS. For information, contact *K.O.A.* Box 10, Site 12 RR 1, Calgary. Open Apr. 15–Oct. 15; *Sunalta Trailer Parks Ltd.* Sub P.O. 55, Calgary, T3B 0H0. Apr. 1–Oct. 31.

HOSTELS. Canadian Youth Hostels Association, 1414 Kensington Rd., N.W. Year-round accommodation in near downtown area. Members to $9.00, non-members to $12.00, per night single.

YMCA/YWCA. Both the YMCA and YWCA have large facilities. Each offers complete Y-club amenities. **YMCA,** 332–6th Ave. S.E. **YWCA,** 320–5th Ave. S.W. Although the YWCA is for women only, they will accept children (boys under 7) on an overnight basis.

Restaurants

Alberta is cattle country and Calgary is the absolute heart of it all. That means beef, stranger! It doesn't really matter what kind of beef you order just so long as it's steak—and a Calgary cut at that. Of course beef is not as cheap as mutton; but the melt-in-your-mouth smoothness and that special taste of Alberta-sweet-grass-fed-and-grain-finished steak shouldn't be missed. Yes steak is the staple; yet Calgary is loaded with ethnic restaurants and gourmet menus. If there are such things as "Syrian Smunchcakes" or "Madagascar Magoosh," you'll find them in one of the hundreds of Calgary eateries. Naturally the fast-food takeouts and franchised chomp-stops are in abundance so that you can survive while you save for that one big steak-bloat.

All price categories quoted are for a complete meal for two. Tips and drinks are not included. Price categories are *Inexpensive:* under $25.00, and *Moderate:* $25.00 to $35.00.

Inexpensive

Karouzo's, 2620–4th St. N.W. The city's finest pizza. **Keg'n Cleaver,** three locations and all tops. Steaks and prime rib specialty. **Mad Trapper's,** 602–11th Ave. S.W. From buffalo to frogs and then some. **Old Spaghetti Factory,** 628–9th Ave. S.W. Italian food in turn-of-the-century atmosphere. **Phoenix Inn,** 616–9th St. S.W. Great Chinese chop suey.

Moderate

The Greek Korner Ristorante, 1604–14th St. S.W. Fried squid and pickled octopus among varied dishes. **Long Bar,** 8th Ave. and

1st St. S.W. Historic location and superb buffet with a 50-item dinner menu à la carte. **Mother Tucker's,** 345–10th Ave. S.W. Great homespun food and fresh bread. **Viking Village,** #10, 7640 Fairmount Dr. S.E. Small with large Scandinavian menu.

What to See and Do

MUSEUMS AND GALLERIES

Centennial Planetarium, 11th St. and 7th Ave. S.W. A unique mixture of entertainment, education, thrills, and facts, offering star shows, an observatory, and an aerospace museum. Admission 50¢.

Ft. Calgary, 750–9th Ave. S.E. On 30 acres of prairie, the ruins of the 1875 North West Mounted Police fort are marked for your wandering around enjoyment. Exhibits of artifacts and a superb audio/visual/sensory presentation make a visit more than worthwhile. No admission charge.

Glenbow-Alberta Institute, 120–9th Ave. S.E. (across from the Calgary Tower). This is an excellent museum plus a Class "A" gallery. Its displays of Western Canadiana and native Indian art and artifacts are outstanding. The museum's scope includes international displays and perhaps the finest military exhibits in the country. Admission $2.00, children $1.00.

Heritage Park, 14th St. and Heritage Dr. S.W. Calgary's foremost attraction after the Stampede. An authentic town has been re-established in detail from baked bread you can buy to snooker you can shoot. The town includes a ranch, a railway, an oil well, and a paddlewheeling riverboat within its pre-1914 confines. The town is a delightful combination of museum and hustle-bustle oriented to family fun, nostalgia, and entertainment. Take the whole day to enjoy it properly. Admission $4.00, children $2.00 with extras for a train ride, boat ride, or food.

Military Museum, on Canadian Forces Base Calgary at Richard Rd. and Crowchild Tr. S.W. Dedicated to the men of the two regiments who participated in Canada's wars and peacekeeping operations. Great for military buffs. It is necessary to make an appointment by telephoning (403) 246–7525.

Some Principal Sights and Attractions

Calgary Stampede bills itself as the "Greatest Dad-Burned Show on Earth" and is held during the first two weeks of July each year (in 1986, from July 4 to 13). It consists of top rodeo action, dazzling stage shows, gambling casinos, midways and exhibitions, and total city commitment to fun and activity.

Sam Livingstone Fish Hatchery, 1440–17A St. S.E. Displays showing species and explaining habitats, breeding and location of fish found in Alberta. Free admission.

Zoo and Prehistoric Park, St. George's Island (in Bow River) 620–12th St. S.E. The second-largest zoo in Canada with 300 species of critters, dinosaur life-size display, tropical aviary, and children's zoo. Admission $3.50, children 12–17 $2.00, $1.00 under 12.

Calaway Park. 3 miles west of Calgary on Hwy. 1. 60-acre theme park with 50 rides. About $11.00 per person or a variety of pricing plans available.

PARKS. Calgary has over 11,000 acres of parkland within its boundaries. Some of the most important are *Bowness, Confederation, Edworthy, Glenmore, Patrick Burns Memorial, Prince's Island, Reader Rock Gardens.* The indoor *Devonian Gardens* is a "must see" for visitors. All have no admission charge.

ENTERTAINMENT

Music. *Calgary Philharmonic Orchestra* presents several series from classic to pop each season. *Mount Royal Woodwind Quintet,* performs regularly at the Leacock Theatre at Mount Royal College. *Music at Noon,* a noon time program offered September through April at the W.R. Castell Central Library.

Choral. *Calgary Renaissance Singers and Players* is an unusual group performing at the University of Calgary Theatre. *Southern Alberta Opera Association* presents three operas a year at the Jubilee Auditorium. *Devonian Gardens* features regular entertainment from concerts to impromptu sessions.

Theater. *Alberta Theatre Projects,* at the Canmore Opera House in Heritage Park. Excellent group offering five plays per year. *Calgary Theatre Singers* present old-time favorites and musicals. *Loose Moose Theatre* offers innovative productions at the Pumphouse Theatre. *Lunchbox Theatre* performs irregularly in Bow Valley Square at noon hour. *Story Book Theatre* gives matinees every weekend at the Pumphouse Theatre. *Theatre Calgary* is a top professional organization with two series each season at the QM Centre.

Dance. *Alberta Ballet Company* is an excellent young company performing primarily at the Jubilee Auditorium.

Bars and Clubs. Calgary is an entertainment-loving city with hundreds of spots featuring professional talent. One notable completely in the Western character of Calgary is *Ranchman's* with two locations: 1117–1st St. S.W. and 9311 Macleod Tr. S. It features many popular artists along with drinking, dining, and dancing.

Sports. There is a wide variety of sport in this city for spectators and participants alike. Aside from **rodeo,** Calgary is immensely proud of its Canadian **Football** League *Calgary Stampeders* and National **Hockey** League *Calgary Flames.* It has pro **soccer** and **baseball** and a host of semi-pro and amateur teams in a myriad of leagues. **Skiing** is also highly popular with two slopes—Paskapoo and Shaganappi right in the city. The mountain runs of Fortress, Sunshine, Lake Louise, and Norquay offer skiing from November to May. Rentals of equipment are readily available in the city, and several bus packages provide economical and popular transportation packages. **Tennis, swimming, jogging,** and **hiking**

facilities are numerous and free. There's lots of area for **cross-country skiing** in the winter. **Racquetball** and **health-exercise** facilities are numerous. And, of course, **horseback riding** is always available. Finally, Calgary has a city-wide **biking** trail that is widely used.

EXPLORING EDMONTON

Edmonton, located smack-dab in the center of Alberta, is this province's capital; and, counting the adjoining communities, has a population of well over 700,000. It is very much a sister city to Calgary, and the similarities are apparent. Like Calgary, Edmonton's downtown section has undergone a modern metamorphosis with old building after old building giving way to new highrises. Thanks to the crude oil business, the benefits of boomtown economics—prosperity and growth—are obvious.

Edmonton has become the service and supply headquarters for the oilpatch, and serves as the gateway to the vast expanse of Canada known simply as the "north." Edmontonians are fully aware of their fortunate position in a world that for the most part continues a difficult struggle for survival. Still, the heads under all the hard-hats have not become fat. They go about their business quietly, doing their best to harvest what they can while the sun is blazing, and steadily move over to make room for those who come seeking a small part of the glory hole. It is the way of Edmontonians —and indeed, all Albertans.

The business core of Edmonton has been constructed on the northern escarpment of the great North Saskatchewan River which performs a wide, meandering bisection of the city. As a result of the additional height, the downtown skyline of Edmonton is an imposing sight especially when viewed from the river valley.

From the viewing gallery of Vista 33 in the Alberta Telephone Tower, you can orient yourself and discover the bird's-eye beauty of this city. At 388 feet above street level, Vista 33 (located south of Jasper Ave. on 100th St.) offers a vast panorama of 2,500 square miles. The northern outlook reveals Edmonton's downtown development, most of which has occurred in the last decade, Commonwealth Stadium and the Municipal Airport. To the east, one can get a great view of the incredible Capital City Recreation Park, a place that seems to have been custom-made for budget-minded tourists. Southward, toward Calgary, shows industrial areas and residential subdivisions as well as more of the scenic river valley. And west, toward the mountains, leads one's eye from downtown highrises, beyond residential areas and on to the parkland country surrounding Edmonton.

To see Edmonton properly, several tours are recommended, each in a different section of the city. Edmonton's downtown area has a number of interesting sights in a relatively small area. It is not that

Edmonton's downtown is small or confined (actually it's fairly spread out and quite large in area), it is simply a fortunate fact that many of the core highlights are close to each other.

Starting at Jasper Ave. and 100 St., walk east two blocks to the stunning new Convention Center, an $84 million complex sunk into the river bank and the home of Canada's Aviation Hall of Fame. Retrace to 100 St. and proceed north to Sir Winston Churchill Square and the Civic Center. Surrounding the square are, counter-clockwise from the southeast corner of 102 Ave. and 100 St., the Centennial Library, The Citadel Theatre, and to the north, the Edmonton Art Gallery, Law Courts Building, and City Hall. To the west is Edmonton Center, a climate-controlled complex of shops, restaurants, office towers and hotel.

Cutting back south on 100th St. once more, brings one back to the main thoroughfare of Jasper Ave. One block west on Jasper is Edmonton's main LRT (Light Rail Transit) station. The head office of Travel Alberta is across the avenue at Capital Sq., 10065 Jasper Ave. (14th fl.). Last, the Beaver House Art Gallery, a gallery and workshop dedicated to Alberta art, is at 10158–103rd St. (3rd fl.).

Settlement began in the North Saskatchewan River valley. In the late 1700's, the Northwest Company and the Hudson's Bay Company—the two great fur trading corporations—leap-frogged their rivalrous, fort-building way along the north shore of the river. At least seven forts over a fifty-year period were constructed. They were located on the north shore in Cree Indian territory rather than the south shore, which was part of the formidible Blackfoot Indian hunting grounds. One of the forts was situated on what is now the Alberta Legislative grounds. Two earlier forts were located on the present Edmonton powerhouse site in the river valley.

The Capital City Park contains something of interest for almost everyone. It lines the river valley of the North Saskatchewan River and has become the crowning physical feature of this city. In its entirety this playground covers 17 miles that includes 33 miles of exploration trails for hiking or biking. Included are facilities for golf, swimming, boating, tennis, winter sports, and the interest of flora and fauna. The Strathcona Science Center offers exhibits, a feature gallery, and free admission. It is located at the far northeast end of this long river-valley park. The striking glass pyramids of the Muttart Gardens feature plant species representing three specific climatic zones, in addition to showcasing special displays. The John Walter Site contains Edmonton's first dwelling plus four other historical buildings. This attraction is in the valley on the river's south shore. Directly across the water is the Alberta Legislative Centre. Finally, traces of gold can still be panned out of the gravel of the river. In 1897 gold fever struck and Edmonton experienced a rush. It lasted only three weeks, for all that could be gained were traces that were eagerly left for the river's sturgeon when news arrived of the great Klondike strike of '98.

On the river's south shore is the former town of Strathcona, which amalgamated with Edmonton in 1912. The site still contains many original buildings and streetscapes characteristic of a turn-of-the-century town. The Old Strathcona Foundation produces a walking-tour map that is always available at the Edmonton Visitor's Bureau. Strathcona also contains the University of Alberta where group tours may be arranged.

PRACTICAL INFORMATION FOR EDMONTON

Transportation

AIR. Edmonton is served by two airports: the International (*Air Canada, American, CP Air, Northwest Orient, Pacific Western, United, Wardair,* and *Western*); and the Municipal (*Pacific Western* and *Time Air*).

BUS. *Greyhound* and *Red Arrow Lines* provide service from other centers. An airporter service ($6.50 one way) transports from the International Airport to uptown hotels. *LRT* and street buses provide excellent get-around service for $1.00.

OTHER. *Taxis* cost $1.20 initially, then $1.00 for each additional mile. *Bicycle* rentals are available.

FOR MORE INFORMATION

Edmonton Convention and Tourism Authority, # 104, 9797 Jasper Ave., Alberta T5J 1N9. *Travel Alberta,* Box 2500, Edmonton T5J 2Z4.

Accommodations

Edmonton's upper-grade hotels are expensive; but fortunately there are many adequate properties that cater to the budget-minded traveler. Reservations are recommended, especially during "Klondike Days," July 17–26, in 1986. Persons wishing to visit Edmonton during this time would be wise to write Travel Alberta and request an *Alberta Accommodations Guide* (free), then prebook and confirm accommodation well in advance.

Price categories for double-occupancy are: *Inexpensive:* under $40.00, and *Moderate:* $40.00 to $60.00.

Inexpensive

Algonquin Motor Lodge, 10401 Mayfield Rd., T5P 4C8. TV, pool, sauna; family rates. **Bonaventure Motor Hotel,** 12520 St. Albert Tr., T5L 4H4. Air conditioning, phones, TV, tavern. **Chateau Motel,** R.R. 1 S., T6H 4N6. Kitchenettes, laundry, TV; no charge for children in same room. **Laurentian Motor Inn,** 18245 Stony Plain Rd., T5S 1A9. **Relax Inn,** 2 locations. *Southside:* 10320–45th

Ave. T5S 1A7. *West End:* 18320 Stony Plain Rd. T5S 1A7. Pool, TV, phones, dining. **Rosslyn Motor Inn,** 13620–97th St., T5E 4E2. Pool, dining, drinks, air conditioning, TV, phones. **Southgate Motor Inn,** 4805 Calgary Trail T6H 4T1. Kitchenettes, pool, coffee, air conditioning, TV, phones, mini-golf.

Moderate

Capilano Motor Inn, 9125–50th St. Pool, Jacuzzi, dining, tavern; family rates. **Hotel Vega,** 10815 Jasper Ave., T5J 2B1. Waterbeds, dining, entertainment, TV, phones; no charge for children in same room. **Mayfield Inn,** Mayfield Rd. and 109 Ave. T5T 4B6. Pool, TV, sports facilities, pub, dinner theater; family plan. **Renford Inn On Whyte,** 10620 Whyte Ave., T6E 2A7. Whirlpool, dining, entertainment, air conditioning, TV, phones. **Riviera Motor Hotel,** 5359 Calgary Tr., T6H 4J9. Dining, entertainment, TV; no charge for children in same room. **Royal Park Apartment Hotel** 9835–106 St., Edmonton, T5K 1C3. 50 suites, kitchens, laundry. Daily and weekly rates. **Sandman Inn,** 17635 Stony Plain Rd., T5S 1E3. Air conditioning, dining, entertainment, pool, TV; no charge for children in same room.

CAMPGROUNDS. Shakers Acres, Box 59, Winterburn, T0E 2N0 (on Hwy. 16, west at Winterburn overpass). 178 sites with food service, indoor pool, laundry and showers, groceries. Open year round. **Half Moon Lake Resort,** (May–Sept.) 21524 Township Rd., Sherwood Park, T8E 1E5. 200 sites, full facilities, beach. **Glowing Embers,** Box 2000, Winterburn, T0E 2N0. 273 sites, laundry, store, hook-ups. **Klondike Valley,** Box 2, Site 3, R.R. 1, Edmonton, T6H 4N6. 160 sites, laundry, groceries, showers, firewood, playground.

HOSTELS. Edmonton Youth Hostel, 10422–91st St., T5H 1S6. Up to $9.00 per night for CHA members or $12.00 per night for nonmembers.

YMCA/YWCA. YMCA, 10030–102A Ave., T5J 0G5. $12.00 for single. **YWCA,** 10305–100th Ave., T5J 0G5. Accommodations from $7.00,

OTHER. *University of Alberta,* 44 Lister Hall, U. of A., T6G 2H6. Student residences are available from May through August only. (The residences involved are located at 87th Ave. and 116th St.)

Restaurants

Given Edmonton's location in the middle of beef-producing Alberta, visitors should have no difficulty in finding large portions of good steak. There are steakhouses in all price ranges, and with all types of atmospheres—from formal to family dining. Edmonton has become a highly cosmopolitan city. Several years ago, steak was the best, if not the only bet for dining out. However, in the last decade, ethnic and haute-cuisine restaurants have proliferated. Edmonton now boasts that it has ". . . an enchanting potpourri of cultures and tastes . . . you can eat in over twenty-four different languages . . ." And several restaurants are proving that classical cooking is not synonymous with high prices.

Discovering just how diversified the Edmonton palate is can be an exciting and satisfying part of your visit. You don't have to be afraid to try ethnic eateries here. Local patrons tend to have educated palates, and even a hopeful imitation is not likely to succeed.

All price categories quoted are for a complete meal for two. Tips and drinks are not included. Price categories are: *Inexpensive:* under $25.00, and *Moderate:* $25.00 to $35.00.

Inexpensive

Good World Restaurant, 10777–97th St. Chinese. **The Merryland,** 7006–109th St. Korean and informal. **Mother Tucker's,** 10184–104th St. Salad bar, prime rib, apple pie. **The Pyrogy House,** 12510–118th Ave. and 10346 University Dr. Two locations and sensational Ukrainian. **The Red Ox Inn,** 9420–91st St. Informal home-cooking. **Swiss Chalet,** 17008–107 Ave., 4975–98 Ave., and 5020–97 St. Great barbecued chicken and ribs. **Strathcona Gasthaus,** 8120–101st St. Hearty German fare. Cash only but worth a visit.

Moderate

Ashoka Curry House, 9570–111th Ave. East Indian curries. **Bistro Praha,** 10168–100A St. Large portions, informal surroundings. **Cucci's,** 99th St. and Jasper Ave. Continental fare. **Dagwood's Deli.** 10310 Jasper Ave. Smoked meat and other deli delights. **Hawkeye's,** 10065 Jasper Ave. Varied, from shrimp to pizza. **Red Diamond.** 7500–82 Ave. Cantonese. Consistent quality. **San Remo,** 290 Saddleback Rd. Italian, with a special 4-course dinner on Sunday. **Steakboard.** 10220–103 St. Salad bar, good steak. **Trapper John's Trading Post,** 10415–104 Ave. Campfire ribs, goldmine chicken, fool's gold. **The Courtyard,** Four Seasons Hotel. Excellent variety and quality.

What to See and Do

MUSEUMS AND GALLERIES

Fort Edmonton Park, Whitemud Fwy. and Fox Dr. (exit on south end of Quesnell Bridge). 178-acre site consisting of the reconstruction of an 1846 fort, a farm, and a "living" town featuring specific dated streets that trace Edmonton's history. Adults $4.00, children and Senior Citizens $2.50, preschoolers free.

Provincial Museum of Alberta, 12845–102nd Ave. Wildlife, Native history and culture, geology, fossils, dinosaurs, and Alberta's pioneer past. Free.

Strathcona Science Park, south of Hwy. 16 east on 17th St. A collection of displays which describe and interpret how Alberta's natural resources are put to use; plus the evidence of man's existence in prehistoric times featuring an actual "dig" for artifacts to 3000 B.C. Admission is free.

Ukrainian Museum of Canada, 10611–110th Ave. Costumes, Easter eggs, dolls and tapestries are displayed. Free.

GALLERIES. Beaver House, 10158–103rd St., Alberta art. Free admission. **Edmonton Art Gallery,** 2 Sir Winston Churchill Sq., offers extras in the way of concerts, films, and theater. Free. **Ring House Gallery** at the University of Alberta (south of the Faculty Club off Saskatchewan Dr.). Free.

Some Principal Sights and Attractions

Klondike Days, held during the last two weeks of July, is an extravaganza that takes place all over the city including the river. The focal point of the action is at Northlands Park, where the Klondike Days Exposition features gold-panning, horse racing and casino gambling, in addition to all the fun of a summer fair. Free entertainment in the downtown area includes bathtub races, a costume promenade, raft races and daily parades.

In August, **Heritage Days** celebrates the city's cultural diversity. It is followed by **Summerfest** with free puppet shows in Churchill Square, Jazz City, Folk and Theatre Festivals. For full and revised information, contact *Edmonton Convention and Tourism Authority,* #104, 9797 Jasper Ave., Edmonton, Canada T5J 1N9.

Muttart Conservatory, 98th Ave. and 96A St. (east end of James McDonald Bridge). Unique glass pyramids offering plant species representative of specific world climatic zones. Adults $2.00. Children $1.00.

Polar Park, on Hwy. 14–14 miles east of Edmonton. The first of its kind, Polar Park is concerned with the preservation and breeding of animal species indigenous to the cold-climate countries of the world. Adults $3.00, children under 6 free.

Queen Elizabeth Planetarium, and **Edmonton Space Sciences Center** (opened spring 1984), 134th St. and 111th Ave. in Coronation Park. Multi-media productions of astral activities. Admission is $3.50 for adults, children (5–15) $2.50.

Valley Zoo, Buena Vista Rd. and 134th St. Story-book fairy tales form the theme for the exhibition of 500 birds and animals. Adults $2.25, children $1.00.

Fantasyland, West Edmonton Mall. This is one of the largest indoor amusement parks, in one of the world's largest shopping centers. Rides, petting zoo, aquarium, and ice rink! Adults $1.50, children under 16 $1.00.

ENTERTAINMENT

Music. Edmonton has both the *Edmonton Symphony Orchestra* and *Edmonton Opera Society,* which perform regularly.

Theater. *The Citadel Theatre,* with its impressive facilities in downtown Edmonton, is one of Canada's top-rated companies. Its productions feature internationally known players. Additionally, Edmonton enjoys a healthy array of amateur companies. One of Canada's most successful dinner theaters is at the *Mayfield Inn.*

Bars and Clubs. Edmonton takes a back seat to no city when it comes to night entertainment. Night clubs, cabarets, taverns, lounges, and that infamous Alberta watering hole—the beer parlor—combine to provide a constant offering of local and international artists.

Sports. Pride, joy and ecstasy could describe an Edmontonian's feeling for its three major professional teams, the *Eskimos* (CFL **football**), the *Oilers* (NHL **hockey**), and the *Trappers* (pro **baseball**). Yet, besides these clubs, there are hundreds of others, semipro and amateur, actively engaged in a myriad of competitive sports. Recreational participation in sports is a civic preoccupation. As a result, Edmonton is able to offer opportunities and facilities that are perhaps unequaled in Western Canada.

EXPLORING ALBERTA'S ROCKIES

Alberta's backbone is the great, jagged sawtooth of the Canadian Rockies that extend along the western border with British Columbia. These mountains, along with their forested valleys, high alpine lakes and meadows, yield a playground of sightseeing and recreational opportunities that are world renowned.

Five National Parks—Waterton, Banff, Jasper, Wood Buffalo, and Elk Island—plus an immense Alberta Forest Reserve combine to organize and preserve this area for the enjoyment of millions of annual visitors.

Waterton National Park

Waterton National Park adjoins the Glacier National Park in Montana. Together, they form what is known as the International Peace Park.

Waterton is a jewel. Small, only 203 square miles, it provides a maximum of scenery in a minimum of space that is an inspiring combination of short-grass prairie, high peaks, and glacial water. A naturalist's dream world, Waterton is rich in birds and animals, and the slower pace of the park gives the time to relax and enjoy. It has wisely been designed for hiking and many, many trails meander past some 40 lakes and ponds and twice that many streams.

The hiking trails in the park range from easy walking tours such as Red Rock Canyon, to difficult hikes. For example, the Linam Lakes Trail is 3.5 miles long and for the most part is not too difficult. Yet, a climbing permit is needed because of a 300-foot perpendicular cliff that must be scaled to reach the lakes. The lakes, at 7,000 feet, have excellent fishing, for not many anglers reach them.

A really good trail for families who wish to remain close to the town is the Krandle Lake Trail. It can be traversed in as little as one hour's time, although two campsites invite an overnight stay. Full information regarding all the park's trails and sightseeing opportunities can be found at the park information center located at the entrance to Waterton town. Also, park wardens offer a free interpretive program of conducted walks, field trips, fireside talks, and slide and film presentations. Queries by mail should be directed to: *Superintendent, Waterton Lakes National Park, Waterton Park, Alberta TOK 2M0.*

Banff National Park

Seventy miles west of Calgary on the Trans-Canada Hwy. lies Banff National Park and over 2,500 square miles of some of the world's most spectacular scenery.

The town of Banff has a population of 4,627 people and numerous elk, deer, chipmunk, and various other critters. The town lies nestled in the valley of the Bow River encircled by imposing mountains—Rundle, Cascade, Norquay, and Sulphur. It is a year-round resort. In winter, the slopes of Mt. Norquay excite skiers of all ages and abilities. A few miles away, Sunshine has the best snow conditions in the Canadian Rockies with an average of 400 inches per season. Skiing begins at Sunshine in November and can last to the end of May.

In all seasons, Banff is a playground. Most visitors come to simply wander, see and relax. The atmosphere of Banff is soothing. Its days are warm and its evenings are refreshingly cool.

Banff town offers a wide array of facilities for visitors—shops, cabarets, attractions, restaurants, and accommodations. Recreation in the form of canoe trips on the river, horseback riding on forest and alpine trails, bicycling on footpaths, or hiking and climbing occupies a great deal of the vacationer's holiday. Rental of all necessary equipment is readily available and moderately priced.

Several activities are on the "must" list for any Banff visit. Both the Luxton Museum and the Natural History Museum are worthwhile. A trip to the summit of Sulphur Mountain via gondola, or to the top of the Mt. Norquay via chair lift, is a good idea and reasonable in cost. So is a dip in the Upper Hot Springs pool to enjoy the warm, sulfurous waters. A drive through the gorgeous Banff Springs Hotel golf course, or a 1½-hour hike along the tumbling waterfalls of Sundance Canyon, are each well worth taking—and neither costs a cent.

Visitors to Banff, who have never explored deeper into the Canadian Rockies, may feel that nature simply could not be more beautiful. That would be a mistake. The scenery of the Rockies does indeed become more lovely. The 1A Hwy. to Lake Louise is 30 miles of nature at its best. Many hiking trails lead off of this leisurely "by-way highway" allowing direct access to the forest, streams, and ponds. One of the most popular hikes is at Johnston's Canyon; it winds its way to a spectacular falls approximately a mile into the forest.

Lake Louise is considered one of the natural wonders of the world. On any average summer's day the cold, green water provides a perfect mirror image of the 11,365-foot Mt. Victoria and its glacier. Two adjacent mountains, the Beehive and Mt. Fairview, complete the famous portrait by forming a "V" in the center of a pictorial wonder.

Perhaps the most stunning stretch of highway in Canada is the 144-mile long "Icefield Parkway" that runs north and south through Banff and Jasper National Parks, connecting the Trans-Canada Hwy. with the Yellowhead Hwy. Scaling two passes on its way, this drive approaches the uppermost limits of timberline. Wildlife is in abundance the entire length and the grandeur of the panorama is beyond description. The drive is further enhanced by many stunning scenic viewpoints. All of them should be taken advantage of, especially the Peyto Lake one (access via a secondary road from Bow Summit) that gives a dramatic view of serene Peyto Lake and the majestic Mistaya Valley 800 feet below.

Jasper National Park

Jasper National Park begins at the northern boundary of Banff National Park. It is rich in history and the effects of glacial activity is extensive. Its passes, formed by great natural upheavals, and the valleys carved by massive ice flows were traversed by explorers and fur traders crossing the Rockies.

It boasts more than 600 miles of hiking trails and a profusion of alpine meadows and deep-blue lakes. It is a paradise to those who enjoy hiking, photography, fishing, and just plain looking. Most of the park's larger lakes offer good boating and canoeing, with rentals and cruises available.

Access to the park is gained by traveling west from Edmonton via the Yellowhead Hwy., or north from Banff National Park via the Icefield Pkwy.

The Columbia Icefield, located on the Icefield Pkwy. 60 miles south of Jasper townsite, is the largest body of ice in the Rockies, covering 150 square miles. The Columbia Icefield feeds many glaciers. Visible from the highway is the Athabasca Glacier. Seasonally it both retreats and advances. The rate of melt at its toe is greater than its downward flow; thus the net result is that it retreats at the rate of approximately 30 feet per year.

Athabasca Falls is one of the more popular and certainly most spectacular scenic diversions in the entire Rockies. The Falls is accessible from Hwy. 93A, a scenic loop that joins the Parkway north of the Columbia Icefield.

The Jasper townsite (population 3,422) vicinity was a wilderness throughout the 1800's. Still, there was a regular traffic of explorers, traders, Indians, and missionaries traveling to and from the Columbia River across the Continental Divide. Today, Jasper is a busy town whose main employers are the CN Railroad and the tourism industry. It offers year-round recreational adventures and most amenities urban-oriented visitors expect.

An Adventure Highway

East of Jasper, at Hinton, the Yellowhead Hwy. is bisected by the incredible Forestry Trunk Road—a real adventure route. Much of its surface is gravel, and anyone using it must check out weather and road conditions prior to traveling.

The road runs south to the American border through the picturesque eastern slopes of the Rocky Mountains. It also extends a further 200 miles north of Hinton, and along its entire length Ranger Stations can supply emergency aid and exit roads lead east back to civilization. Many services that are taken for granted along ordinary highway are not present, and it is wise to carry at least minimal survival gear—sleeping bags, ground sheets, large ax, flashlight, extra batteries, waxed matches, fishline and, most important, a first-aid kit containing an ample supply of insect repellent.

There are many provincially maintained campsites so overnighting is not really a problem. This huge forested backcountry provides extensive opportunities for pursuing outdoor interests. Remember, it's for the adventurous.

PRACTICAL INFORMATION FOR ALBERTA

Transportation

AIR. *Air Canada, American, CP Air, Western Airlines, Pacific Western, United, Lufthansa, Wardair,* and *Northwest Orient* all provide service to Alberta. Additionally, numerous charter airlines provide unscheduled flights. Within the province *Time Air* serves on a domestic basis.

RAIL. *Via Rail's* main line passes through the province and with a network of secondary lines throughout.

BUS. Full bus coverage is provided by *Greyhound Bus Lines, Red Arrow, Brewster Transport, Lethbridge Northern Bus Lines, Cardinal Coachlines, Diversified* (PWT), *Yellow Coach* (Grey Goose Lines), and a number of local companies.

CAR. Alberta has a total of 145,583 kms. of rural highways and roads. Of this total, 12,995 kms. are classed as primary highways. Most major and a number of local auto rental firms serve the Alberta market. Rentals of bicycles and motorcycles are possible in major centers.

FOR MORE INFORMATION

Comprehensive literature regarding attractions, accommodations, prices, and maps may be obtained free of charge by mailing a request to *Travel Alberta,* Box 2500, Edmonton, Alberta T5J 2Z4. Travel Alberta will also respond to requests concerning any aspect of tourism: i.e., canoeing, hunting, fishing, skiing, events. This literature may be supplemented by direct requests to any one or all of the 14 tourist zone offices in the province.

Zone 1 "Chinook Country"—Travel and Convention Association of Southern Alberta, 2805 Scenic Dr., Lethbridge, Alberta T1K 5B7.

Zone 2 "The Gateway"—South-East Alberta Travel and Convention Association, Box 605, Medicine Hat, Alberta T1A 7G5.

Zone 3 "Big Country"—The Big Country Tourist Association, 170 Centre Street, Drumheller, Alberta T0J 0Y0.

Zone 4 "Land of David Thompson"—David Thompson Country Tourist Council, 4811–48 Ave., Red Deer, Alberta T4N 3T2.

Zone 5 "Battle River"—Battle River Tourist Association, Box 1515, 6107–48th Ave., Camrose, Alberta T4V 1X4.

Zone 6 "Lakeland"—The Lakeland Tourist Association, Box 874, St. Paul, Alberta T0A 3A0.

Zone 7 "Evergreen Zone"—The Evergreen Tourist Association, Box 2548, Edson, Alberta T0E 0P0.

Zone 8 "Land of the Mighty Peace"—Land of the Mighty Peace Tourist Association, Box 3210, Peace River, Alberta T0H 2X0.

Zone 9 "Jasper"—Jasper Park Chamber of Commerce, Box 98, Jasper, Alberta T0E 1E0.

Zone 10 "The Livin' West"—Calgary Tourist and Convention Association, Hospitality Centre, 237–8th Ave. S.E., Calgary, Alberta T2G 0K8.

Zone 11 "Edmonton"—Edmonton Convention and Tourism Authority, #104, 9797 Jasper Ave., Edmonton, Alberta T5J 1N9.

Zone 12 "Banff"—Tourist Committee, Banff-Lake Louise Chamber of Commerce, Box 1298, 94 Banff Ave., Banff, Alberta T0L 0C0.

Zone 13 "Game Country"—Game Country Travel Association, Box 1254, Grande Prairie, Alberta T8H 4Z6.

Zone 14 "Land of the Midnight Twilight"—Midnight Twilight Tourist Association, #1 Sturgeon Rd., St. Albert, Alberta T8N 0E8.

Accommodations

Alberta is able to offer a good selection of budget-priced accommodation in all areas. Price categories, for double-occupancy, are: *Inexpensive* (I) under $40.00, and *Moderate* (M) $40.00 to $60.00. There is no provincial tax on accommodations, but most hotels and motels charge for local telephone calls.

ADVENTURE HIGHWAY (Forestry Trunk Rd.). *Highwood House*

(M), Box 158, Longview, Alberta T0L 1H0. Rustic log bungalows, store, gas, dining, fishing equipment.

BANFF. *King Edward Hotel* (I), Banff Ave., Box 250, Banff T0L 0C0. Older hotel but clean with dining and tavern. *Spruce Grove Motel* (M), 545 Banff Ave., Box 471, Banff T0L 0C0. TV; kitchenettes extra. *Alpine Motel* (M), 521 Banff Ave., Box 279, Banff T0L 0C0. TV and kitchenettes. *Banff Motel* (M), 222 Lynx St., Box 279, Banff T0L OCO. TV and kitchenettes. *Red Carpet Inn* (M), 425 Banff Ave., Box 1800, Banff T0L 0C0. TV and dining.

Lake Louise Area: *Paradise Lodge* (M), Box 7, Lake Louise T0L 1E0. 27 units, playground, store. *Post Hotel & Pipestone Lodge* (M), Box 69, Lake Louise T0L 1E0. From basin-only rooms to full bath, tavern, and off-season rates.

Icefield Parkway Area: *Num-ti-jah Lodge* (M), Box 39, Lake Louise T0L 1E9. Dining, riding, remote scenic location.

BONNYVILLE. *Southview Motel* (I), Box 1077, Bonnyville T0A 0L0. Kitchenettes, coffee, TV, and phones.

BROOKS. *Plains Motel* (I), Box 1738, Brooks T0J 0J0. Pool, TV, air conditioning, exercise room, coffee.

CAMROSE. *Crystal Springs Motor Hotel* (I), 3911–48th Ave., Camrose T4V 0V5. TV, air conditioning, coffee shop, cabaret; no charge for children in same room.

CANMORE. *Rocky Mountain Chalets* (M), Box 725, Canmore T0L 0M0. 1 and 2 bedroom units and lofts. Kitchenettes, fireplaces.

CARDSTON. *Flamingo Motel* (I), Box 92, Cardston T0K 0K0. TV, phones, air conditioning, coffee, and kitchenettes.

CLARESHOLM. *Golden Pheasant Motor Inn* (I), Box 129, Claresholm T0L 0T0. TV, phones, some suites.

DRUMHELLER. *Dinosaur Motel* (I), Box 730, Drumheller T0J 0Y0. On Red Deer River, air conditioning, kitchenettes, TV, coffee. *Rockhound Motor Inn* (I), Box 2350, Drumheller T0J 0Y0. TV, phones, dining, drinks.

EDSON. *Castle Motel* (I), Box 2098, Edson T0E 0P0. Dining, kitchenettes, TV.

FORT MACLEOD. *Sunset Motel* (M), Box 398, Ft. Macleod T0L 0Z0. Air conditioning, kitchenettes, coffee, TV.

FORT McMURRAY. *Oil Sands Hotel* (I), 10007 Franklin Ave., Fort McMurray T9H 2K7. Air conditioning, dining, tavern.

GRANDE PRAIRIE. *Grande Prairie Motor Inn* (M), 11633–100th

St., Grande Prairie T8V 3Y4. TV, dining, drinks, pool, family rates. *Richmond Hotel*(I), 10437 Richmond Ave., Grande Prairie T8V 2Z6. TV, air conditioning, dining, coffee, kitchenettes.

HINTON. *Hinton Green Tree TraveLodge* (M), Box 938, Hinton T0E 1B0. TV, sauna, dining, kitchenettes, pool, drinks.

JASPER. *Astoria Motor Inn* (I), Box 850, Jasper T0E 1E0. Year round. TV, tavern. *Athabasca Hotel*(M), Box 1420, Jasper T0E 1E0. Dining, lounge, TV, phones. *Mount Robson Motor Inn* (M), Box 88, Jasper T0E 1E0. Dining, pool, TV.

LAC LA BICHE. *Almac Motor Hotel*(M), Box 536, Lac La Biche T0A 2C0. Tavern, dining, TV, phones, kitchenettes.

LETHBRIDGE. *Bridge Townhouse Motel* (I), 1026 Mayor Magrath Dr., Lethbridge T1K 2P8. Coffee, pool, air conditioning, TV. *Sandman Inn* (M), 421 Mayor Magrath Dr., Lethbridge T1J 3L8. Dining, cocktails, pool, TV, dancing. *Lodge Motel*(I), 7th Ave. and Mayor Magrath Dr., Lethbridge T1J 1M7. Waterbeds, pool, kitchenettes, dining, air conditioning. *Lethbridge Lodge Hotel* (M), 320 Scenic Dr., Lethbridge T1J 4B4. Pool and whirlpool, dining, entertainment, dancing, TV, air conditioning.

LLOYDMINSTER. *Lloydminster Motel*(I), 5109–44th St., Lloydminster T9V 0A6. Kitchenettes, family suites, coffee, TV. *Prince Charles Motor Inn* (I), 4820–50 Ave., Lloydminster T9V 0W5. Dining, drinks, entertainment. *Wayside Inn* (M), Box 1250, Lloydminster, S9V 1G1. TV, phones, pool, dining, drinks.

MEDICINE HAT. *Assiniboia Inn* (I), 680–3rd St. S.E., Box 786, Medicine Hat T1A 7G7. Dining, dancing, tavern, air conditioning, TV, phones. *Bel-Aire Motel* (I), 633–14th St. S.W., Medicine Hat T1A 4V5. Kitchenettes, TV, air conditioning, phones. *Continental Inn*(I), 954–7th St. S.W., Medicine Hat T1A 7R7. Air conditioning, dining, entertainment, dancing, TV. *Flamingo Terrace Best Western* (M), Trans-Canada Hwy., Medicine Hat T1A 5E3. Family units and suites, pool, laundromat, racquetball, kitchenettes, dining, TV. *Park Lane Motor Hotel* (I), 780–7th St. S.W., Medicine Hat T1A 4L2. Dining, dancing, tavern, pool, TV, kitchenettes. *Westlander Inn* (I), 3216–13th Ave. S.E., Box 1032, Medicine Hat T1A 7H1. Cabaret, dining, air conditioning, RV. *TraveLodge Motor Inn* (M), No. 1100, Redcliff Dr. S.W., Medicine Hat T1A 5E5. Air conditioning, pool, dining lounge, cocktails, TV; family rates.

RED DEER. *The Red Deer Inn*(I), 4217 Gaetz Ave., Red Deer T4N 3Z4. Dining, bar, air conditioning, TV; no charge for children in same room. *Black Knight Inn* (M), 2929–50 Ave., Red Deer T4N 5E6. Air conditioning, pool, licensed facilities and entertainment. *Red Deer Lodge* (M), Red Deer, T4N 5Y7. Pool, atrium, dining.

ROCKY MOUNTAIN HOUSE. *Tamarack Motor Inn* (I), Box 2860, Rocky Mountain House T0M 1T0. TV, tavern, movies, dining, drinks, whirlpool.

ST. PAUL. *Lakeland Motel* (I), Box 2958, St. Paul T0A 3A0. Air conditioning, kitchenettes, coffee, TV, phones.

SLAVE LAKE. *Sawridge Motor Hotel* (M), Box 879, Slave Lake T0G 2A0. Dining, entertainment, bar, TV; no charge for children under 12 in same room. Wheelchair facilities.

TABER. *The Lodge Motel* (M), Box 1738, Taber T0K 2G0. Pool, kitchenettes, air conditioning, TV, coffee, phones.

VEGREVILLE. *Homesteader Inn* (I), Box 1500, Vegreville T0B 4L0. Dining lounge, bar, dancing, entertainment, TV.

WAINWRIGHT. *Buffalo Springs Motor Inn* (M), Box 1646, Wainwright T0B 4P0. Dining, tavern, air conditioning, TV.

WATERTON LAKES. *Crandell Lodge Motel* (I), Box 114, Waterton Lakes T0K 2M0. Kitchenettes, coffee; some family units. *Aspen (Ponderosa) Windflower Motels* (M), Box 64, Waterton Lakes T0K 2M0. Kitchenettes, coffee, TV; family suites. *Prince of Wales Hotel* (M), Waterton Lakes T0K 2M0. Reservations only May through September; off-season rates. Dining, bar, phones, charming and historic.

WETASKIWIN. *Wayside Inn* (M), 4103–56th St., Wetaskiwin T9A 2G1. Dining, tavern, cabaret, TV, telephones.

WHITECOURT. *White-Kaps Motel* (I), Box 1164, Whitecourt T0E 2L0. Laundromat, coffee, air conditioning, kitchenettes, TV, phones; family plan. *Cascade Motor Inn* (I), 3415 Hi-Way St., Whitecourt T0E 2L0. Dining, air conditioning, coffee, pool, TV, sauna.

Campgrounds

The potential for economical vacations is almost limitless if you decide to camp. In addition to commercial sites, excellent campgrounds with a variety of facilities are available in most of the 60 provincial parks and 5 national parks, at $3.00–$9.00 per night. Alberta Transportation maintains roadside campsites, most of which are free, at least every 50 miles on every major highway. All campgrounds are listed and described in Travel Alberta's *Accommodation Guide*.

Hostels

There are hosteling centers in three cities in Alberta—Calgary, Edmonton, and Medicine Hat. Fourteen more hostels (mainly in the mountain region between Banff and Jasper) bring the total to 17. Overnight fees are $3.00–$9.00 for members and $7.00–$12.00

for nonmembers. Full and complete information may be obtained by writing *Alberta Hostelling Association,* 10926–88th Ave., Edmonton, Alberta T6E 0Z1.

YMCA and YWCA

Both have locations and facilities in Calgary and Edmonton. For more information see the *Accommodations* section under each city listing.

Farm or Ranch Vacations

Alberta has an intriguing variety of country vacation possibilities at farms or ranches. Be catered to, or pitch in and do a little work yourself. There are many options to choose from. Rates vary with the different vacation packages offered. Information on Alberta country vacations may be obtained by writing *Travel Alberta,* Box 2500, Edmonton, Alberta T5J 2Z4, or by telephoning 800–661–8888 toll free, from the U.S. and most of Canada.

Bed and Breakfast

There are more than 75 establishments in Alberta offering home-cooked breakfast and Alberta hospitality as part of an economical holiday. Write to the *Alberta Bed and Breakfast Association,* 4327–86 St., Edmonton, T6K 1A9, or Box 7094, Station E, Calgary, T3C 3L8.

Restaurants

Alberta offers three major types of foods. This is cattle country, and Albertans are fiercely proud of the quality of beef that their grazing lands and grains yield. Thus Alberta's favorite food is steak, followed by seafood and Chinese cuisine.

Restaurants are listed by price category as follows: *Inexpensive* (I), under $25.00, and *Moderate* (M), $25.00 to $35.00. It should be noted that these categories are for two persons without wine or other alcoholic drinks. Tips also are not included, which generally run from 10 to 15 percent, depending upon the degree of good service. Alberta levies no tax on food; however, beer, wine, and liquor are taxed heavily. Therefore, significant savings can be made on dinner costs by eliminating alcoholic beverages.

BANFF. *Banff Cafe* (M). Informal with a broad menu. *Grizzly House Restaurant* (M). Excellent steak, good lobster, fondues. *Paris Restaurant* (M). A long-time favorite serving Continental cuisine. *Phil's* (I). Family restaurant, offering hearty breakfasts.

CLARESHOLM. *The Flying "N"* (I). One of Canada's top ten restaurants and features an extensive menu of home-cooked food served buffet-style.

DRUMHELLER. *The Corner Grill* (I). Seafood tops the list. Try their Dinosaur burger!

EDSON. *The Flame Room* (M). A good, clean family restaurant.

FORT MACLEOD. *The Java Shop* (M). Oven-baked chicken is superb here.

GRANDE PRAIRIE. *Grande Prairie Motor Inn* (M). Excellent prime rib in a small, tastefully appointed dining room.

HINTON. *Husky House* (I). Steak and eggs plus a good, solid truck driver's menu.

JASPER. *Diamond Motel* (M). Good family-type meals. *L&W* (I). Best burgers and pizza in town. *Marmot Motor Lodge* (M). Continental cuisine. *Tekarra Lodge* (M). Good menu. Lamb is the specialty.

LETHBRIDGE. *Majorette Restaurant* (M). Large menu of Western and Chinese cuisine. *Sven Eriksen* (M). Family dining. Hearty portions of home cooking.

MEDICINE HAT. *Golden Dragon* (M). Pleasant and quiet. Oriental menu. *Heidel Haus* (M). Steaks, dancing, and Old Country décor. *The Ming Tree* (M). Good food, friendly faces, and lots of action.

PEACE RIVER. *Traveller's* (I). Daytime smorgasbord.

RED DEER. *Anthony Henday* (M). English menu and style. *Ranch House* (M). Excellent steaks and good salad bar.

WATERTON LAKES. *Kootenay Lodge* (M). Worth several visits. *Tourist Café* (M). Pies are the number one attraction.

What to See in Alberta

Alberta offers just about everything a tourist with a spirit of adventure or an interest in humanities could want—except an ocean. It has though, the longest white-sand beach in the country, at Lesser Slave Lake. A total of five national parks lie in Alberta—Banff, Jasper, Waterton, Elk Island, and Wood Buffalo.

The lay-of-Alberta's-land makes for spectacular geological interest, from alpine to badlands. Its history, though relatively new, is fascinating; thus, museums appear in towns and places all over the province. The culture of its Native peoples is cherished, as a result visits to Native points-of-interest are encouraged. The first inhabitants were the reptiles—dinosaurs; and a most intriguing place to get the story is at Dinosaur Provincial Park north of Brooks. The northern lakes and bush country, the central parkland expanses, the southern prairies, and the western forests and mountains blend together to form a most interesting and exciting environment of nature and people.

Alberta has carved itself up into 14 tourist zones to better aid the traveler in service and information. By writing to Travel Alberta in Edmonton and those particular zones in which your interests most lie, you will be able to obtain the facts necessary to plan a low-cost, informative and fun holiday. See *For More Information* earlier in the chapter for addresses of zones.

Recreation and Sports

There is an absolute kaleidoscope of recreational possibilities in Alberta. Here's just a sampling: trail rides on horseback into remote mountain areas; fishing variety beyond your dreams—river, pond, lake, stream; bicycle touring; backpacking trios; white-water adventures in the prime white-water area in the world; rock climbing; hang gliding; ballooning; fixed-wing gliding; cross-country or downhill skiing; snowmobiling; country leisure vacations. Naturally, all these things cost money; still most are within skimpy budgets and preplanning will lead the way.

British Columbia

Summer or winter, British Columbia has much to offer the visitor, from sailing in the sunny Gulf islands between Vancouver and Vancouver Island, to skiing in the Rockies. From May 1 to Oct. 13, Expo 86 will be drawing hundreds of thousands of visitors to Vancouver, making 1986 a particularly exciting year to visit the province. (For information, contact Expo 86, Box 1986, Station A, Vancouver, B.C. V6C 2X5; 604–689–1986.)

The climate is mild, the mood casual, particularly outside the cities of Vancouver and Victoria. B.C. was true frontier until gold was discovered just over 100 years ago and called attention to the area. Now 2,500,000 people live in British Columbia—most of them in the southern region. As a result, the cities, as well as most of the cultural centers are found there, leaving the broad mass of B.C. for hunters and fishermen, skiers and hikers. There are mountain lakes in the northern area where you can canoe for days without seeing a soul and cross-country skiing trails that offer high adventure. And it needn't cost a king's ransom.

EXPLORING VANCOUVER

Cosmopolitan, prosperous, and outdoorsy, Vancouver commands a magnificent harbor that compares with Cape Town, Rio de Janeiro, Sydney, or Hong Kong. The climate is mild—although maddeningly wet at times—and it is possible to play a game of golf in the morning, ski on Grouse Mountain in the afternoon, and have a swim in English Bay before dinner. As Canada's third largest city, with a population of 500,000 and another one million in close proximity, it has a wide range of things to do, and much of the city can be explored on foot.

Stanley Park

For many travelers, Stanley Park, just a half-hour stroll from the center of the city, is what makes Vancouver unique. The 1,000-acre park is the largest natural park in North America. It was noted by Captain George Vancouver, the first white man to see it, when he sailed into the inner harbor in 1792 to a cordial welcome from 50 Indians in canoes. Paddling out from their villages, the Indians

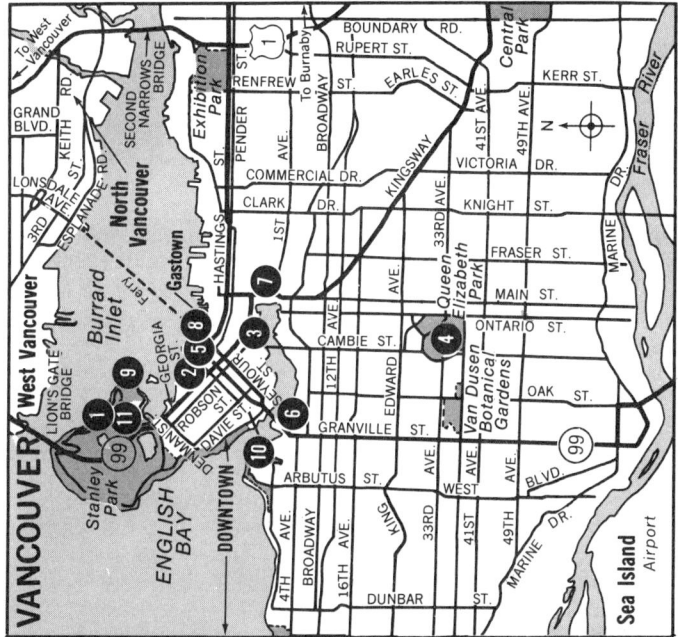

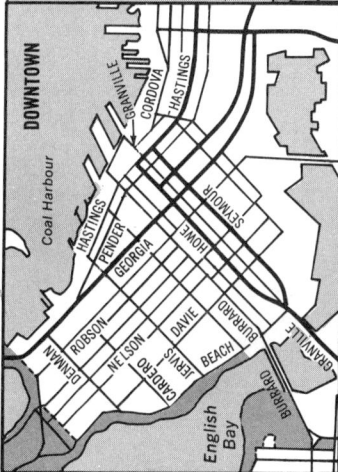

Points of Interest

1) Aquarium
2) Art Gallery
3) B.C. Place Stadium
4) Bloedel Observatory
5) Chinatown
6) Granville Island
7) Railroad Station
8) Seabus Terminal
9) Totem Poles
10) Vanier Park, including the Maritime Museum, Macmillan Planetarium, and the Centennial Museum.
11) Zoo

showered the Englishmen with handfuls of soft white feathers plucked from waterfowl. The visitors camped for one night on what is now Vancouver's waterfront business area and Canada's most expensive real estate, and sailed out again, leaving the Indians undisturbed until the gold rush 100 years later. Although the park still retains its majestic forest, manmade amusements are sprinkled throughout and there are good beaches. There are several restaurants with attractive locations throughout the park, but they are expensive. Stanley Park's natural beauty renders it irresistible to picnickers, so if you want to eat, take provisions. There are picnic tables at several locations, otherwise you can just plonk yourself down under a tree and tuck in. There is a good selection of food shops at Robson and Denman Sts., close to the main park entrance off Georgia St. Not far inside the park you'll come to HMCS Discovery on Deadman's Island. The name derives from an Indian legend in which 200 men exchanged their lives for those of their wives and children, who were being held by an enemy tribe. The Squamish Indians called the site of the slaughter the "island of the dead men." The only blood spilt these days is at Brockton Oval where first-class rugby is played, but if you prefer something gentler there is cricket just over the fence. The cricket is free, the rugby $2.00 admission, but you can watch matches comfortably by leaning on the fence, for which no charge is made. There is also rowing in Coal Harbor. The Vancouver Rowing Club, headquartered in a delightful wooden building set on piles just at the entrance to the park, is an unpretentious place having reciprocity with many North American clubs and universities. Check with the manager at (604) 687–3400.

Some of the park's other features include a zoo, and a children's zoo complete with small animals and a miniature railway. The aquarium is famous for its killer whales, who put on shows in their outdoor pool. It's open summertime from 9:30 A.M. to 9:00 P.M.; winter hours 10:00 A.M.–5:00 P.M. Adults are $5.00, youths (13–18) $3.75, children (5–12), and seniors $2.50; families of up to five are $13.00. For show times call (604) 682–1118.

There are many other things to see in the park. Prospect Point, which looks out over Lions Gate Bridge, was built in the 1930's by the Irish Guinness brewing family to open up its real estate holdings on the North Shore. There is also a memorial to the *Beaver,* the first steamship to sail in these waters, which sank in 1888 near the point after 53 years of service, her paddlewheels flailing valiantly. Brockton Point, where a lighthouse now stands, had been a burial site for the early pioneers. Around the corner is Lumberman's Arch, three giant logs dedicated to B.C.'s loggers. It stands on the site of the Musqueam village of Whoi-Whoi, from where the Indians paddled out to welcome Captain Vancouver in 1792.

Getting around the park is easy. You can walk, jog, run, cycle, take a bus, or go by car. There are plenty of parking lots, but you can't stay overnight in the park. Between April and October, on Sundays and holidays, you can take a city bus round the park. A special ticket—adults $1.00, children 55 cents—allows you to get on and off the bus as you please. It leaves from the Stanley Park loop on Lost Lagoon. You can rent a bike at Stanley Park Rentals, 676 Chilco St., near Lost Lagoon (604–681–5581). A 10-speed bike costs $5.00 an hour, a five-speed $4.00, a three-speed $3.50, a tandem $7.00. You have to pay a $20.00 deposit. You can also rent roller skates. There is a designated bike route round the park. For the fleet of foot, the seawall promenade is about 11 kms. (7 miles) long.

Crisscrossing the park are various trails, some of which are a lovely—and highly recommended—stroll away from the cars, bikes, and roller skates. You'll see lots of different types of trees and birds. In the summer there are open-air shows at Malkin Bowl and, as the company is largely amateur, the tickets are cheap, with children under 14 half-price. For further information call the Park Board office at (604) 681–1141.

Gastown

Gastown is where Vancouver began, back in the 1860's. Many of the city's early stores were established there, as well as a popular hotel run by "Gassy Jack" Deighton, for whom the area is named. The area went into decline but was revived in the 1960's as a tourist spot, sprinkled with boutiques and restaurants, and has become quite lively at night.

Chinatown

The center of Chinatown is Pender St., from Shanghai Alley to Gore St. Vancouver's Chinatown is the second biggest in North America after San Francisco and provides good value for food and just plain browsing. To get there from the city center take a Hastings St. bus—$1.00—and get off at Main St., or you can walk from Gastown.

Granville Island

This has, in recent years, become quite a large tourist attraction in Vancouver. Granville Island has an excellent produce market, an attractive mix of stores and arts and crafts places, two theaters, restaurants, and pubs. Its delightful location beside False Creek is always busy with commercial and pleasure traffic. You'll find Granville Island under the south end of the Granville St. bridge. It's a short bus ride from the center and it can be biked easily.

Otherwise

Other areas in Vancouver are the Granville St. Mall, touted as a pedestrian area but best avoided, and Robsonstrasse, a street with many European-style shops. It is worth a browse, but don't go looking for bargains. Fourth Ave., over the city bridges, has an eccentric variety of secondhand clothes shops, health-food bars, and arts and crafts shops. Look out for B.C. Place Stadium, at the north end of the Cambie St. bridge.

The Environs of Vancouver

Grouse Mountain is only a short trip from Vancouver. To get there take the Lions Gate Bridge to North Vancouver and up to Grouse Mountain. Buses are available, but it is bikable in about 1½ hours. Grouse has an aerial tram and the view from the top is superb; on a clear day you can see from Mount Baker in Washington State to Vancouver Island. At minimum you will see the entire Lower Mainland, with Vancouver harbor and Stanley Park in the foreground. It's a good spot for photographers; there are wooded nature trails and you might even catch some hang-gliding. Open 10:00 A.M. to 10:00 P.M. daily, call (604) 986–6262 for prices and general information. Nearby is the Capilano suspension bridge, the Capilano River salmon hatchery. Park and Tilford Gardens, near the Second Narrows Bridge, were in limbo at press time. For information, call 987–9321. In the opposite direction—out at Horseshoe Bay—is the ferry terminus for Nanaimo, on Vancouver Island, and a pleasant little spot in its own right, with little outboard runabouts for rent for around $20.00 for the first hour, $6.00 an hour thereafter, including gas and fishing rods. And yes, the salmon fishing is excellent.

The cheapest and quickest way to cover a lot of ground is to take a Gray Line tour (604–669-2431). Pick up a brochure at any hotel or information center, but to give you an idea, there are bus trips to the North Shore which include a Seabus ride, a harbor cruise, an excursion up Indian Arm, a tour to Shannon Falls that includes a memorable ride on the Royal Hudson steam train, a visit to Victoria, even a three-day gold rush tour that includes a ride on the Hell's Gate aerial tram.

PRACTICAL INFORMATION
FOR VANCOUVER

Transportation

A taxi into the city from the airport will run $15.00–$20.00, not bad if you've got three or four sharing, but at certain times (and depending on your arrival area) they cannot be found. Make sure the driver uses the meter. The *Hustle Bus* (604–273–0071) goes downtown for $5.25, but the drivers will let you off on the way if you wish. For those on their way to the airport, the bus can be flagged down at the corner of Granville and Broadway, or Granville and 41st. Cheapest way is to take a city bus (75 cents); catch the Mid-Way Connector (#100 or #800) to 71st Ave. and Granville, then transfer to a #25 Victoria, which goes right down Granville into the downtown. For bus information call (604) 324–3211.

TAXIS can be phoned, flagged down, or picked up at stands. They are reasonable for short trips but pricey for longer rides.

TRAINS have three stations. *Via Rail* trains come into the terminal at Main Ave. and Terminal Sta., which is serviced by city buses, as well as the old CPR terminal on the waterfront at Granville Sq. There's also the *British Columbia Railway* (BCR), which comes into the station at West First St., North Vancouver. Buses to the North Vancouver terminal leave the bus depot at Dunsmuir and Cambie Sts. at 6:40 A.M. daily, and a bus meets the arriving evening train.

The BCR goes to Whistler Mountain (and on to Prince George). There are special combination tickets for the train and lift for about $25.00. Call BCR at (604) 984–5246 for details.

PARKING in Vancouver is difficult and expensive in the downtown area. Best bets for daily parking are the big store lots—such as Woodward's in Gastown and the Hudson's Bay parking lot off Seymour or Richards Sts. Parking at Granville Island is poor.

BUSES in Vancouver are plentiful and inexpensive. A $1.00 fare will take you a long way, and $2.00 from White Rock, near the U.S. border, to Grouse Mountain. For information call *Metro Transit* at (604) 324–3211, or check the transit guides on bus shelters. The *Seabus,* an alternative to the bridges if you want to go to the North Shore, is fun and only $1.00. *Greyhound* bus inquiries can be made at (604) 280–9439, and the cheapest way to Victoria and Vancouver Island (bar cycling) is to sail by bus from downtown Vancouver to downtown Victoria. Buses leave the depot at Dunsmuir and Cambie Sts. 10 minutes before every hour, from 5:50 A.M. to 8:50 P.M. (every two hours in winter), adult fare $14.25.

FERRIES play a big role in these parts. Sailings are frequent and inexpensive, but you can get left behind if you travel on Thursdays, Fridays, and Sundays. If you're in an over-height vehicle such as a camper, be prepared for one- or two-ferry wait. When you get on board make a note of where you leave your vehicle—these ferries are big! There are sailings from Tsawwassen, 32 km. (20 miles) south of Vancouver, and Horseshoe Bay, in West Vancouver. Tsawwassen ferries go to Swartz Bay near Victoria (1 hour 40 minutes) and the Gulf Islands. The Horseshoe Bay ferries service Nanaimo, the Sunshine Coast, and Bowen Island. For sailing times call (604) 669–1211. One-way fare from the mainland to Vancouver Island is $19.00 for a car and driver. Other passengers are $4.00. Children (5–11) are half-price; bikers $2.00.

FOR MORE INFORMATION

For more information call the *Greater Vancouver Convention and Visitors Bureau* at (604) 682–2222, or visit *Tourism B.C.* at Robson Sq. (604–668–2300). The daily newspapers publish what's on lists and the monthly *Vancouver Guideline Magazine* is recommended for its thorough approach.

Accommodations

Reservations at Vancouver hotels are strongly recommended May through September. Prices for double-occupancy: *Inexpensive:* $45.00 or less, and *Moderate:* $45.00 to $70.00. There are many hotels and motels outside the city center—in Burnaby and Richmond, for example—but prices are not generally any lower.

Inexpensive

Ambassador Hotel, 773 Seymour (604–684–2436), modest rooms, central location, parking. **Kingston Hotel,** 757 Richards (604–684–9024), clean rooms, coffee shop, sauna, English-style pub. **Niagara Hotel,** 435 Pender (604–681–5548), downtown, coffee shop and parking.

Moderate

Abbotsford Hotel, 921 West Pender (604–681–4335), good downtown location, nice atmosphere. **Avalon Motor Hotel,** 1025 Marine Dr., North Vancouver (604–985–4181), near bridge. **Buchan Hotel,** 1906 Haro (604–685–5354), good location in West End, handy for Stanley Park. **Greenbrier Apartment Hotel,** 1393 Robson (604–683–4558), another good Robson St. location, has provision for wheelchairs. **Sylvia Hotel,** 1154 Gifford (604–681–9321), delightful ivy-covered old hotel, large rooms, right on the water, best value.

The **Downtown YMCA** is at 955 Burrard; a double is $39.00. It has parking, a dining room, and an indoor pool. The **YWCA** is at 580 Burrard; double rooms range from $38.00 to $41.00. There is a coffee shop, indoor pool, but no parking. Phone numbers are YMCA (604) 681–0221 and YWCA (604) 683–2531. The **Vancouver Hostel** of the Canadian Hostelling Association has a superb location on Jericho Beach. Members pay $7.50 a night, nonmembers $9.50. Phone: (604) 224–3208. There is a cafeteria as well as facilities for self-cooking. To get there by bus take the Fourth Ave. bus to Jericho Park. Continue west on 4th Ave. to Discovery St. and turn right. The hostel is the large white building on your left. Also it's close to the Jericho Sailing Center, base for many small sailboat clubs, including university organizations. Visitors can sometimes hitch a ride, maybe even borrow a boat if they can prove competence.

Restaurants

Inexpensive in Vancouver means about $15.00 for two; *Moderate* is $20.00 to $30.00. Chinese food is the best bargain, and as Vancouver has the second biggest Chinatown in North America—after San Francisco—the selection is excellent. There is a 7 percent tax on restaurant meals costing more than $7.00. Markups on wines are generally 100 percent of the liquor store prices. Some restaurants allow you to bring your own wine, but as this is technically illegal we can't list the premises here. If you like the idea of BYOB, you'll have to ask when you get to Vancouver; just don't ask a policeman.

Inexpensive

Vegetable Patch, 1484 W. Broadway, at the corner of Granville St., lives up to its name with good, fresh fare. **Old Spaghetti Factory,** 53 Water St., Gastown, serves simple dishes with family appeal. **P.J. Burger's,** 2966 W. 4th, Kitsilano, does good hamburgers and special milk shakes. **White Spot** is a local hamburger franchise with numerous locations and provides an alternative to *McDonald's.* Any Chinese restaurant will give you a good meal for a few dollars, but avoid those that advertise "Chinese and Canadian food" or Chinese and any other combination. Don't miss **The Only,** 20 E. Hastings.

Moderate

Kamei Sushi, 811 Thurlow, serves superb Japanese cuisine with style. **Las Tapas,** 131 W. Esplanade, North Vancouver, where you'll get an assortment of Spanish snacks. **Heaven and Earth,** 1754 W. 4th St., for hot dishes and good tandooris. **Village Chalet Restaurant,** 1050 W. Queens, North Vancouver; nothing pretentious but nutritious Canadian cooking with a touch of the Continent. **My Tan,** 1481 W. Broadway; large helpings of spicy Vietnamese food and friendly service. **Fresgo Inn,** 1138 Davie; fast food with a home cooked touch.

What to See and Do

MUSEUMS AND ART GALLERIES

The following are in Vanier Park, at the south end of the Burrard St. Bridge. Call (604) 736–7736 for program information on any of them.

Vancouver Museum. Has sections on local history, the lumber industry, a railway coach and a collection of Indian artifacts. Open 10:00 A.M. to 5:00 P.M. daily. Adults $2.50, children and seniors $1, families $5.50.

Planetarium. It is upstairs in the same building housing the Vancouver Museum. Call (604) 736–7736 for details on the programs, which run Tuesday to Saturday. Children under 8 are not admitted for evening shows. There's a cafeteria on the main floor, with breakfast available from 9:30 A.M. Admission $3.50.

Just outside is the **Gordon Southam Observatory,** which is open to the public Tuesday to Sunday from 3:00 P.M. to 10:30 P.M. It's free.

Maritime Museum and St. Roch. Immediately to the west are the Maritime Museum and a fine old RCMP patrol vessel, the *St. Roch.* She was the first ship to circumnavigate the North American continent and has been through the Northwest Passage both ways. Admission to both museums is adults $1.75, children 75 cents.

To get to **Vanier Park** board #22 Macdonald bus on the west side of Burrard. Get off at Cypress and walk four blocks north. Return downtown via the #22 Knight bus.

Hastings Mill Store Museum. The first store and post office built in Vancouver is now a small museum. Open 10:00 A.M.–4:00 P.M. daily from June to September and from 1:00 P.M.–4:00 P.M. weekends the rest of the year. It was the only building to survive the great city fire of 1886. Admission is by donation. Phone: (604) 228–1213.

University of British Columbia Museums. UBC *Museum of Anthropology* has a collection of Indian art as well as artifacts from other cultures. It is a striking building with huge totems outside. Open Wednesday to Sunday, 11:00 A.M. to 5:00 P.M., Tuesdays until 9:00 P.M. Adults $2.50, most others $1.00. Tuesdays free. Phone: (604) 228–3825.

There are also museums at the UBC's Department of Biology (604–228–3344), Geology (604–228–5586), Zoology (604–228–4665). The *Geological Sciences Museum* is open Monday to Friday, 9:00 A.M. to 4:30 P.M., the *Biology Museum* 9:00 A.M. to 5:00 P.M., and there's also an *Entomology Museum* open 9:00 A.M. to 4:00 P.M. Phone: (604) 228–3379.

To get to UBC take a #10 bus anywhere along the Granville Mall southbound. The bus terminates at UBC, and to return take a #14 Hastings bus.

The Museums of Archeology and Ethnology at Simon Fraser University has a collection of Indian artifacts. Open 10:00 A.M. to 4:30 P.M., Monday to Friday, noon to 3:00 P.M. weekends. Phone: (604) 291–3325. To get there take a #14 Hastings bus on Granville Mall northbound and transfer at Kootenay Loop to 35 Westridge bus for SFU.

Heritage Village Museum. Re-creation of a turn-of-the-century B.C. town. There's a pioneer log cabin, a blacksmith, a herbalist, and so on. Nearby is a small-scale steam railway. The village is open Tuesday to Sunday 11:00 A.M. to 4:30 P.M., but is closed December 20 to March. The model train fare is 75 cents. Admission to the village is $3.00, children $1.50. Phone: (604) 294–1231.

Arts, Sciences and Technology Centre, 600 Granville. Phone: (604) 687–8414. Optical illusions, electricity shows, popular mechanics, computer know-how. Open Monday to Saturday

10:00 A.M.–5:00 P.M., Sunday 1:00 P.M.–5:00 P.M.; closed Monday and Tuesday during winter. Adults $3.00, others $1.50.

ART GALLERIES

Vancouver Art Gallery, 800 W. Georgia (604–682–5621), has the finest collection of Emily Carr's work, also other Canadian and European paintings. The gallery is open Tuesday to Saturday, 10:00 A.M.–6:00 P.M., Sunday 1:00 P.M.–6:00 P.M. Admission $2.00, seniors, students and children $1.00.

Atelier Gallery, 3039 Granville, at W. 14th Ave. (604–732–3021). Originals by Canadian artists, prints by international masters. Open Tuesday to Saturday, 10:00 A.M.–5:00 P.M.

Bau-Xi Gallery, 3045 Gallery, 3045 Granville (604–733–7011). Contemporary Canadian artists. Open Monday to Saturday 9:30 A.M.–5:30 P.M.

Equinox Gallery, 1525 W. 8th Ave., 3rd fl. (604–736–2405). International graphic artists. Open Tuesday to Saturday, 9:30 A.M.–4:30 P.M.

Kenneth Heffel Fine Art, 2247 Granville (604–732–6505). Works by the Group of Seven and contemporaries, housed in historic building. Open Tuesday to Saturday, 10:00 A.M.–6:00 P.M.

Nova Gallery, 1972 W. 4th Ave. (604–732–1812). Photography. Open Tuesday to Saturday, 1:00 P.M.–6:00 P.M.

Paperworks Gallery, 1944 West 4th Ave. (604–732–7033). Graphics and prints, some of them relatively inexpensive. Open Tuesday to Saturday, 11:00 A.M.–5:00 P.M.

Krieger Galleries, 775 Homer (604–681–3485). Canadian and U.S. artists, limited edition prints. Open Monday to Saturday, 10:00 A.M. to 6:00 P.M.

Some Principal Sights and Attractions

Chinatown. North America's second largest Chinatown has numerous restaurants, curio chops, and Oriental stores and the world's thinnest office building. It's within walking distance from most downtown points.

Gastown. Where Vancouver began now has antique-type shops, restaurants, smart stores, and nightspots, some of which have endeavored to catch an Old World flavor. Within walking distance of most downtown points.

Granville Island Public Market. Located at the south end of False Creek under the Granville St. Bridge, the market offers fresh produce, fish, meats as well as other foodstuffs and plants. Open 9:00 A.M.–6:00 P.M. daily except Mondays. Parking difficult, especially at night. It is bikable, and for the bus take a #20 Granville bus on the west side of Granville Mall. Alight at Granville and Broadway and transfer to 51 Granville Island bus.

Queen Elizabeth Park. A flower-lover's delight, in two former stone quarries. Houses the Bloedel Conservatory, a triodetic dome filled with tropical plants. Highest point within the city limits. Bring your camera. Board #15 Cambie bus on west side of Burrard St., get off at 33rd Ave. Return by #19 Cambie bus. Park open 10:00 A.M.–9:30 P.M. daily in summer, until 5:30 P.M. in winter. Adults $2.00, children (6 to 18) $1.00. For information call (604) 872–5513.

Stanley Park. See details listed earlier. To get there take a #11 Stanley Park bus from the north side of Pender St. Returns over the same route as #12 Powell or #24 Nanaimo.

University of British Columbia. Nitobe Gardens (604–228–3928), near to the Museum of Anthropology, has delightful Japanese gardens. Open 10:00 A.M. to 6:00 P.M. daily, but closing 3:00 P.M. in winter months. Adults 50 cents, children (10 to 16) 10 cents.

VanDusen Botanical Gardens (604–266–7194). The city's largest collection of plants, trees, flowers, and shrubs. Also a horticultural library and gift shop. Open daily 10:00 A.M. to 9:00 P.M. during the summer, and until 4:00 P.M. in winter. Adults $3.00, children (6 to 18) $1.50. Take a #17 Oak St. bus from the west side of Granville Mall.

SPORTS

In winter there is **skiing** at Grouse Mountain (604–984–0661), Cypress Bowl (604–929–3911), and Mt. Seymour (604–929–2358), all on the North Shore. Cypress Bowl and Mt. Seymour both have **snowshoeing, tobogganing,** and **cross-country skiing,** which is free, but check locally for trails and conditions.

Golf. Several good courses, busy but inexpensive. Call the Park board at (604) 681–1141 for information.

ENTERTAINMENT

Theater and opera. Vancouver's largest theater is the *Queen Elizabeth Theatre,* located between Cambie and Hamilton Sts. immediately north of Georgia St. Its programs include plays, opera, concerts, dance, and musicals. Box office number is (604) 683–2311, or call the Vancouver Ticket Center at (604) 687–4444, which is in the same building, for tickets for performances at this or any other theater. Next door to the Queen E, as it's known, is the *Queen Elizabeth Playhouse* (604–683–2311). *The Arts Club* (box office: 604–687–1644) has two theaters, at 1181 Seymour St., and at Granville Island. Also on Granville Island is the *Waterfront Theatre* (604–685–6217). The *Vancouver East Cultural Center* (604–254–9578), 1895 Venables, is an eastside theater that has quickly become respected for its wide variety of quality programs. As for the universities, UBC has its *Frederic Wood Theatre* (604–228–2678) and Simon Fraser University the *SFU University Theatre* (604–291–3514). *City Stage* (604–688–1436), 842 Thurlow, is an innovative, downtown theater; occasionally does lunchtime shows.

Dance. Vancouver has the reputation for having the best dance of any city in Canada. There's the *Anna Wyman Dance Company* (604–926–6041), *Paula Ross Dance Company* (604–732–9513), and *Pacific Ballet Theatre* (604–669–5954) to name a few.

Music. The *Vancouver Symphony Orchestra* (604–689–1411) plays in the splendid Orpheum Theatre (604–683–2311), 884 Granville. Performances are broadcast on the CBC. The *Vancouver Opera Association* (604–682–2871) performs at the Queen Elizabeth Theatre. The *Festival Concert Society* (604–736–7661) puts on Sunday Coffee Concerts at the Queen Elizabeth Playhouse, Sundays at 11:00 A.M., at which local and touring artists perform. The cost is $2.00. The *Recital Hall* at UBC (604–228–3113) generally has something on; otherwise there is the *Bach Choir* (604–921–8012), the *Purcell String Quartet* (604–291–3221), the *New Music Society* (604–669–0909), the *Chamber Choir* (604–732–6026), or the Cantate Singers (604–224–1187).

Cinema. Seat prices have been climbing relentlessly in the past few years, but bargains can be had at the *Hollywood* (604–738–3211), 3123 W. Broadway, and the Ridge (604–738–6311). *The Varsity* (604–224–3730) has an international film festival every summer; otherwise check SFU's *Images Theatre* (604–291–4754) or the *National Film Board Theatre* (604–732–6119).

Nightlife. A consistently good spot is the *Hot Jazz Society* (604–873–4131), 2120 Main Street. Open Tuesday to Saturday from 8:30 P.M. Nonmember admission from $2.50 to $5.50. *Town Pump* (604–683–6695), 66 Water St., Gastown, has live rock groups, and many visiting performers come to the *Commodore,* 870 Granville. *Savoy Cabaret* (604–687–0418), 6 Powell St., Gastown. Gets good music acts. Another lively spot is *The Bombay Bicycle Club,* at the Abbotsford Hotel (604–681–4335), 921 West Pender.

Vancouver's pub scene is improving with popular places such as *Bridges* on Granville Island, *Bimini* and *Jerry's Cove* in Kitsilano, *Stamp's Landing* in False Creek. The *Pelican Bay Bar* at the new Granville Island Hotel is the current "in" meeting place, but beware of dress code and line-ups. Most hotel bars, by the way, are open until 1:00 A.M., while the newer "neighborhood pubs" generally shut at 11:00 P.M.

EXPLORING VANCOUVER ISLAND

The island is a mixture of the old and the new, the urban and the wild. The old is best represented in Victoria, the province's oldest established community, which still preserves much of its British and Victorian heritage. Here you'll see red double-decker buses and probably want to walk through the lobby of the charming old Empress Hotel.

In Victoria the things to see are the harbor and the elegant Legislative Buildings. You should also have afternoon tea at the Empress Hotel and visit the world-famous Butchart Gardens. Drive or cycle north to Campbell River, one of the best salmon-fishing spots in the world (and boat rental is surprisingly cheap), and you can go right up to Hardy Bay and catch a ferry for Prince Rupert (and on to Alaska). Over on the West Coast are the golden sands of Long Beach and the West Coast Trail, created as a lifesaving device for shipwrecked seamen but now a (very tough) hikers' trail. In the middle there are spectacular mountains, and at the top the wild Cape Scott. Specially recommended is the *Lady Rose* out of Port Alberni, and the *Uchuck* out of Gold River. Both are coasters which poke into coves and logging camps on the West Coast. Check Tourism B.C.'s *Travel Information and Accommodation Directory* (free from Tourism B.C.) for details.

EXPLORING BRITISH COLUMBIA

Lower Mainland

North from Vancouver is the Sunshine Coast, easily and cheaply reached by ferry. The farmlands of the Fraser Valley run to the east, climbing to Hope and the spectacular Fraser Canyon.

On your way to the Sunshine Coast stop at Horseshoe Bay and try your luck at salmon fishing. A boat with gas, rods and bait will cost less than $40.00 for several hours excellent (maybe even profitable) fishing. Try Sewells Marina or Bay Boats. Going east from Vancouver the Hope Hwy. goes close to charming Harrison Hot Springs and swings north to the canyon, where you'll find the breathtaking Hell's Gate Airtram, adults $5.50, children and seniors $3.25. Phone: (604) 689–5300. South of Vancouver is Fort Langley, original capital of the crown colony of B.C. There's a museum, adults $1.00, children 50 cents, families $3.00. Whistler Village offers superb skiing, and in summer there's golf, boating, fishing, tennis, hiking, and great mountain scenery; on the way you'll find several provincial parks. Lastly, the Gulf Islands—particularly Saltspring—enjoy better than average weather, are pleasant to visit, and are fine for biking.

Okanagan-Similkameen

In the spring, the Okanagan hillsides are crowded with blossom as the fruit trees come to life, by summer the sandy beaches are busy, the summer and fall brings out the roadside fruit stands, and winter brings snow carnivals.

Many U.S. visitors drive into this area on U.S. 97 and enter south of Osoyoos. You are soon into delightful lake country and the casual little towns of Penticton, Summerland, Kelowna, and Vernon. There's a game farm south of Penticton, sternwheelers moored at Penticton and Kelowna, and a restored mission near Kelowna. Ski hills lie outside Osoyoos, Penticton, Vernon, and Kelowna.

Kootenay-Boundary

This is a land of mountains and valleys, from the peaks of the Rockies, Purcells, and Selkirks to the long sweep of the Arrow and Kootenay Lakes and the Columbia River. As such it has strong appeal to those who enjoy the outdoors, and its many lakesides and parks have lots of room for tenters.

The highway east of Osoyoos goes to Castlegar, then up to the silver town of New Denver, which once rivaled San Francisco. Now it's a sleepy little place, a turning-off point for the road to Kaslo, a delightful little spot where hang-gliders soar over an old stern-wheeler. North of Cranbrook and Kimberley you'll find hot springs at Fairmont (as well as Radium, Nakusp, and Ainsworth) and the road to Yoho National Park.

Thompson-Columbia

This is pure scenery, a land for hikers and skiers. Here you'll find Mount Robson, the highest park in the Canadian Rockies, the ice-fields of Glacier National Park, the waterfalls of Wells Gray, and rolling ranchland and fishing lakes of the high country.

Here it's worth digging a little deeper in your pockets and renting a houseboat on the Shuswap Lakes. Kamloops is the major city. Merritt, to the south, is a fun cowboy town. Beyond the Shuswap Lakes is Revelstoke, and beyond that lakes and parks to satisfy the most ardent outdoorspeople. There is camping space galore, and if Yoho isn't big enough, there's always Banff National Park over the border in Alberta. In the winter there's cross-country skiing, and for those who want to break out financially, helicopter skiing.

Cariboo-Chilcotin-Yellowhead

This is the big country, getting north too, where travel costs are climbing, but it is a region that gives the visitor an idea of the size and grandeur of the province.

Families can stay not too expensively at lakeside lodges while enjoying the natural setting and the quiet of these outdoors. At Bowron Lake Provincial Park a round-trip circuit of 73 miles (117 kms.) of wilderness gives canoeists a chance to test their skill and energy. The Bella Coola Hwy. leads to the spectacular coastal scenery of the Bella Coola Valley, and farther north, the Yellowhead Hwy. runs into Prince George and points the visitor toward Prince Rupert and ferries back south to Vancouver Island. If you're in a touristy mood, there's Barkerville with its restored gold-rush flavor. In winter, this is great country for cross-country skiing or snowshoeing.

PRACTICAL INFORMATION FOR BRITISH COLUMBIA

Transportation

Air travel within B.C. is easy, but like elsewhere, hardly cheap. **Train** services are limited and the trend is for a steady cutting back. **Car** or **tour bus** are the recommended ways to travel. Also work **ferries** into your plans wherever possible. They are frequent, cheap, and provide a great sightseeing platform.

FOR MORE INFORMATION

Contact *Tourism B.C.,* at 1117 Wharf St., Victoria, (604) 387–1642 or local visitors' bureaus in any other area.

Accommodations and Restaurants

A room at the inn is hard to find almost anywhere in B.C. unless you book in advance, but easier and cheaper spring and fall. The provincial park sites are particularly good value, but there is no advance reservation system and occupancy is limited to 14 days. Each campground contains a number of campsites consisting of a parking spur, tent space, table and fireplace. Recreational vehicles and trailers up to 20 ft. (6 meters) can be accommodated, although no hook-ups are provided (private operators provide the latter). Firewood is supplied and there are good toilet and refuse facilities. There is a nightly charge of a few dollars and campgrounds are normally gated between 11:00 P.M. and 7:00 A.M. Do not confuse campgrounds with picnic grounds, where camping is not permitted. There are 130 provincial campgrounds in B.C., and a full list is contained in Tourism B.C.'s *Accommodation Guide,* available free at any tourist office.

As for hotels and motels outside of Vancouver, for double-occupancy $40.00 or less is *Inexpensive,* and $41.00 to $70.00 *Moderate.* The cautious budget travelers will be wise to stay in housekeeping units or to camp where they will be cooking for themselves and avoiding restaurants wherever possible.

VANCOUVER ISLAND. *Casa Linda Motel* (I), 364 Coldstream Ave., Victoria (604–474–2141), some units with kitchens. *Cheltenham Court Motel* (I), 994 Gorge Rd. W., Victoria (604–385–9559), good-value cottages, coffee shop. *Cowichan Valley Inn* (M), 6457 Norcross Rd., Duncan (604–748–2772), opposite B.C. Forest Museum, near shopping, fishing, and golf. *Ingraham Hotel* (I), 2915 Douglas St., Victoria (604–385–6731). The restaurant here is inexpensive and open daily. *Schooner Restaurant* (M), Campbell St.,

Tofino (604–725–3444), has good fresh seafood, particularly crab. *Rod and Reel Resort* (I), R.R. 2, Campbell River (604–923–5250), housekeeping cottages, boat and bait rentals. *Vista Del Mar Motel* (M), 920 South Island Hwy., Campbell River (604–923–4271), housekeeping units, next to store, boat launch nearby.

LOWER MAINLAND. *Blue Star Motel* (M), 28044 Fraser Hwy., Aldergrove (604–856–8125), quiet country atmosphere, pets okay. *Glencoe Motel* (I), Box 181, Harrison Hot Springs (604–796–2574), sleeping and housekeeping units, opposite mineral pool. *Harrison Lakeshore Motel* (M), Esplanade Ave., Harrison Hot Springs (604–796–2441), large units facing lakefront, heated pool.

OKANAGAN-SIMILKAMEEN. *Bel Air Cedar Motel* (I), Hwy. 97 S., R.R. 1, Oliver (604–498–2443), family units, swimming pool. *Boundary Motel* (I), R.R. 2, Osoyoos (604–495–6050), close to border, off-season rates. *Log Cabin Motel* (M), 3287 Skaha Lake Rd., Penticton (604–492–3155), log-cabin housekeeping units. *Majestic Motor Inn* (M), 152 Riverside Dr., Penticton (604–493–6616), swimming pool, close to beach. *Willow Inn Hotel* (M), 235 Queensway, Kelowna (604–762–2122), downtown, close to park and lake. *Western Budget Motel* (I), 2679 Hwy. 97N, Kelowna (604–860–4990), big picnic area, pets welcome.

KOOTENAY-BOUNDARY. *Byng Hotel* (I), 21 Cranbrook St., Cranbrook (604–426–4279), downtown, licensed dining room. *Jones Boys Marine Motel* (M), Box 700, Kaslo, lakeside housekeeping units, boat launching ramp. *Lucerne Motel* (I), Box 86, New Denver (604–358–2228), licensed dining lounge. *Nakusp Hot Springs Cedar Chalets* (M), Box 172, Nakusp (radio phone N 695800), fishing, hiking, and ski trails nearby, close to hot springs. *Sandman Inn* (M), 405 Cranbrook St., Cranbrook (604–426–4236), central, big beds, indoor pool. A word of caution—should you decide to explore the old silver mining town of Sandon, don't expect to find a friendly inn; Sandon is a ghost town.

THOMPSON-COLUMBIA. *Anglemont Estates* (M), Box 48, Anglemont (604–955–2211), lodge overlooking Shuswap Lake, private beach and golf course. *Copper Valley Motel* (I), Box 670, Merritt (604–378–5331), central location, swimming pool. *Mountaineer Inn* (M), Box 217, Valemount, sleeping and housekeeping rooms, quiet spot. *Plaza Motor Hotel* (I), 405 Victoria St., Kamloops (604–372–7121), dining room, pub, parking, and family plan. No pets. *Sandman Inn* (M), 550 Columbia St. at 6th, Kamloops (604–374–1218), sleeping and kitchenette units, handy to town. *Regent Motor Inn* (M), 112 East First St., Revelstoke (604–837–2107), renovated, bridal suite, family rates.

CARIBOO-YELLOWHEAD. *Billy Barker Inn* (M), 308 McLean St., Quesnel (604–992–5533), free parking, recommended restaurant. *Casbar Motel* (I), Box 4039, Quesnel (604–992–6622), two miles north of Quesnel, double beds. *Esther's Inn* (M), 1151 Commercial Dr., Prince George (604–562–4131), restaurant, indoor pool. *Lakeside Motel* (I), 1505 Cariboo Hwy. S., Williams Lake (604–392–4181), restaurant nearby, peaceful setting. *Parkside Resort Motel*(M), 11th Ave. and McBride St., Prince Rupert (604–624–9131), close to city center, car storage. *Jacob's Inn,* 1401 Queensway, Prince George (604–563–9236), sleeping and housekeeping units, water beds extra. *Roblyn Motel* (I), 3755 John Hart Hwy., Prince George (604–962–7081), family atmosphere, housekeeping units. *Sandman Inn*(M), 1650 Central St., Prince George (604–563 –8131), full restaurant facilities, pool. *Totem Lodge Motel*(M), 1335 Park Ave., Prince Rupert (604–624–6761), near terminals of Kelsey Bay and Alaska Ferries and airport, car storage. *Valley View Motel* (I), 1523 Cariboo Hwy. S., Williams Lake (604–392–4655), sleeping and housekeeping units overlooking private lake.

What to See

Barkerville, the gold-rush town which once had a bigger population than San Francisco, became a ghost town and is now a major tourist attraction.

Glacier National Park, between Revelstoke and Golden, is a wonderland of mountains, glaciers, and rugged peaks.

The **Hell's Gate Airtram** in the Fraser River canyon. See Lower Mainland section for details. Visit the **B.C. Forest Museum** in Duncan, open daily 10:00 A.M. to 5:30 P.M., May 15 to September 15, adults $2.00. Phone: (604) 748–9389.

Kootenay National Park, entered from the west at Radium Hot Springs. Vermillion Pass is the main attraction.

Mount Revelstoke National Park boasts some of the most splendid scenery in Canada.

Pacific Rim National Park, on the west coast of Vancouver Island, where you'll find the famed Long Beach.

Port Alberni, where you find the *Lady Rose,* a coaster with an intriguing itinerary; day trips; call (604) 723–9774.

Saltspring Island, most popular of the sunny Gulf Islands that lie between Vancouver and Vancouver Island.

Yoho National Park. Good campgrounds and views of glaciers and waterfalls.

A last word—don't forget to wear your seat belt in B.C. It is mandatory under law.

French-English Tourist Vocabulary

DAILY EXPRESSIONS

Can anyone here speak English?	Y a-t-il quelqu'un qui parle anglais?
Do you speak English?	Parlez-vous anglais?
Do you understand?	Comprenez-vous?
Don't mention it	Pas de quoi
I beg you pardon	Pardon? (pahrr'dong)
Good morning . . . day . . . afternoon	Bonjour
Good evening . . . night	Bonsoir
Goodbye	Au revoir
How are you?	Comment allez-vous?
How much . . . many?	Combien?
I don't know	Je ne sais pas
I don't understand	Je ne comprends pas
Yes	Oui
No	Non
Please speak more slowly	Parlez plus lentement, s'il vous plaît
Stop	Arrêtez
Go ahead	Continuez
Hurry	Dépêchez-vous
Wait here	Attendez ici
Come in!	Entrez! (ahn'tray)
Sit down	Asseyez-vous
Thank you very much	Merci bien
There is, there are	Il y a
Very good . . . well	Très bien
What is this?	Qu'est-ce que c'est? (kes-kuh-say)
What do you want?	Que voulez-vous?
Please	S'il vous plaît (seevooplay)

I'm sorry	Je regrette
You're welcome	Je vous en prie
What time is it?	Quelle heure est-il?
What is your name?	Comment vous appelez-vous?
With pleasure	Avec plaisir
You are very kind	Vous êtes bien aimable

DAYS OF THE WEEK

Sunday	Dimanche
Monday	Lundi
Tuesday	Mardi
Wednesday	Mercredi
Thursday	Jeudi
Friday	Vendredi
Saturday	Samedi

COMMON QUESTIONS

Is there . . .	Y a-t-il . . .
—a bus for . . . ?	—un autobus pour . . . ?
—a dining car?	—un wagon-restaurant . . . ?
—an English interpreter?	—un interprète anglais?
—a guide?	—un guide?
—a good hotel at . . . ?	—un bon hôtel à . . . ?
—a good restaurant here?	—un bon restaurant ici?
—a sleeper?	—une place dans de wagon-lit?
—time to get out?	—le temps de descendre?
—a train for . . . ?	—un train pour . . . ?
Where is . . .	Où est . . .
—the airport?	—l'aéroport?
—a bank?	—une banque?
—the bar?	—le bar?
—the barber's shop?	—le coiffeur?
—the bathroom?	—la salle de bain?
—the ticket (booking) office?	—le guichet?
—a chemist's shop (drugstore)?	—une pharmacie?
—the movies (cinema)?	—le cinema?
—the cloakroom?	—le vestiaire?
—the British (American) Consulate?	—le consulat d'Angleterre (d'Amérique)?
—the Customs office?	—la douane?
—a garage?	—un garage?
—a hairdresser? (barber)	—un coiffeur?
—the lavatory?	—le lavabo?
—the luggage?	—les bagages?

—the museum? — le musée?
—the police station? — le gendarmerie?
—the post office? — le bureau de poste?
—the railway station? — la gare?
—the theater? — le théâtre?
—a tobacconist? — un débit de tabac?

When . . . Quand . . .
—is lunch? — le déjeuner est-il servi?
—is dinner? — le dîner est-il servi?
—is the first (last) bus? — le premier (dernier) autobus part-il?
—is the first (last) train? — le premier (dernier) train part-il?
—does the theater open? — ouvre-t-on le théâtre?
—will it be ready? — sera-t-il (elle) prêt(e)?
—does the performance begin (end)? — la séance commence-t-elle (finit-elle)?
—will you be back? — rentrerez-vous?
—can you return them? — pouvez-vous me les rendre?
—can I have a bath? — pourrais-je prendre un bain?

Which is . . . Quel est . . .
—the way to . . . street? — Par où va-t-on à la rue . . . ?
—the best hotel at . . . ? — le meilleur hôtel de . . . ?
—the train (bus) for . . . ? — le train (autobus) pour . . . ?

What is . . . Quel est . . .
—the fare to . . . ? — le prix du billet à . . . ?
—the single fare? — le prix d'aller?
—the round trip (return) fare? — le prix d'aller et retour?
—the fare (taxi)? — Je vous dois combien?
—the price? — le prix?
—the price per day? per week? — le prix par jour? par semaine?
—the price per kilo? (2.2 pounds) — combien le kilo?
—the price per meter? (39½ inches) — combien le mètre?
—the matter? — Qu'est-ce qu'il y a?
—the French for . . . ? — Comment dit-on . . . en français?

Have you . . . Avez-vous . . .
—any American (English) cigarettes? — des cigarettes américaines (anglaises)?
—a timetable? — un indicateur?
—a room to let? — une chambre à louer?
—anything ready? (Food) — quelque chose de prêt?
How often? Combien de fois?

How long?   Combien de temps?

DAILY NEEDS

I want . . .   Je désire . . . Je voudrais . . .
  —my bill   —l'addition (la note)
  —to buy   —d'acheter
  —cigars, cigarettes   —des cigares, cigarettes
  —a dentist   —consulter un dentiste
  —a dictionary   —un dictionnaire
  —a doctor   —consulter un médecin
  —something to drink   —prendre quelque chose à
                               boire
  —something to eat   —manger quelque chose
  —some American (English)   —des journaux américains
    papers   (anglais)
  —a haircut   —me faire couper les
                               cheveux
  —a shave   —me faire raser
  —to go to   —aller à (au) . . .
  —a porter   —un porteur
  —to see . . .   —voir . . .
  —to send a telegram   —envoyer un tétégramme
  —some stamps   —des timbres
  —a taxi   —un taxi
  —to telephone   —téléphoner
  —the waiter   —parler avec le garçon
  —some beer   —de la bière
  —change for . . .   —la monnaie de . . .
  —water   —de l'eau
  —my key   —ma clé
  —razor blades   —des lames de rasoir
  —a road map   —une carte routière
  —a soap   —du savon

MENU TRANSLATOR

Meats (Viandes)

Agneau	Lamb	Jambon	Ham
Bifteck	Steak	Lapin	Rabbit
Boeuf	Beef	Lard	Bacon
Charcuterie	Pork cold cuts	Mouton	Mutton
Châteaubriand	Rump steak	Porc	Pork
Côte	Chop	Rosbif	Roast beef
Entrecôte	Rib steak	Saucisse	Sausage
Gigot d'agneau	Leg of Lamb	Veau	Veal
Gibier	Wild game		

Poultry (Volaille)

Canard	Duck	Oie	Goose
Caneton	Duckling	Pintade	Guinea hen
Coq	Young cock	Poulet	Chicken
Faisan	Pheasant		

Offal (Abats)

Cervelles	Brains	Langue	Tongue
Foie	Liver	Rognon	Kidney

Fish (Poisson)

Anguille	Eel	Perche	Bass
Maquereau	Mackerel	Saumon	Salmon
Morue	Cod	Truite	Trout

Shellfish (Coquillages, Crustaces)

Crevettes	Shrimp	Homard	Lobster
Ecrevisses	Crawfish	Huîtres	Oysters
Escargots	Snails	Langouste	Spiny rock lobster
Fruits de mer	Mixed shellfish	Moules	Mussels
Grenouilles	Frogs' legs	Palourdes	Clams

Vegetables (Légumes)

Aubergine	Eggplant	Epinard	Spinach
Chou	Cabbage	Haricots	Beans
Cresson	Watercress	Haricots verts	Green beans

Desserts (Desserts)

Beignets	Fritters	Glace	Ice cream
Gâteau	Cake	Tarte	Pie

CANADA

BEAUFORT
SEA

QUEEN
ELIZABETH
IS.

DISTRICT

ALASKA

YUKON
TERRITORY

Dawson

Inuvik
Fort McPherson

Victoria
Is.

N O R T H W E S T   T E R

Yukon R.

Whitehorse

Mackenzie R.

Great
Bear Lake

DISTRICT OF
MACKENZIE

DISTRICT OF
KEEWATIN

ROCKY MTS.

Fort Nelson

Peace R.

Great
Slave Lake

Slave R.

Uranium City

Lake
Athabaska

Wollaston
Lake

Churchill

Prince Rupert

Athabaska R.

Prince George

BR.
COLUMBIA

Jasper

ALBERTA

Edmonton

Reindeer
Lake

MANITOBA

Flin Flon

Fraser R.

Lake Louise
Banff

Calgary

SASK.

Prince Albert

Saskatoon

Lake
Winnipeg

Vancouver I.

Victoria

Vancouver

Lethbridge

Medicine Hat

Trans Canada

Saskatchewan R.

Hwy.

Regina

Winnipegosis
Lake

Winnipeg

O

Lake
of the Wood

Columbia R.

PACIFIC
OCEAN

Red River

UNITE

0   200   400

Scale of Miles

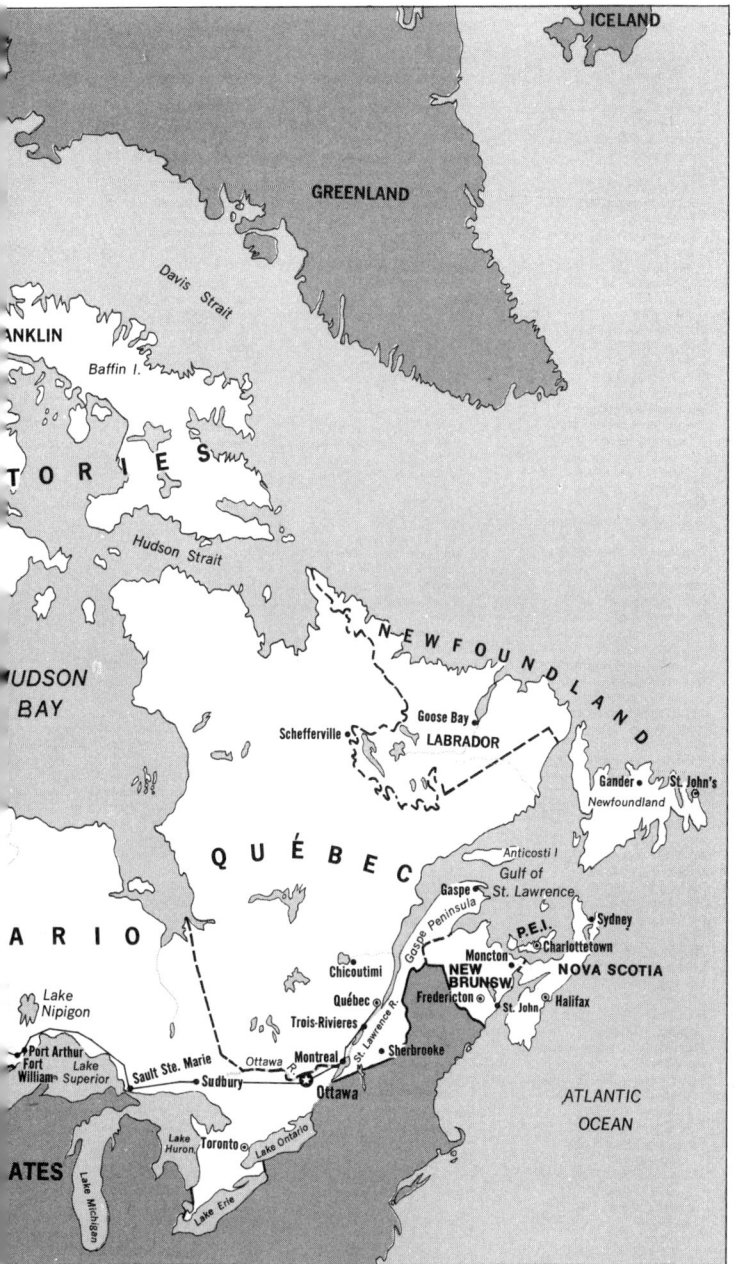

INDEX

GENERAL INFORMATION
(See individual provinces for more specific information)